PHILOSOPHY OF THE TOURIST

PHILOSOPHY OF THE TOURIST

HIROKI AZUMA

Translated by
JOHN D. PERSON

URBANOMIC

Published in 2022 by
URBANOMIC MEDIA LTD,
THE OLD LEMONADE FACTORY,
WINDSOR QUARRY,
FALMOUTH TR11 3EX,
UNITED KINGDOM

Originally published in Japanese as
Genron 0—Kankōkyaku no tetsugaku (Tokyo: Genron, 2017)
© Hiroki Azuma © Genron Co., Ltd
This English language translation © Urbanomic Media Ltd.
All rights reserved.

Publication of this book
is supported by the Suntory Foundation
Support for Overseas Publication program.

BRITISH LIBRARY CATALOGUING-IN-PUBLICATION DATA

A full catalogue record of this book is available
from the British Library

ISBN 978-1-915103-00-0

Distributed by The MIT Press, Cambridge, Massachusetts
and London, England

Type by Norm, Zurich
Printed and bound in the UK by
TJ Books, Padstow

www.urbanomic.com

CONTENTS

Preface

This text appeared in Japan as a belated preparatory issue (no. 0) of the journal of criticism *Genron* launched by our company Genron in November 2015, while also being the final issue (no. 5) of the 'bookazine' *Shisō Chizu β*, also launched by Genron in January 2011, arriving after a three-and-a-half-year gap, and is also a book of philosophy that I wrote during winter 2016–2017. Whether we call it a book, a magazine, or a monograph is a matter of channels of circulation, and isn't really what is essential.

It is a work of philosophy. And although I am a critic, I do think about philosophy. My first work was published in 1993. It was an essay on the Soviet anti-establishment writer Aleksandr Solzhenitsyn. During the intervening quarter-century, I have thought about many different things. I have especially thought about the nature of the philosophy truly needed in the twenty-first century world, a world inhabited by the internet, terrorism, and a great deal of hate. My conclusions at this particular moment in time are recorded in this book.

Over the past quarter of a century, I have engaged in a diverse range of projects, ranging from philosophy and social analysis to subculture criticism and fiction. For that reason, my work has been received in diverse ways, and at times has been subject to unproductive misunderstandings. The present book was also written in order to correct this situation. It is therefore constructed in a manner that makes connections between my previous works. This book can be read as a sequel to *Ontological, Postal*, or *Otaku: Japan's Database Animals*, or *General Will 2.0*, or *Weak Links*. You might even be able to read it as a sequel to my novel *Quantum Families*.

In writing this book I came to sincerely and freely embrace my own style of 'criticism' for the first time in nearly twenty years. I had always felt a sense of guilt at being a critic. I worried that no one really benefited or gained in happiness by my writing a work of criticism. That sense of disillusionment has dissipated. Having finished writing this book, I feel the freedom of writing as never before.

The development of this book was a winding path. It was originally intended to be published in 2013 as the fifth issue of *Shisō chizu β* and delivered to the subscribing members (fourth season) of our company. At the time, it was planned as part of a bookazine with several contributing writers, not as a monograph.

The publication of that bookazine became impossible for several reasons. But, having already collected subscription fees, we needed to deliver a book or magazine of the same value. So I decided to publish a preparatory issue based on a transcript of myself speaking on the topics discussed in this book, to mark the launch of *Genron*. That was the plan that became the starting point for the Japanese version of *Philosophy of the Tourist*. Production of that book proceeded, with the goal of publishing it by autumn 2015 at the earliest and the end of that year at the latest. By summer we had finished recording the material and began the editorial process. Soon we had a manuscript, and I had completed about half of the revisions.

But that's when the true complications really began. By December 2015, we had launched *Genron* ahead of the publication of this book, intended as a preparatory issue. The magazine was received favourably. Moreover, through our Genron Café and School, our company became more well known. In the midst of these changes, I grew sceptical of the plan for this book. More than anything, I didn't like the fact that it was based on a transcript. True, many works of criticism and non-fiction today are transcripts, and it seemed as if this trend was here for the duration. But once *Genron* had launched, it didn't seem like I should be chasing that kind of trend. So in the winter of 2016, I threw out the manuscript and decided to write a new book from scratch. The manuscript for this book was written over the three months that followed.

The idea of 'misdelivery' is key to the argument of this book. And the book itself is a product of this very misdelivery.

Without the fact that our company had collected subscription fees for the final issue of *Shisō chizu β* and couldn't deliver on its publication, this book would have never been imagined. Moreover, had I not decided on a whim to build a company seven years ago, completely changing my life trajectory, I probably wouldn't have written this kind of book. Had I not made that decision, I probably would have quit writing books altogether, having never felt the freedom of criticism again. Indeed, for the past ten years I have repeatedly said that I have no intention of writing any more books. Had I set out to write a book from the start, I most likely would not have been able to write one at all.

Misdeliveries create society and they create solidarity. For that reason, we must actively expose ourselves to misdeliveries. That is the thesis I propose in chapter 4, and the very existence of this book serves as a good example.

With that said, the real premise behind all of the above is that misdeliveries can cause many problems for people. The production of this book forced a great burden on many. I would like to sincerely apologise to our fourth and fifth season subscribing members who waited not months but years for this publication, as well as the printing company and booksellers who were yanked around by the ever-changing plan and impossible schedule. I placed a burden on my staff as well. I hope the contents of this book pass muster as repayment.

Criticism can still accomplish a great deal. At the very least, it can discuss grand things. I hope that such a message will be misdelivered to as many readers as possible.

1 March 2017

Preface to the English Translation

As noted in the preface to the original Japanese edition, this book travelled a winding road to publication. It was the first issue of a magazine created for the supporting members of Genron, a company that I founded in 2010 and continue to run today, while also being an independent monograph. In the first form it was entitled *Genron 0*, in the second *Philosophy of the Tourist*.

The company Genron is not known in the English-speaking world. This English edition is simply titled *Philosophy of the Tourist*. Thus, all of the above may not necessarily seem of interest to readers. However, this context is crucial to understanding my philosophy.

To this day I am known outside of Japan as a postmodern thinker well-versed in pop culture and information society. In other words, it seems that I am thought of as a scaled-down version of Slavoj Žižek, who 'analyses' contemporary culture and politics using 'cutting-edge theory'.

However, such an image is vastly different from the reality today. I began my career as a critic in Tokyo in 1993. The influence of postmodernism was still powerful at the time, and I began writing in such an atmosphere. So in my early years I published works in a pedantic prose reminiscent of Žižek, and this image still lingers in Japan as well. But even in works dealing with pop culture, such as *Animalizing Postmodern* (published in English as *Otaku: Japan's Database Animals*), I was never satisfied with simply analysing symbols and iconography. I have always been drawn to the people behind them.

Because I was educated in the era of the postmodern, I still often use the terminology of the postmodern. The philosophers I reference tend to be European or American. But this is simply a reflection of the limits of my knowledge, and my arguments and interest themselves are quite different from postmodernism as it is commonly understood. I continue to work in philosophy today so that I can live well and so that those interested in my work can live well. Philosophy is nothing more than a tool to live well. A postmodernist would never utter such words. And in the past, neither could I. But I no longer have any hesitation in doing so.

True, I used to be an academic. I received my doctorate from Tokyo University with a dissertation on Jacques Derrida. But I no longer have any academic affiliation. In these ten years since founding Genron and leaving the university, my standpoint and my readership have changed dramatically. Today, I am more widely read outside of the academic world. And I write in order to satisfy my readers. *Philosophy of the Tourist* is one of my books written under these circumstances. These changes are known to readers in Japan, but they are not known abroad. I suspect that readers of this translation will likely be researchers and students who prefer books of philosophy and the humanities.

That is inevitable, and a product of my own shortcomings. But in truth, I hope that this English edition, too, reaches a general readership of those who have never even heard of postmodernism, as was the case with the Japanese edition.

Of course, this book is a book of philosophy, and I do use some of the specialised language of the field. However, the ideas proposed here have nothing to do with 'cutting-edge theory'. In fact, this book does not adopt the jargon that became popular in the world of philosophy and theory in the 2010s, such as Anthropocene, singularity, and so on. While the focus on the tourist might itself be particular to the twenty-first century, the issues I raise are highly classical in nature. Moreover, the arguments developed here are in fact more deeply tied to my own actual struggles over the past decade to raise funds, build a company, hire workers, and deliver the voice of philosophy to the general public than to the arguments of the philosophers I cite. On this point, more than anything, the concept of the tourist proposed in this book developed out of these practical experiences, and the theory is nothing more than what I discovered after the fact. Academic types might feel disappointed to hear this, but I think that this has always been how philosophy works.

This is the second translation of *Philosophy of the Tourist*. A Korean translation has already been published (August 2020) and a Chinese translation is currently in preparation. Two translations in five years since its publication is not a bad pace for a Japanese book in the humanities, but two major events occurred in the interim: the COVID-19 pandemic and the Russian invasion of Ukraine.

These two events not only changed the face of the world, they also greatly changed how this book is read. The theme of this book is the tourist. Before the pandemic, 'tourist' was a word brimming with hope. Over a billion people crossed national boundaries as the entire world placed great expectations on the growth of the tourism industry. Of course, there were concerns about cultural appropriation, overtourism, and environmental issues. But in spite of this, the simple fact that billions of people speaking different languages with different cultural and religious backgrounds are starting to easily cross national boundaries on their own for private reasons, crisscrossing the earth, appeared to be a premonition of the emergence of a new global society. For this very reason, this book attempted to reinterpret the emergence of tourists as something that deconstructs what Carl Schmitt defined as the division between friend and enemy—that is, the traditional realm of politics.

However, now the situation has changed completely. When the pandemic broke out in 2020, countries around the world, regardless of ideology, quickly responded by closing their national borders, with the so-called liberal democratic countries leading the charge. Cities were locked down and surveillance technologies were mobilised. Citizens and non-citizens, non-infected and infected, negative testers and positive testers, those who have the right to appear in public and those who don't—the division between friend and enemy once again became the basis of social order. International flights ceased and the tourism industry was dealt a devastating blow. No longer the hope of global solidarity, the tourist was now the object of alarm and expulsion as a vector threatening the health of citizens. These conditions appeared to ease to some extent by late 2021, raising hopes that the era of tourism was returning, but then came the war. The world became divided between the Ukrainian cause and the evil of Russia. Social media erupted and the possibility of nuclear war even became the topic of daily discussion. It will likely take a long time before the international movement of tourists returns to its former proportions and light-hearted nature. And even were this to happen, perhaps some countries and regions would no longer be able to be tourist destinations.

For that reason, some of you reading this book may find its arguments to be overly optimistic and outdated. Today the world is organised by the opposition between friend and enemy and the place of the tourist is limited. In such times, what use is a philosophy that sees in the tourist the deconstruction of friend and enemy?

That impression is only half correct. I wrote this book in the 2010s. It is probably influenced by the euphoric psyche of the 2010s. It may not be welcomed in the 2020s.

But the 2020s will not go on forever. The pandemic and the war will someday end. The opposition between friend and enemy is not absolute, and the world will no doubt move toward a global society once again. I believe that the arguments of this book will have a renewed value when that day comes. The tourists of the 2010s were no doubt defeated by the pandemic and war. But that does not mean that the philosophy of the tourist is unnecessary. Instead, when this storm has passed, we must build anew a stronger philosophy of the tourist that can withstand pandemic and war.

Finally, the discussion in this book is not complete. Part 2, entitled 'Philosophy of the Family', is presented as 'An Introduction'. What this signifies is that, at the time of writing, not only was the discussion of Part 2 incomplete, it was not clearly enough connected to Part 1. That is a shortcoming of this book.

I am currently writing a sequel that corrects this shortcoming and develops the discussion presented here, while also connecting it to another book entitled *General Will 2.0*, which has also been translated into English. The first half has already been published as an independent article in *Genron 12* as 'The Philosophy of Corrigibility, or, On a New Publicness'. There I link the concept of the tourist to the discussion of the family through reference to Ludwig Wittgenstein and Saul Kripke, while also proposing a new reading of Richard Rorty and Hannah Arendt. Although I am still writing the second half, I should be able to publish it by early next year.

In truth, as the author I would like you to read that sequel soon. The connection to academic debates has been strengthened, and more importantly the aim of this book will become much easier to understand. Unfortunately, far fewer books are translated from Japanese to English than vice versa. So its future translation likely hinges on how this book is received—and moreover, translations take time. Either way, I hope that by the time I am discussing its translation, the era of the tourist has showed some signs of returning.

I would like to thank the translator John Person, Robin Mackay of Urbanomic, and the philosopher Yuk Hui who introduced me to Robin.

John is the translator of *General Will 2.0*, and one of my most trusted English translators. My prose is not complex. And yet translating my Japanese, which discusses philosophical content without necessarily using specialist terms with fixed translations, must be rather difficult. My thanks to him for always taking it on.

I met Yuk at a symposium in Hangzhou in the autumn of 2016. Since then, we have become friends and I have been greatly stimulated by our exchanges. He has published a book with Urbanomic, *The Question Concerning Technology in China*, and I was fortunate to be introduced to Robin through him. Urbanomic is known even in Japan as a unique publisher that serves as a beacon in the field of contemporary philosophy. I am honoured to be included in its catalogue.

The English translation of this book received the assistance of the Suntory Foundation through its Support for Overseas Publications program. In 1999, my first book, *Ontological, Postal* (which has not been translated into English) received an award from the Suntory Foundation. I would like to thank the Foundation for supporting me once again.

18 April 2022

PART ONE

PHILOSOPHY OF
THE TOURIST

1. Tourism

1

Back in 2014 I published a short book entitled *Weak Links*[1] in which I proposed a three-way classification system: villager, nomad, and tourist. I argued that, in order to live prosperously, it is important to be neither a 'villager', who is committed only to a single community, nor a 'nomad', who doesn't belong to any community, but a 'tourist' who, while belonging to a particular community, sometimes visits others.

The book garnered unexpected acclaim, probably because the way I framed the tourist as a third way beyond 'inside' and 'outside' allowed it to be interpreted as a lifestyle choice or a kind of self-improvement. And, to be honest, the publisher advertised it in that way too.

But seasoned readers of philosophy and criticism probably felt that it was a fairly commonplace idea. Although I didn't say so in the book, my theory of the tourist was inspired by numerous debates in philosophy and criticism, such as Masao Yamaguchi's famous schema of 'centre and periphery'.[2]

Even prior to that, the critic Kōjin Karatani, whose work has inspired me greatly, proposed something very similar. Some time ago he was arguing that 'communities' are no good because they are closed, and that the 'Other' who comes from the 'outside' is necessary.[3] My line of thinking might be read as an updating of Karatani's arguments on the topic. In that regard, in essence *Weak Links* didn't propose anything new.

1.   H. Azuma, *Yowai tsunagari—kensaku wādo o sagasu tabi* [*Weak Links: A Journey to Find Search Words*] (Tokyo: Gentōsha, 2014).

2.   See M. Yamaguchi, *Bunka to ryōgisei* [*Culture and Duality*] (Tokyo: Iwanami Gendai Bunko, 2000) and *Chi no enkinhō* [*Perspectives of Knowledge*] (Tokyo: Iwanami Shoten, 1978).

3.   [See for example K. Karatani, *Tankyū I* (*Investigations I*) (Kōdansha Gakujutsu Bunko, 1992). Azuma's first publication as an author appeared in a journal edited by Karatani, *Hihyō kūkan* (*Critical Space*), in 1993. Azuma returns to Karatani's work in Chapter 5 of the present book—trans.]

But if it's essence we are talking about, philosophy is a field in which nothing essentially new has happened since the days of Ancient Greece. As a book on philosophy, perhaps the essence of *Weak Links* is that it presented an old theme in a new style—in other words, its novelty lay in its design rather than its essence. If I may pursue this tangent a little further, I would add that this distorted relation in which the essence is actually inessential and the inessential is actually the essence is an issue that has long been addressed by philosophy; we might even say that this incommensurability between essence and non-essence is itself the 'essence' of philosophy. This was precisely the argument of Jacques Derrida, whose work I studied as a student.

In any case, the essence of my theory of the tourist in *Weak Links* is somewhat more concentrated in its inessential style. What I tried to do in that book was to link concepts such as the 'Other' and the 'nomad'—concepts that had often been articulated in a leftist, literary, political, and somewhat romantic language—with the commercial, utilitarian, and vulgar word 'tourism'. As far as I know, *Weak Links*, along with the present book, are the first to attempt such a thing. It is possible that my theorisation of the tourist is 'essentially' the same as existing theories of the Other. And yet saying that 'tourists are important' sounds quite a different note to saying that 'the Other is important'. I think that this difference in nuance is quite important today, and this book was written in order to provide a theoretical foundation to establish the significance of that difference.

We will encounter the names of many philosophers and thinkers in the pages that follow. There is a common characteristic among so-called 'liberal intellectuals' of the humanist tradition over the past seventy years or so, both those that I mention in this book and those I do not: they have all deployed various types of rhetoric and logic to tell us to 'respect the Other'. Of course, if we look closely, there are numerous differences as to how they understand 'the Other'. For example, the German Jürgen Habermas said that the concept of the Other proposed by the French Derrida is far too abstract, while the American Richard Rorty argued that such a debate itself obscures the true Other.[4]

4.   See J. Habermas, 'Beyond a Temporalized Philosophy of Origins: Jacques Derrida's Critique of Phonocentrism', in *The Philosophical Discourse of Modernity*, tr. T. McCarthy (Cambridge, MA: MIT Press, 1987). The original German book was published in 1985. For Rorty's attempt to overcome Habermas's critique of French philosophy, see R. Rorty, *Contingency, Irony, and Solidarity* (Cambridge:

Still, we can say that all of the influential thinkers agree on one point: that we should all regard others, and those outside of the community, with respect. This was likely an ethic that emerged as the lowest common denominator from a humanity that had produced a harrowing number of deaths through the consecutive wars brought on by the rise of nationalism in the first half of the twentieth century. We simply cannot continue to think only of our own country—until recently this has been the basic principle of human society (at least, the one that can be spoken about in public).

However, this situation is changing rapidly. People are no longer so receptive to the simple imperative to 'respect the Other'. I do not deal with concrete political situations very much in this book, but I would like readers to keep in mind that it was written between 2016 and 2017, a period during which England decided to leave the EU, Donald Trump rose to the US Presidency campaigning on 'America First', and Japan was engulfed in a storm of hate speech.[5] By 2017, people were beginning to cry out: 'We are tired of being with others'. They were beginning to say that they wanted to start by thinking of themselves and their own countries. The liberal message that the Other must be respected was no longer reaching anyone.

This is why I want to venture a theory of the *tourist* instead of a theory of the Other. From here on, I will seldom use the word 'Other', as it is weighed down by too much baggage. As soon as I invoke the Other, I will lose a significant number of readers as the arguments of this book become assimilated into a particular ideology.

Still, the issue that I am exploring here is ultimately that of the Other. And this is a strategy of sorts on my part. By using the word 'tourist' instead, I hope to speak to those who insist that they are tired of being with others—that

Cambridge University Press, 1989). Although Rorty focuses mainly on the clash between Habermas and Foucault, his argument also applies to Habermas's clash with Derrida. A very rough summary of the differences between the three thinkers' views on 'the Other' would be as follows: Habermas (modernist) argues that one can come to an understanding with the Other through reason, while Derrida (postmodernist) argues that the Other in fact refers to a being with which we cannot come to an understanding, and Rorty (pragmatist) argues that there is no sense in deepening our definition of the Other in the first place, and that we must apply different approaches in different situations. I return to Rorty in Chapter 4 below.

5.   [In 2016 Japan's National Diet introduced a Hate Speech Act to comply with the UN's Convention on the Elimination of Racial Discrimination, as a result of national soul-searching following several cases involving hate speech coming to court—trans.]

they just want to be with their friends, and are sick of being told to respect others—and ask them: But don't you enjoy being a tourist? I would like to use that question as an entry point to drag them through the back door into the liberal imperative to 'respect the Other' once again.

The aim of this book, then, is to imagine a new philosophy (of the Other) that begins with the tourist.

A cautionary note is in order here. I am definitely a tourist (I enjoy travelling with my family on long vacations), but I am not a scholar of tourism. Neither am I involved in the tourism industry (although, as I will discuss later, I run a company which conducts an annual tour of Chernobyl in Ukraine). I have not conducted any fieldwork study of tourists either. My writing on tourism in this book is a philosophical exploration, an exploration of the *concept* of tourism.

As such, although the title of this book is *Philosophy of the Tourist*, it has little to do with the actual tourism industry. I do not explore the conditions of that industry, nor do I analyse the psychology of tourists.

This is a book of philosophy. As you will notice if you read on, it is a book of philosophy that proposes some quite abstract arguments. Just as Derrida uses the word 'postal' without writing about post offices or stamps, and Karatani uses the word *kōtsu*, a common word for transportation, without writing about trains and highways,[6] here we will not discuss hotels and casinos even though we use the word 'tourism'. Such is the style of this book.

So if you were expecting a book that would be useful for business or Tourism Studies, now might be a good time to put it aside. The 'tourist' in this book is nothing more than a name given to a new concept for the purpose of pushing forward a certain philosophical tradition.

At the same time, this doesn't mean that I am uninterested in concrete, actual tourism.

In truth, I'd like to talk about that too. I'd like to talk passionately about the artificiality of Dubai, the popular appeal of Caribbean cruises, and the perfection of Disney World. It would be a lot of fun to talk about the attractiveness of the Sri Lankan resort designed by Geoffrey Bawa. (These are all places that I have travelled to in the past few years.) But the vocabulary of conventional philosophy and thought contains a huge barrier that one runs into simply by attempting

---

6.   [Translators of Karatani often translate *kōtsū* as 'intercourse'—trans.]

to speak about the experience of being a tourist. Readers, especially those accustomed to reading books in the humanities, may have felt a little uneasy with the notion that I would be talking about Dubai and Disneyland. While talking about resorts and theme parks is fine, isn't it a bit different from philosophy? It might be business, or sociology, or journalism, but we can't call it philosophy. This intuition itself is the barrier.

Before being able to talk concretely about tourism, we would need to investigate what this barrier is—and destroy it if necessary. Because of such limitations, this book remains in the realm of abstract deliberation on the concept of tourism.

In which case, maybe it is not so much a philosophy of tourism as a conceptual preparation that aims to make such a philosophy of tourism possible, or an introduction to a philosophy of tourism. Either way, philosophical thinking about tourism requires this kind of preparatory work.

2

Let us now begin our discussion.

Although I began this book with a series of complicated caveats, it is a straightforward fact that my suggestion that we need a philosophy of the tourist coincides with a tourism boom around the world.[7]

Japan has become quite impoverished over the past quarter century. The Japanese no longer spend money like they used to; the tourism boom in Japan is now long past. So, some Japanese readers may be scratching their heads when I say that there is a tourism boom. But even those readers have probably heard of the term 'explosive buying [*bakugai*]'. Between 2014 and 2016, it was the substantial consumption of Chinese tourists that rescued Japanese tourist sites. And it's not just the Chinese; overseas tourists visiting Japan increased markedly.

Figure 1 overleaf presents statistics from the Japan Tourism Agency. These figures show how the number of tourists from abroad increased while that of domestic tourists dwindled. In 2015, the number of tourists from abroad reached 19,740,000 and it was estimated that this would rise to 24 million in 2016. In 2010, the year before the Tōhoku earthquake, this figure stood at 8,610,000, so this

---

7. [As noted in the preface, this book was published in 2017 before the outbreak of the COVID-19 global pandemic. Japan closed its borders to tourists early in the pandemic and as of the time of this translation—early 2022—no plans have been announced to reopen its borders to tourists—trans.]

estimate represents an expected threefold increase over six years. The Japanese government has aggressively subsidised the tourism industry in an effort to drive these numbers up in the hope of reaching 40 million in the near future.

This is not a phenomenon unique to Japan. It is true that both private and public sectors in Japan have concentrated their efforts on welcoming tourists. The 'Cool Japan' national brand strategy and the Olympics have featured heavily in their campaigns, and the above statistics reflect the fruits of those efforts. But the increase in tourists, especially those crossing national boundaries, is a global trend.

Figure 2 shows the results of a study conducted by the UN World Tourism Organization. The figures represent inbound tourists, that is, tourists who cross national boundaries, for each country.

The graph shows us that the total number of inbound tourists has more than doubled over the past twenty years, increasing from 527,000,000 in 1995 to 1,184,000,000 in 2015. Moreover, it shows a constant increase, interrupted only by the 9/11 terrorist attacks and the 2008 financial crisis. These numbers represent only international tourists, so they do not include domestic tourism within the Chinese market, which likely also increased substantially. The growth trajectory would become even steeper if we included those figures. The Japanese tend to think of tourism as an older form of consumer activity associated with the years between the high growth era and the bubble economy of the second half of the twentieth century. But in reality it is one of the most promising growth industries of the twenty-first century, and this is one of the major factors behind the Japanese government's efforts to invest in tourism.

The world today is swarming with tourists as never before. If the twentieth century was the age of war, perhaps the twenty-first century will become the age of tourism.

If so, then philosophy should take up the issue of tourism. This rather obvious intuition constitutes the starting point of this project.

So what will the age of tourism be like? In order to answer this question, we would need to define tourism.

But this is not as easy as it sounds. The main Japanese textbook on Tourism Studies offers only the broad definition 'travel for pleasure', a definition so

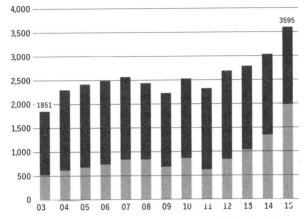

Figure 1. Outbound Japanese tourists (darker area above) and inbound foreign travellers to Japan (lighter area below), 2003–2015 (millions). Source: World Tourism Organization (UNWTO), <http://www.mlit.go.jp/kankocho/siryou/toukei/in_out.html>.

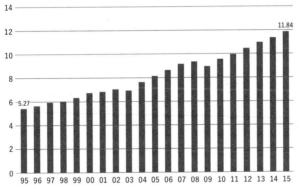

Figure 2. Foreign tourists visiting Japan, 1995–2016 (hundreds of miillions). Source: Japan National Tourism Organization (JNTO), <http://cf.cdn.unwto.org/sites/all/files/pdf/annual_report_2015_lr.pdf>, 15.

vague that it borders on the useless.[8] The aforementioned UN World Tourism Organization defines the visitor engaging in tourism as 'a traveller taking a trip to a main destination outside his/her usual environment, for less than a year, for any main purpose (business, leisure or other personal purpose) other than to be employed by a resident entity in the country or place visited'.[9] This definition is extremely clear, but so formal that it excludes any detailed understanding of its content. In the present age, many cross national borders in search of employment (immigrants), and the number of people entering other counties in flight from war or disaster (refugees) is also on the rise. The definition above was created to differentiate tourists from these other travellers, and while it may be useful for collecting statistics, it is less so for thinking about tourism.

Philosophers sometimes examine etymology when they run into a problem like this. Starting with the Japanese compound word 観光 [kankō], which combines the characters signifying 'to view' and 'light', it is known that usage of this word began in the Meiji era (1868–1912) as a translation of the English word 'tourism' and other European words sharing the same etymological root. This compound has its origins in the I Ching or Book of Changes, and originally meant 'observing the radiance of the country'. This etymology is therefore not too useful in thinking about the concept of tourism.

How about the etymology of the English word, then? Today 'tour' refers to travel. However, the dictionary tells us that this usage is actually relatively new.[10] 'Tour' is a word with roots in the Old French word 'tor [turn]', and it was not until the mid-seventeenth century that it came to refer to travel. British aristocrats of that era customarily embarked on a journey of self-cultivation around the European continent during their youth, especially the Italian penin-sula, in order to deepen their self-awareness as inheritors of European culture. This came to be known as the 'Grand Tour'.[11] It was not until the early nineteenth century that the 'ism' of 'tourism' emerged.

---

8.   N. Okamoto, Kankōgaku nyūmon (Tokyo: Yūhikaku Aruma, 2001), 2.

9.   S. Satake, 'Tsūrizumu to kankō no teigi', in Osaka Kankō Daigaku kiyō (Tokyo: Kaigaku jyusshūnen kinengō, 2010), <http://library.tourism.ac.jp/no.10SinichiSatake.pdf>. [The English definition above is drawn from the glossary of the UNWTO, <https://www.unwto.org/glossary-tourism-terms>—trans.]

10.   Definition from the Oxford English Dictionary.

11.   For more on the grand tour, see A. Okada, Gurando tsuā (Tokyo: Iwanami shinsho, 2010).

Tourism is a modern phenomenon, there is broad consensus among scholars on that point. Although I said above that Tourism Studies lacks a clear definition of its object, there are of course individual works that offer valuable insights. Among them is *The Tourist Gaze* by John Urry and Jonas Larsen, who state that 'acting as a tourist is one of the defining characteristics of being "modern"'.[12] People have been travelling for a long time, and have also embarked on pilgrimages and adventures. But tourism has only existed since the advent of modern society. Although it might make sense as a figure of speech to say that second-century Roman aristocrats 'toured' the Euphrates or that fifteenth-century Venetians 'toured' Palestine, it would not be entirely accurate.

What then is the characteristic of modern tourism that differentiates it from premodern travels that are not considered tourism?

Urry and Larsen argue that the distinguishing factor is the emergence of the masses,[13] a phenomenon inextricable from the Industrial Revolution. They argue that there were practices similar to modern tourism in Rome and Venice. The Roman Empire had an extensive travel infrastructure and periodically tours to Palestine were organised in Venice. But they catered only for the very wealthiest Romans and Venetians. In contrast, the tourism that emerged in modernity was not limited exclusively to a wealthy class (the figures cited above testify well enough to the mass appeal of tourism). This is the differentiating factor.

For tourism to become tourism, the way of life among the working class had to undergo dramatic changes into something that included leisure, through the transformation brought on by the Industrial Revolution which, in turn, gave the working class more consumer power. In other words, mass society and consumer society were necessary for tourism to flourish. While the terms 'mass society' and 'consumer society' are generally used in reference to the twentieth century, their initial buds can be found in the mid-nineteenth century, and tourism grew out of these same buds. As Urry and Larsen argue, '[o]ne effect of the economic, demographic and spatial transformation of nineteenth-century towns was to

---

12.   J. Urry and J. Larsen, *The Tourist Gaze 3.0* (London: Sage, 2011), 4.

13.   They write: 'The mass tourist gaze was initiated in the backstreets of the industrial towns and cities in the north of England. This chapter is devoted to examining why this industrial working-class came to think that going away for short periods to other places was an appropriate form of social activity. Why did the tourist gaze develop among this industrial working-class in the north of England? [...] The growth of such tourism represents a kind of "democratization" of travel'. Ibid., 31.

produce self-regulating working-class communities, communities relatively autonomous of either the old or new institutions of the wider society. Such communities were important in developing forms of working-class leisure.'[14] From these new forms of leisure there emerged a new industry, that is, tourism. In tracing these developments, Urry and Larsen look to the construction of seaside resorts in England starting in the 1840s. Swimming became popular among workers in the nineteenth century, leading to the rapid urbanisation of seaside villages such as Brighton. These were also a substitute for the spas that had developed in the eighteenth century and remained dominated by the upper class. At the time, submersion in water was still associated more with medical and therapeutic benefits than with pure pleasure.

In the twenty-first century tourism has become more diverse, taking on many forms aside from mass tourism—eco-tourism and study tours, for example. Although these developments have somewhat obscured the origins of tourism, mass tourism was its original form.

The mass character of tourism can also be read through the histories of certain individuals. One of the key figures in its development is Thomas Cook (travellers from Japan to Europe some time ago might remember the *Thomas Cook International Timetable* with its distinctive red cover).

The entrepreneur Thomas Cook's lifespan (1808–1892) overlaps with the Victorian Age. Cook was the first person to plan group tours (mass tourism) using the railroad, and is said to have invented most of the devices that are the basis of the tourism industry today, such as roundtrip tickets, hotel coupons, travellers' checks, and guidebooks. His group tour business began in 1841, offering services for a trip of just over ten miles, and developed rapidly through the late nineteenth century. It expanded into overseas travel in the 1850s and offered the first world tour in 1872. It wielded significant political influence, supporting England's occupation of Egypt in the 1880s, by which time Cook's son had taken over the reins of the business. By the 1890s it had developed into one of the largest and most iconic companies of the British Empire, with eighty-four branches and eighty-five agencies worldwide. The Thomas Cook Group, which still bears its founder's name, continues to be a leading travel agent today.

---

14.   Ibid., 34.

Cook's operations began in the northern regions of England, home to two of the central industries in the Industrial Revolution, coal and textiles. His clients were neither aristocrats nor intellectuals, but those denizens of the middle class and working class who were rapidly gaining consumer power. He was precisely the kind of entrepreneur that responded to the social changes indicated by the authors of The Tourist Gaze. In fact, one of Cook's early business operations involved offering inexpensive day trips to seaside beaches like those analysed by those authors.

Importantly, Cook's business operations were inextricable from his passion for enlightenment and social progress. He publicly announced that he never worked for profit alone.[15] For example, Cook offered tours to Scotland, which at the time was still on shaky political terms with England, and turned visits to the country-house estates of provincial aristocrats into a business. He was also a devout Christian and a passionate advocate for the temperance movement—indeed, the first services he ever offered were for travel to a temperance movement conference. We also cannot overlook the fact that Cook's business was closely related to the development of a new transportation technology: the railroad. His rise as a businessman overlaps precisely with the era during which railroads spread throughout England, and his tourism business expanded together with the railroad companies; as the railroads expanded, so too did the roster of tour destinations. This link between tourism, enlightenment, and technology reached its zenith at the Great Exhibition, the first World's Fair held in London in 1851, an important event symbolic of the development of mass society and industrialisation in the mid-nineteenth century. Thomas Cook transported 160,000 people to London for the Exhibition.

Cook truly believed that the masses could be enlightened and that society could be improved through tourism. The history of modern tourism begins with this belief.

For that reason, Cook's activities at times invited jeers from establishment aristocrats and intellectuals. One biography describes these clashes as follows: 'they [aristocrats] resisted opening their country houses [...] and they did not hesitate to speak about the uneducated boorishness of the groups led by Cook. [...] They expressed an almost physical aversion to the "masses" that loudly

---

15.   H. Hirukawa, Tomasu Kukku no shōzō [A Portrait of Thomas Cook] (Tokyo: Maruzen, 1998), 180.

barged in. [...] This was in fact Cook's goal.' In the 1860s, Cook succeeded in sending a group tour to Italy, the destination of those grand tours monopolised by aristocrats throughout the eighteenth century. This should serve as ample proof of Cook's aim to overturn established values and, as one might expect, he was harshly criticised for it by a high-ranking government official (of his own country) who viewed tourists as wicked people who would tarnish the reputation of the British with their terrible manners.[16] Indeed, the image of British tourists in Paris and Rome had become the object of ridicule in the conservative media—a state of affairs not so different from Japanese laughing at Chinese tourists a hundred and fifty years later.

To summarise the basic points so far, tourism is 'travel for pleasure' in which someone 'tak[es] a trip to a main destination outside his/her usual environment', 'for any main purpose (business, leisure or other personal purpose) other than to be employed by a resident entity in the country or place visited'. But more fundamentally, it is a phenomenon tied to the birth of mass society and con-sumer society. Tourism is an activity associated with the new lifestyle created by new industries and transportation technologies, and one that tends to clash with the old establishment.

Assuming that this tourism will continue to spread across the world, what is its significance for our civilisation? How will tourism change our world? These are the questions that come to mind in imagining a philosophy of tourism.

But we immediately run into obstacles when we begin to consider these matters. This is because scholarship has rarely considered such questions. And even where it has, it has invariably provided negative answers.

Allow me to explain by giving a broad overview of research on the topic. In Japan, the study of tourism is a practical field. As I noted earlier, the main textbook

---

16.   Ibid., 146–47, and 152 on. Near the passage cited above, Hirukawa writes that Cook's greatest enemy was the typical British 'snobbery' exemplified by this high-ranking official (153). In a book entitled *Otaku: Japan's Database Animals* (tr. J.E. Abel and S. Kōno, Minneapolis and London: University of Minnesota Press, 2009), I cited Alexandre Kojève in juxtaposing this word 'snobbery' with the 'animal'. I will examine the latter term more closely in Chapter 2 below, but Hirukawa's note is interesting in light of that juxtaposition. Tourists were animals. Tourism was an industry that supported animals. Snobbery was a way of life that clashed with animals. Hence snobbery became the greatest enemy of tourism.

on the subject defines tourism only as 'travel for pleasure'. That is probably
enough for practical studies; I do not mean to deny this. But it is clear that such
a definition will not assist us in our deliberations.[17]

How about outside of Tourism Studies? Or in the Anglophone world?

The best known position is given by Daniel Boorstin's argument in his 1962
book *The Image*, the third chapter of which is entitled 'From Traveler to Tourist'
and features his now famous criticism of tourists. *The Image* is known as a critique
of contemporary culture through the key concept of the 'pseudo-event' (false
events created by the mass media), and according to Boorstin, tourism too is
a prototypical 'pseudo-event': 'Both for the few adventuring travelers who still
exist and for the larger number of travelers-turned-tourists, voyaging becomes
a pseudo-event. [...] We look into a mirror instead of out a window, and we see
only ourselves.'[18] For Boorstin, travelling is good because it encounters the real,
and tourism is bad because it fails to encounter anything real. This criticism is
so simplistic that many have taken it to task since, including scholars of tourism
such as Dean MacCannell in his 1976 book *The Tourist*. However, without a doubt
Boorstin's juxtaposition of travel with tourism has served as the model for an
undervaluing of tourism that persists to this day.[19]

Tourism Studies does not explore the essence of tourism. And those outside
of Tourism Studies can only apprehend tourism as a superficial phenomenon.

---

17.   A new academic association called the Japan Society for Tourism Studies has recently been
founded in Japan. Its charter states: 'What is sought from the study of tourism in Japan is progress
in theoretical scholarly research. We cannot deny the fact that the study of tourism in Japan to
date has been weak in the realm of scholarly discussion and analysis owing to its practical character.'
Japan Society for Tourism Studies, 'Gakkai no kiroku [*Record of the Society*]', 2012, <https://jsts.sc/
archive>.

18.   D.J. Boorstin, *The Image: A Guide to Pseudo-Events in America* (New York: Harper Colophon,
1961), 117.

19.   Cf. D. MacCannell, *The Ethics of Sightseeing* (Oakland, CA: University of California Press, 2011),
Appendix. Although I will only briefly mention it here, the American historian Eric Leed's *The Mind of
the Traveler* also incorporates this juxtaposition between 'travel' and 'tourism' to the detriment of the
latter. What is particularly interesting in the context of the discussion in this book (particularly the
themes that emerge from Chapter 2 onward) is that Leed superimposes the birth of tourism onto
the death of Hegelianism and the concept of the 'Other': 'Perhaps this is only to say that our time
is the bitter end of the dialectic, and a time of sorrow for those who have defined their identities in
terms of outer and opposing worlds of others. [...] Hegel is dead, buried, and incorporated into the
contemporary consciousness, the modern mind of the traveler.' E.J. Leed, *The Mind of the Traveler:
From Gilgamesh to Global Tourism* (New York: Basic Books, 1991), 288. Tourism is born following the
death of Hegel. The flipside of this is that tourism cannot be understood without killing Hegel. We will
tackle this issue head-on in the following chapter.

No one, then, has explored the essence of tourism. This, in brief, was the broad situation in the history of Tourism Studies. But evidence of change began to emerge in the 1990s.

Urry and Larsen's *The Tourist Gaze* served as the impetus for this shift. First published as a book authored by Urry in 1990, a far more robust third edition was published with Larsen as co-author in 2011 (including responses to critics of the first edition, as well as new lines of inquiry taking into consideration the emergence of the internet). Inspired by Foucault, *The Tourist Gaze* frames the birth of tourism as the birth of 'the gaze', and incorporates the fruits of post-modernism and Cultural Studies, making it an influential text for later research.

But even this book begins with a note of caution:

> Tourism, holidaymaking and travel are more significant social phenomena than most commentators have considered. On the face of it there could not be a more trivial subject for a book. And indeed since social scientists have had plenty of difficulty in explaining weightier topics, such as work or politics, it might be thought that they would have great difficulties in accounting for more trivial phenomena such as holiday-making.[20]

This passage remains in the third edition. In other words, tourism was still seen as a 'trivial' subject for scholarship in 1990 (and even in 2011!), and scholars of tourism outside of more practical fields still felt the need to defend themselves against such a perspective.

What is even more tragic (or perhaps comical) is that Urry and Larsen themselves, the architects of a theoretical foundation for Tourism Studies, express a negative view of contemporary globalised tourism. In the final chapter of *The Tourist Gaze 3.0*, entitled 'Risks and Futures', having explored topics such as the relation between terrorism and tourism and the destruction of ecosystems, Urry and Larsen close with a harsh critique of the tourism industry in Dubai: 'The decline and fall of Dubai may thus be the start of a much more general decline in the significance of the tourist gaze. Will there still be relatively widespread and common "tourist gaze" operating away in 2050?'[21] Although the passage

---

20.   Urry and Larsen, *The Tourist Gaze 3.0*, 3.
21.   Ibid., 240.

is written in interrogatives, they are clearly rhetorical. The authors believe that even if the twenty-first century becomes an era of tourism, this tourism will necessarily take on an altered form.

Simplistic critiques of tourism like Boorstin's no longer pass muster today. There are, to be sure, more careful explorations of the various functions of tourism. Nevertheless, even scholars of tourism struggle to find anything positive about the dynamism of tourism's deep relationship to capitalism.

Why then is the world becoming increasingly covered with tourists? Is it because humans are stupid? Will humanity blithely drift into the end of history surrounded by tourism, shopping malls, and theme parks, protected in the womb of postmodernism?

I don't think so. And that is what leads me to imagine a philosophy of the tourist.

3

Tourism was born in the nineteenth century, and then blossomed in the twentieth century. The twenty-first century may become the age of tourism. It is high time for a philosophical exploration of the meaning of tourism. This is the original starting point of this book.

And yet once we embark upon this task, it becomes apparent that it is rather difficult to speak philosophically about tourism, especially in a positive manner. In order to construct a philosophy of the tourist, we must first destroy this obstacle. The deliberative process of this book begins with that task.

We will confront this obstacle head on, determining its identity in Chapter 2 and poking a hole in it in Chapter 3. The first part of the book comes to a close with Chapter 4 as we determine the contours of the future tourist that we can see on the other side of that hole. We will begin a different deliberative process in Part 2.

Chapters 2 and 3 are written in the rigid prose of philosophical scholarship, which is uncharacteristically 'serious' for me. I refer to thinkers including Voltaire, Kant, Schmitt, Kojève, Arendt, Nozick, and Negri, exploring their texts one by one. This format was unavoidable, given the fact that I call this a book of philosophy. At the same time, for readers unaccustomed to the roundabout rhetorical methods of philosophy, this format might obscure the overall flow and aim of the book as a whole.

Thus, before ending Chapter 1, it may be helpful to articulate straightforwardly and in a broader context what exactly I am trying to achieve with this philosophy of the tourist. There are three goals.

The first is to build a new framework for thinking about globalism.

Tourism is inextricable from globalism. Stated differently, it is inextricable from the act of crossing national borders. This is something that has not changed since Thomas Cook invented tourism. Tourism abroad was Cook's objective from the very beginning of his enterprise.

Debates over the pros and cons of tourism are therefore inextricable from debates over the pros and cons of globalism, a matter much discussed around the world at the time of writing. Given that this book was written in such a context, what position does it take with regard to globalism? As one might guess from its project of constructing a philosophy of the tourist, it certainly does not equate globalism with evil. Rather, it argues that the fact that deliberations in the humanities have hitherto only been able to grasp globalism as an evil reveals their limitations.

Allow me to explain. Since I will enter into more theoretical discussions in the next chapter, here I will provide a simple note about my understanding of the fact of globalism. Is globalism good or evil? What comes to my mind when I think about the issue is a video produced by the BBC in 2010 that is still available to view online. Figure 3 is a graphic based on a scene in that video. This scene shows a plot graph that measures average lifespan on the vertical axis and per capita income on the horizontal axis. The conditions of a variety of developed and developing countries are plotted on the graph, with the size of circles representing the population. In other words, countries with high income (wealthy) and long lifespans (healthy) are plotted in the upper right. The graph moves as time progresses.

Interested readers should view the actual video, but in short, what is striking is the fact that, as time progresses from the start of the twentieth century, the disparities between countries almost always shrink and all countries shift toward the upper right—that is, toward wealthier and healthier positions. Of course,

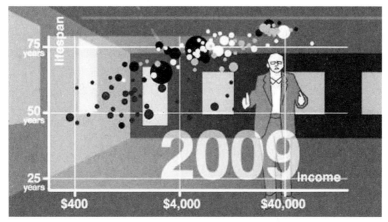

Figure 3. Graphic based on *Hans Rosling's 200 Countries, 200 Years, 4 Minutes: The Joy of Stats*, BBC, 2010.

there are exceptions, such as the two World Wars. There are also countries that fall towards the lower left, Japan immediately after the Second World War being a good example. But these are the exceptions. The shrinking of disparities in lifespan beginning in the 1970s is especially dramatic, almost breathtakingly so. Humanity is certainly becoming wealthier and healthier.

Of course, this is merely a simplified popular TV presentation. We might take issue with some of its assumptions and ask, for example, whether per capita income reflects true wealth. However, it is also true that an image of the world emerges from the video that is quite different from the one-sided criticism of globalism typically in circulation, especially in leftist media.

Globalism certainly strengthened the concentration of wealth. Wealth disparities also expanded within developed countries. At the same time, wealth disparities between counties are shrinking. How should we understand this? Should we take issue with this because people in our own country are being sacrificed for the wealth of those elsewhere? Or are we to affirm these trends because humanity as a whole is becoming wealthier?

Whether we take it positively or negatively, one thing we can say for sure is that the world is rapidly becoming more homogeneous. As the same BBC video points out (by pulling cities out of countries and plotting them on the chart as if they were countries themselves), today the economic disparities between countries are becoming smaller than the economic disparities between urban and rural areas within those countries. Using an expression from Thomas Friedman's bestseller from the 2000s, we might say that at the present time, the world is becoming flat.[22] We live in an age where we can all see the same ads, listen to the same music, buy the same clothes at shopping malls that carry the same brands no matter what country we go to, whether it is the United States, Europe, Asia, or what was previously the Soviet Union. The sudden increase in tourism is inextricable from this change. Exploring the philosophical meaning of the tourist is akin to exploring the philosophical meaning of this 'becoming flat'.

Writing in this way may invite the ire of some readers who might accuse me of affirming the violence of capital. However, as you will see if you read to the end of the book, I do not wish to present a simplistic affirmation of capitalism. I invite you to see from the discussion to follow how thinking about the tourist can become a stepping-stone for 'resistance'.

My second aim is a little more abstract than the first: I would like to offer a framework for people and society in terms of non-need (chance or contingency) rather than need (necessity).

People do not engage in tourism primarily because they *need* to. We can already see this in the aforementioned textbook definition ('travel for pleasure') and the statistical standard of the UN World Tourism Organization ('for any main purpose other than to be employed'). Travel undertaken out of need for livelihood or work is not tourism. Tourism involves going somewhere, on a whim, to a place that you have no need to go to, seeing things you do not need to see, and meeting people you do not need to meet. This is why tourism can only develop in wealthy, post-Industrial-Revolution countries where productive forces have increased and the middle class and working class, not just a segment of the wealthy class, can spend a certain amount of money on things that are unnecessary for subsistence.

---

22.   T.L. Friedman, *The World is Flat: A Brief History of the Twenty-first Century* (London: Picador, 2005). The entrepreneur Ken Suzuki, who I will mention in Chapter 2, argues that the world became 'smooth' rather than 'flat', meaning that although borders have disappeared, this does not mean that all aspects of the world have become homogeneous. Rather, whether we are discussing economics or politics, conditions are now such that we must understand relations as continuous. Although I agree with this understanding, I use the more well known expression 'flat' here. See K. Suzuki, *Nameraka na shakai to sono teki* [The Smooth Society and Its Enemies] (Tokyo: Keisō Shobō, 2013).

This non-necessity (contingency) of tourism is deeply related to the issue of urban culture. Urry and Larsen pay special attention to the fact that the birth of tourism is contemporaneous with the *flâneur*, a figure that famously drew the attention of the German critic Walter Benjamin.[23]

As Benjamin describes, in early-nineteenth-century Paris the glass-roofed shopping destinations known as *arcades* became popular. The arcade is an outdoor space, but one covered with a roof, and *flâneur* is the term for those who passively stroll through this space which is neither outdoors nor indoors, peering into the shop windows they pass by along the way. The flâneur did not exist before the emergence of the arcade. As the sociologist Mikio Wakabayashi has observed, the arcade is the distant origin of the shopping mall (although the architectural origin of the mall is generally held to lie in the United States of the 1950s), and the flâneur is the distant relative of the shoppers who stroll through malls today.[24] Now, the tourist is precisely that figure who enters into the landscape of their destination as a flâneur. The destination holds no vital necessities for the tourist. There is nothing they need to buy or anywhere they need to go. For the tourist, everything at their destination is a commodity and an exhibit that is the object of their neutral, passive—that is to say, contingent— gaze. The tourist gaze is none other than a gaze that views the entire world as an arcade or shopping mall.

Above I referred to the Great Exhibition in London in which Cook participated. This Exhibition actually has a deep relation to the arcade.

The 1851 Great Exhibition is known as an important event, symbolic of the fact that the centre of gravity of English society had shifted from the aristocracy to the middle classes, and that the locus of value had shifted from beauty to production. Although I will refrain from a detailed analysis here, a particularly popular attraction at the Fair was a massive glass building called the

---

23.   Urry and Larsen, *The Tourist Gaze 3.0*, 161–62. Though I was not able to address this in the main text, Urry and Larsen also point out that the birth of tourism was contemporaneous with the birth of photography (in fact, this is the main theme of their book). Photography, too, is an important theme for Benjamin. Tourism, photography, and the flâneur were all born in the same era and are internally connected. Indeed, tourism is a Benjaminian theme *par excellence*.

24.   M. Wakabayashi, 'Tayōsei, kinshitsusei, kyodaisei, tōkasei [Diversity, Homogeneity, Enormity, Transparency]', in M. Wakabayashi (ed.), *Mōruka suru toshi to shakai* [*The Mall-ization of Cities and Society*] (Tokyo: NTT Shuppan, 2013), 213 on.

Crystal Palace.[25] Constructed of iron beams and glass, with its interior exhibiting industrial products from around the world, as Benjamin once said, this massive building (whose interior layout was itself an imaginary world tour) was also a kind of ideal form of the arcade.[26] The Great Exhibition in London was built to be a haven for the tourist-flâneur.

Tourists *drift* through their destinations like flâneurs. And they take in the appearance of the world through a chance gaze. Like window-shopping consumers, they are drawn to things they encounter by chance, and visit with people they meet by chance. For that reason, sometimes they discover things that residents of their destination do not want them to see. In this book I was not able to explore issues of culture and representation, such as the relation between tourism and the city, visual sensation, or mechanical reproduction, but this 'drifting' (chance) character is crucial to grasping the essence of the tourist. Therein lies the limitation of the figure of the tourist, as well as its possibilities. I will take up this issue from another angle in Chapter 4, below.

Moreover, the image of the arcade and that of the Crystal Palace is also deeply related to nineteenth-century political thought. It is well known that the great imaginative socialist Charles Fourier used the arcade as a model for designing the building for his ideal community of 'phalanges'. In other words, Fourier saw the shopping mall as a utopia, or at least thought it could serve as a foundation for such a utopia. The emergence of the arcade, a new space for consumption where a new class of people supported by new industries and new technologies congregate, provided a new utopian image for contemporary socialists. In Chapter 7, in opening my exploration of a new tourist subjectivity, I refer to the way in which Dostoevsky targeted this image in his *Notes from the Underground*.

And finally, the third aim is even more abstract than the second: I would like to develop a new intellectual discourse beyond the limits of 'seriousness' and 'frivolity'.[27]

---

25.   On the cultural significance of the Crystal Palace, see M. Matsumura, *Suishōkyū monogatari* [*Story of the Crystal Palace*] (Tokyo: Chikuma Gakugei Bunko, 2000).

26.   W. Benjamin, *The Arcades Project*, tr. H. Eiland and K. McLaughlin (Cambridge, MA: Belknap Press, 1999), e.g. 158.

27.   Differentiating what should 'seriously' be discussed and what should not is an extremely political process, and it is possible that some issues cannot be discussed without resetting this 'seriousness' itself. I have written about this difficulty in discussing the debate between Norihiro Katō and Tetsuya

Allow me to explain. Scholars only think about serious matters. That is what it means to be a scholar in the first place. But tourism is a frivolous activity. Thus, it is difficult for scholars to 'seriously' take it up as an object of research. Beginning in the next chapter, I will undertake an intellectual historical study of the difficulties of a philosophy of the tourist, but this, in layman's terms, is the basic difficulty. It's also related to the contorted relation between the essential and inessential that I referred to earlier.

It is my understanding that scholars in the humanities are now facing a moment where they must go beyond the dichotomy of 'serious' and 'frivolous'.

The example of terrorism will help to explain my point. It seems obvious that terrorism is a perfect example of something that we should consider 'seriously'. It also seems that it is the polar opposite of the 'frivolity' of tourism. But are they really that far removed from one another?

It seems to me that they are surprisingly close. In the final chapter of *The Tourist Gaze 3.0*, Urry and Larsen warn that the development of the tourism industry concurrently means a rise in the risk of terrorism, noting that '[t]ourist places can [...] attract tourists and terrorists'.[28] Terrorists disguise themselves as tourists and at times attack tourist destinations. In the mid-2010s, one of the greatest challenges concerning terrorism is that terrorists themselves are becoming tourist-like.

Here I am thinking about the new types of terrorists known as 'homegrown terrorists' and 'lone wolves' in developed countries who plot to commit crimes on their own, outside of any organisation. They have no ideology. Their targets aren't necessarily politicians or financiers. Instead they attack the general public, those that live happily in the twenty-first-century world itself. They target the descendants of the working classes who paid an entrance fee to the London Great Exhibition and strolled around the arcades of Paris without paying a thing.

These incidents happen frequently. Around the time I was writing this, in November 2015, there was a mass shooting at a concert venue and restaurant in Paris. In June 2016 a nightclub in Florida was attacked, while in the same month there was an explosion in an airport lobby in Istanbul, followed by an incident in

---

Takahashi concerning Japan's responsibility in the postwar period. See H. Azuma (ed.), *Genron 3* (Tokyo: Genron, 2016), 22. [For Takahashi's critique of Katō, see Chapter 6 of R. Calichman (ed.), *Contemporary Japanese Thought* (New York: Columbia University Press, 2005)—trans.]

28.   Urry and Larsen, *The Tourist Gaze 3.0*, 221. Italics removed.

Nice that July where a terrorist drove a truck into a crowd of tourists returning from a fireworks festival. In December of that year there was a similar incident where a truck rammed into a Christmas market in Berlin, and on New Year's Day there was another mass shooting at a nightclub in Istanbul. None of these cases featured any kind of political event, nor were there VIPs among the targets. Neither are these war-torn areas. If the suspect is identified (although in most cases they themselves are killed during the incident), authorities search for motives and dig up connections to Jihadism (radical Islam) or anti-immigration sentiments, but in reality the motive is typically nothing more than the fact that they were passionate consumers of internet videos.

The more we 'seriously' consider their motives, the more we find ourselves running around in circles. Since their actions involve actually killing people and even killing themselves, they are absolutely 'serious'. There is nothing more 'serious' than the death of a person. But when we trace their motives, we run into a shallowness that is hard to take 'seriously'. Readers who have viewed the execution videos uploaded by Islamic State (IS), edited like Hollywood movies, are probably familiar with this feeling of being suspended between 'seriousness' and 'frivolity'. And today terrorists are being born around the world, inspired by these videos.

At stake here is the fact that political thinking fundamentally cannot process these acts that can be called neither 'serious' nor 'frivolous'. This is because, as we will discuss further in Chapter 2 through a reading of the works of Carl Schmitt, the essence of the political lies in differentiating between friend (people of our nation) and enemy (terrorist) by means of a public standard. In the context of our discussion here, civil means 'serious'. Schmitt's point was that politics is fundamentally a 'serious' act.

But the terrorists we are discussing here do not have a 'serious', in other words a civil and political, goal. It will be extremely difficult for governments to uncover these plots no matter how much they ramp up intelligence activities. Since they do not have 'serious' goals to begin with, it is impossible to grasp their intentions. The attempt to 'seriously' understand the motives of such terrorists itself serves only to further obscure their activities. Thus, we need to set aside the boundaries between 'serious' and 'frivolous' if we are to articulate the principle behind their behaviour. We need to fundamentally doubt the premise that behind every political act there is a political will and decision. Moreover, we need to fundamentally rethink the relation between the touristic and the political. This set of issues has informed the writing of this book on the philosophy of the tourist.

To get a little ahead of myself for a moment, the 'Underground Man' from Dostoevsky's aforementioned novel probably constitutes a more accurate representation than Schmitt's 'enemy' of these terrorists who seem to be neither serious nor frivolous. The twenty-first-century terrorist is more Dostoevskian than Schmittian—that is to say, more literary than political.

For while politics stipulates the demarcation between 'serious' and 'frivolous', literature can explore the very line that separates them. In that sense, this book also highlights the need to reincorporate literary thinking into political thought. The tourist is our name for that which is neither political nor literary, but both at the same time.

Supplement: On Derivative Works

1

The sections that follow are supplementary. Most readers will find it more useful to move straight onto Chapter 2.

But given the character of this book, I assume there are some readers who are familiar with my previous work. And I would wager that some of them are puzzled by the fact that I should start writing about tourists in the 2010s, or are somewhat sceptical about the relationship between this book and my other activities in recent years.

For that reason, I decided to add a couple of supplementary explanations that link the conception of this book with my past work. Those uninterested in my work in general may skip this supplementary section entirely. Several passages later in the book will refer to my discussion here, but you can understand the overall argument without going into the details.

Let's speed through these supplementary points as quickly as possible. The first has to do with the theoretical background.

It is true that I only recently began to use the term 'tourist'. But I have been thinking about 'frivolous beings' such as tourists for quite a long time. In fact, I once used the term 'derivative works' to refer to a similar phenomenon.

Allow me to explain. Some readers of a certain generation still think of me as a critic familiar with otaku subculture (despite the fact that I am quite unfamiliar with recent trends, since I have not watched much anime or played many games over the past few years). This association has its roots in a book that was published in 2001 entitled *The Animalizing Postmodern* [*Dōbutsuka suru posutomodan*], published in English translation in 2009 as *Otaku: Japan's Database Animals*.

In this book I focused on the production of 'derivative works' by otaku. 'Derivative works' are creative activities in which otaku take certain characters and settings from a particular manga and anime, and create a different story separate from the 'original' for their own pleasure. For example, some lovers of *shōnen* manga (mostly women) create pornographic works by depicting their favourite characters performing sexual acts (many such works exist). Although derivative works are nothing more than amateur publications, and their circulation is limited to booths at fairs and speciality bookstores, they are so influential that we cannot talk about otaku culture from a certain period on without considering their significance. Interested readers may consult *Otaku: Japan's Database Animals*—although the examples are dated, essentially things have not changed much.

In the context of this book, we could say that these derivative works have a 'touristic' character. This is because they are a 'frivolous' activity that takes a specific work, removes a portion of it, and creates a completely different reading from what the author intended, without assuming any responsibility in relation to that author. This is structurally similar to tourism, where tourists arrive at a destination, enjoy it in a way completely different from how the locals intended, and return home having enjoyed a somewhat one-sided satisfaction.

What the two have in common is their *irresponsibility*. Tourists do not assume any responsibility toward locals, just as derivative works do not assume any responsibility toward the author. Tourists visit a destination and return home having consumed only what they want to consume, completely unrelated to the realities and hardships of the locals. Creators of derivative works, too, consume only the parts they like and leave the rest, without any regard for the original author's intentions and hard work.

As such, just as tourists are hated by the residents of tourist destinations, derivative works are sometimes hated by authors and fans of the original works. Although derivative works have become far more familiar today, and negative incidents involving original authors have become infrequent, I have heard at least one author expressing anger about their works being reread as pornography. This anger is similar to that expressed by local residents toward tourists. To take this one step further, there is also a similarity in the ironic process by which tourists and derivative works are initially reviled, but later become accepted, and eventually locals and authors alike even become economically reliant upon them. No matter how much one might hate derivative works and want to deny them, the market for original works can no longer economically function without them, just as many local economies are reliant upon tourists.

An interesting slang term, 'original-chū', has emerged online.[1] It refers to people who claim that the world view of the original is the most important element in adapting a work. Adapting a work into a live action drama or film, even more so an animation, is to some degree a derivative creation, that is to say, it always involves some changes in relation to the original. For example, sometimes the personality of the characters is different or the ending might be changed. When that happens, original-chū tend to complain that it is 'not like the original'.

This resistance from original-chū is similar in structure to the discomfort felt by locals regarding the images cherished by tourists. For example, let's say that some foreigners spend some time in Japan and return home having focusing exclusively on geisha, Fujiyama, and Akihabara, snapping ample photos along the way. From our perspective here in Japan, their photos are nothing more than a 'derivative Japan' that takes away from a diverse reality only the images the holidaymaker prefers. We laugh at them and say that they 'know nothing about Japan'. This is precisely the attitude of an original-chū. Just as locals reject tourists, original-chū reject derivative works. At the same time, just as the local economy does not function without tourists, the joy of original-chū cannot exist without derivative works (spin-off dramatisations and live action films), because they are precisely what allow the authors of the original to earn a living. In reality, even if they are 'not like the original', live action dramatisations and films broaden the readership and market for the original work.

In *Otaku*, I paid close attention to this reality, arguing that, in thinking about contemporary society and culture, we cannot ignore 'otaku who create derivative works'. This is what led me to the concept of 'database consumption'.[2] Keeping in mind this parallel between the relation of the original artist to the

---

1. [The term applies to media consumption the popular slang term 'chūni-byō', literally 'middle-two syndrome' or 'eighth-grader syndrome' if translated into American educational terms. It is often used to poke fun at delusions of self-importance on the part of both consumers of popular media and characters in media creations. 'Original-chū', then, refers to fans of media creations obsessed with canonical narratives—trans.]

2. [See Azuma, *Otaku: Japan's Database Animals*, and the short glossary entry at <https://jmpc-utokyo.com/keyword/database-consumption/>—trans.]

derivative work and the relation of locals to tourists, it should be easy to connect my theory of subculture with the theory of the tourist developed in this book.

Allow me to extend this discussion a little further. In 2007 I published a sequel to *Otaku* entitled *The Birth of Gamic Realism* [*Gēmu-teki riarizumu no tanjō*].[3]

While *Otaku* focused on social analysis, in the sequel I focused on the analysis of works. I believe that from a certain point onward (roughly 1995), otaku content began to more or less internalise the assumed emergence of derivative works from its very inception. Once the market for derivative works had reached a certain level, authors started to consider the possibility of their works being re-read through derivative works, and found that it made commercial sense to design the characters with this in mind. As a result, the narratives and characters circulating in the market begin to exhibit some very specific tendencies: character settings and design incorporated more *moé*[4] so that they could easily be used for derivative works, and narratives became fragmented into 'databased' parts from the very beginning, making the work more prone to spinoffs. In one genre of games, the anticipation of derivative works (re-readings) led to the popularity of a time-loop motif in which the same incident repeats itself again and again.

We might say that this is a common phenomenon in postmodern society, not limited to otaku culture. In contemporary society, there are hardly any instances where a work is evaluated and circulated based solely on its own value. All works are consumed in a manner that incorporates the 'gaze of the other', that is, considerations such as 'How do other consumers evaluate this work?' or 'If I valued this work, how would other consumers consider my evaluation?'

Theoretically speaking, this is the same phenomenon that John Maynard Keynes talked about with the example of the beauty contest, and which René Girard referred to as 'triangular desire' and social systems theory calls 'double contingency'. We can easily understand its essence without using these terms if we simply think of the 'Like' button on Facebook. People don't necessarily just

---

3.   H. Azuma, *Gēmuteki riarizumu no tanjō* [*The Birth of Gamic Realism*] (Tokyo: Kōdansha gendai shinsho, 2007)—trans.

4.   [Passionate feelings of devotion among readers, players, or viewers, aroused by particular alluring characteristics of characters, settings, or even objects—see Azuma, *Otaku: Japan's Database Animals*, and the short glossary entry at <https://jmpc-utokyo.com/keyword/moe/>—trans.]

naively push the 'Like' button on posts they like. Rather, they actively push the 'Like' button on posts the 'Liking' of which might boost their reputation among others. For this reason, when we examine the network as a whole, people tend to avoid polarising topics such as politics, while 'harmless' content such as photos of cats and food gather many 'Likes'. Today we live in a world where a mechanism of 'desiring the desire of others' wields an unprecedented amount of clout.

In *The Birth of Gamic Realism* I argued that this condition calls for a new critical perspective. The commonsense order of things in which there could be an evaluation of a work prior to its environment of consumption is no longer tenable. Since the work itself weaves in the environment of consumption at its very inception, the analyst must bear this in mind when examining it. We need a 'meta-perspective' to analyse a 'meta-work'. The creation of original works with derivative works in mind is a perfect example of such a condition.

In the realm of philosophy, Jean Baudrillard famously argued in the 1970s for the need for such a 'metacritique' (theory of simulacra). However, he did not provide a concrete method. While the suggestion of postmodernists such as Baudrillard was eventually systematised in the Anglophone world, giving birth to Cultural Studies, in Japan, the corresponding analysis of 'meta-perspective' came not from criticism or contemporary thought, but from outside of it. Eiji Otsuka's 1989 work *Theory of Narrative Consumption* and Shinji Miyadai's 1993 work *Deconstructing the Myth of Subculture* are two trailblazing examples.[5] My work builds upon these foundations.

Whether it be novels, film, or manga, lovers of creative works tend to focus on interpreting the work itself, setting aside the analysis of its environment for consumption as a 'sociological' affair. However, in today's world, the gesture of cutting the inside of the work (the work itself) off from its outside (the environment of consumption) and carrying out a 'pure' critique and study of the former is no longer tenable. Neither criticism nor study can exist if we do not understand the dynamism by which the exterior is woven into the interior. In *The Birth of Gamic Realism* I called the focus on this dynamism an 'environmental-analytical' interpretation.[6]

---

5.   E. Otsuka, *Teihon Monogatari Shōhi-Ron* [*Theory of Narrative Consumption*] (Tokyo: Kadokawa, 1989); S. Miyadai, *Sabukaruchō Shinwa Kaitai* [*Deconstructing the Myth of Subculture*] (1993) (Tokyo: Kadokawa Bunko, 2001).

6.   Azuma, *Gēmuteki riarizumu no tanjō*, 154ff.

To translate this into the vocabulary of the present work, in research on com-munities and regional studies today, an analysis by way of the tourist gaze is crucial from the very beginning. At times, such studies have been approached via a progression that begins with an 'idyllic land' which is then discovered by tourists, and gradually loses its idyllic character in exchange for financial profit. But is this really accurate? In today's consumer environment, derivative works do not proceed from an original work that precedes them. The author of orig-inal works anticipates the emergence of derivative works from the beginning. That being the case, could we not say that the order of there first being 'idyllic' locals, followed afterward by tourists, is also reversed? Are places everywhere not already internalising the tourist gaze into their community and cityscape design? In other words, is not the world itself becoming a theme park? This is an issue that requires serious consideration.

The word 'postmodern' became favoured in French thought during a certain period. Because French thought briefly became popular in Japan in a peculiar way (New Academism) and very quickly faded after that fad had passed, there are some in Japan who are turned off by this word, snicker at the mere use of the term, and deem arguments that incorporate it to be obsolete.

But most of these people tend not to be particularly knowledgeable about the debates concerning the postmodern, and are only reacting to its status as a fad. Although the word will appear from time to time in this book, I hope the reader will consider it to be nothing more than a cultural historical concept that refers to the era after the 1970s. It is a fact that the shape of contemporary society changed greatly during that era (I discuss this in Chapter 6), and the period that follows must be differentiated using some word or other. The French called it postmodern, and that's all there is to it. There are many scholars who, although they use a similar concept, employ a different expression. For example, sociologists outside of the Francophone world such as Ulrich Beck and Anthony Giddens use the term 'reflexive modernization' to refer to a very similar condition.[7] 'Reflexive' refers to the meta-attitude whereby, in deciding on how to act, people are always conscious of how others will perceive their actions; in other words, it refers to 'desiring the desire of others'. We live in a society where 'desiring

7.   U. Beck, A. Giddens, and S. Lash, *Reflexive Modernization: Politics, Tradition, and Aesthetics in the Modern Social Order* (Stanford, CA: Stanford University Press, 1994).

the desire of others' is becoming ubiquitous. In that sense, the postmodern has not ended at all. In fact, we live in an era in which this condition is deepening.

In the postmodern or reflexive modern world of the twenty-first century, nobody can make original works without weaving in the possibility of derivative works, and nobody can build communities without weaving in the tourist gaze. The theory of the tourist proposed in this book is based on this condition.

The creators of derivative works are tourists in the world of creative content. Flipping this over, we might say that tourists are *creators of derivative works in reality*.

2

My second supplementary remark has to do with the relationship between this book and my activities over the past few years. In 2013 I published a book entitled *Fukushima Nuclear Power Plant No. 1 Tourism Plan*.[8] It is a book that suggests that, since Fukushima has gained international 'fame' as a result of the 2011 nuclear disaster, we could perhaps take advantage of this situation by making the affected area a 'mecca' for dark tourism, on the model of Hiroshima and Auschwitz.

'Dark tourism' is a concept introduced by a British scholar of tourism about fifteen years ago, and refers to new initiatives to make 'tragic sites' of wars and disasters into tourist destinations.[9] It became a subject of discussion in Japan after the 2011 earthquake, and there is now even a magazine devoted to the topic. In 2013, the same year as the Fukushima book, I had already published a *Chernobyl Dark Tourism Guide*.[10] There I discussed the fact that tourism was developing in Chernobyl, Ukraine, which in 1986, like Fukushima, suffered a nuclear accident, and provided reference information on the rebuilding in affected areas. *Fukushima Nuclear Power Plant No. 1 Tourism Plan* was published as a follow-up to the Chernobyl guide.

As some readers may be aware, publication of this book met with a significant backlash. The title 'Tourism Plan' was heavily criticised. Moreover, there was

---

8.   H. Azuma (ed.), *Fukushima Daiichi Genpatsu Kankōchika Keikaku* [*Fukushima Nuclear Power Plant No. 1 Tourism Plan*] (Tokyo: Genron, 2013), published as the second part of *Shisō Chizu β 4*.

9.   See J. Lennon and M. Foley, *Dark Tourism: The Attraction of Death and Disaster* (London: Continuum, 2nd Edition 2000).

10.   H. Azuma (ed.), *Cherunobuiri daaku tsūrizumu gaido* [*Chernobyl Dark Tourism Guide*] (Tokyo: Genron, 2013). This book was published as the first part of the journal *Shisō Chizu β 4*.

also significant criticism of the idea that I, a Tokyoite with no connection to Fukushima, would publish a book like this. What was particularly decisive was the fact that the sociologist and Fukushima native Hiroshi Kainuma changed his attitude and turned into a critic after the book was published, despite having participated in the project and contributed to the volume. Because of the strong criticism directed against me at the time, some readers may still have an impression of Hiroki Azuma as the person who profited off the affected areas with his 'tourism plan'.

Since the book you are now reading contains the word 'tourist' in its title, I cannot silently pass over the existence of this other book published only four years prior to it, whose title also includes the word 'tourism'. Therefore I would like to provide a simple supplementary explanation about the relationship between this book and that plan.

As you can see from the above, most of the criticism against *Fukushima Nuclear Power Plant No. 1 Tourism Plan* had nothing to do with the content of the book. Much of it was a misunderstanding stemming from the title of the book or slander based on nefarious associations imagined by critics; in other words, it did not merit a response. To combat this type of slander, all that was necessary was to show that we did not receive a penny of public funds or assistance from the electrical companies in our research and publication of the plan.

It may then seem that the only response I need to make is to the criticism by Kainuma. However, since Kainuma barely referred to the content of the tourism plan, the point of disagreement is hard to pinpoint. Still, if we review the public letters we exchanged in the newspaper *Mainichi Shimbun* in 2015 and the book *Introduction to Fukushima Studies* that Kainuma published around the same time, a point of contention emerges.[11]

In essence, Kaimuma argues that we must stop amplifying the image that equates Fukushima with the nuclear disaster. There are many aspects to Fukushima aside from the nuclear disaster. The victims were residents of Fukushima before the disaster, and many people continue to live there, without any relation

---

11.   H. Azuma and H. Kainuma. 'Datsu "Fukushima-ron"', *Mainichi Shimbun* (web version), 2015, <http://mainichi.jp/correspondence>; H. Kainuma, *Hajimete no Fukushima-gaku* [*Introduction to Fukushima Studies*] (Tokyo: Iisuto Puresu, 2015).

to the nuclear disaster. If we are to get involved in the affected areas, should we not first consider their everyday lived experience? Does not the mention of 'tourism' trample upon their feelings?

I can very well understand this argument. It is natural that the people of Fukushima would see the equation of Fukushima with nuclear disaster as a type of violence. Fukushima is a large prefecture; for example, although both are in Fukushima, the Hamadōri region is nearly a hundred kilometres away from the Aizu region. Many regions in Fukushima Prefecture were barely affected by the nuclear accident, even though they are also part of Fukushima. Kainuma believes that people must first be educated about this fact, and I am in agreement with him on this point.

The question in my mind is this: Was it not because such an education is limited that this idea of the tourist destination became necessary? In other words, why would Kainuma criticise me when my suggestion was always precisely to pursue this type of education?

Let's think of this from the perspective of tourism as a derivative work of reality. In the words of this book, the fact that Fukushima is painted over with the image of the nuclear accident is akin to the image of Fukushima being rewritten as a 'derivative work' with the image of the disaster at its centre, quite apart from its original reality (the original work). The derivative creation of Fukushima, that is 'FUKUSHIMAization', is sometimes referred to as an act of reputational damage.[12] Six years on from the disaster, more people are aware of this reputational damage, and domestically the number of people who associate Fukushima with the nuclear accident is declining. But outside of Japan things are not so simple. Although many in Japan remember 'Fukushima prior to the nuclear accident' (original work), this is not the case outside of Japan. There are many outside of Japan who had never heard of Fukushima before the nuclear accident (the derivative work).

It is easy to imagine the implications of this when we think of what the word 'Chernobyl' signifies to us today. Chernobyl, too, had a long history prior to its

---

12.   [In the Japanese original text, the words I render here as 'Fukushima' and 'FUKUSHIMA' are written in *kanji* and *katakana* respectively. Inscribing place names that are typically written in *kanji* in *katakana* renders them both alien and conceptual, a device commonly used in discussing, for example, Hiroshima and Nagasaki in relation to the legacy of the atomic bombs. Thus, writing 'FUKUSHIMA' in *katakana* immediately associates it with other sites of nuclear catastrophe—trans.]

accident. It also possesses a rich natural landscape. Chernobyl today has greatly recovered from the standpoint of nuclear contamination. More than thirty years have passed since the accident. But how many of us can imagine 'Chernobyl in reality'? I would venture to guess that most do not get beyond images such as 'Infertile Land Contaminated by Radiation' or 'Cursed Land Where Deformed Children are Born'. That being the case, it is reasonable to assume that something similar will happen with Fukushima. Internationally, FUKUSHIMA, like Chernobyl, has become synonymous with nuclear accidents and radioactive contamination. It is a fact that Fukushima has become this kind of a special place-name, no matter how much the victims dislike it.

What kind of attitude should we take up in facing this reality, then? Of course, I too believe that we should resist the fiction of FUKUSHIMA. I attempted something similar with Chernobyl. Since the publication of *Chernobyl Dark Tourism Guide,* my company has led annual tours of areas to which access was formerly barred, including inside of the nuclear power plant. The tours have been held four times to date, with over a hundred participants. The participants frequently comment that Chernobyl was far more 'ordinary' than they had imagined.[13] In other words, there was a daily life there that was unrelated to the derivative work 'Infertile Land Contaminated by Radiation'. In that sense, I can say that my activities share in Kainuma's call not to whitewash Fukushima with the image of the nuclear accident.

But I think a more complex strategy needs to be devised regarding Fukushima. This is why I published *Fukushima Nuclear Power Plant No. 1 Tourism Plan.*

Today, only a derivative work regarding Fukushima (FUKUSHIMA) circulates in the world. This reality must be unbearable for those who hold dear the original (the Fukushima that we have known). Kainuma appeals to this unbearable feeling. We might say that he is taking the position of the *original-chū*. We must respect these feelings. At the same time, it is also true that we cannot remove derivative works from this postmodern world. Illusions regarding FUKUSHIMA will continue to be reproduced. Could we not then take advantage of this circulation of derivative works/FUKUSHIMA and guide at least a few people

---

13.   K. Ōyama, 'Cherunobuiri wa 'futsū' datta [Chernobyl was "ordinary"]', *Daily Portal Z,* 2016, <https://portal.nifty.com/kiji/161118198099_1.htm>.

to the original/true Fukushima? In other words, rather than just disseminating information about Fukushima that is irrelevant to the nuclear accident, could we not envision a programme in which we disseminate the attractiveness of Fukushima by taking advantage of people's desire to see the accident site or the ruins? This was my proposal.

In order to have people respect the original, we must first confront the derivative works. This might be difficult to understand at first. If you only focus on the logic of it, it might even seem like mere wordplay. But it is a rather simple idea in concrete terms. For example, the reason why I am able to take people to Chernobyl is because they once believed the derivative works regarding Chernobyl ('Infertile Land Contaminated by Radiation'). Who would visit an agricultural region in the outskirts of Ukraine without the nuclear accident and the notion that Chernobyl is 'extraordinary'? In a similar way, Kainuma was able to publish *Introduction to Fukushima Studies* only because of that accident. Why would there be any need to construct a discipline of Fukushima Studies in the first place without the nuclear accident and the circulation of the monstrous FUKUSI IIMA? Sometimes there is no route to the original without derivative works.[14]

I noted earlier that participants in the Chernobyl tour all observe how 'ordinary' Chernobyl is. But this does not signal a disappointment; rather it signals the expansion of their interest. Chernobyl has a long history with records dating back to the twelfth century, and was once a city where half of the population was Jewish. The Polesia region, where Chernobyl is located, is a marshy area with a beautiful forest, while Pripyat, the now abandoned city near the power plant, was a cutting-edge planned city designed to be a utopia representative of the Soviet Union.

Most Japanese do not know about this. Nor are they interested (just as most foreigners have no interest in the actual Fukushima). And they harbour immature illusions about Chernobyl. But we shouldn't just unilaterally cast blame on them for that. Instead, we should use it to our advantage. For even if their reasons

---

14.   In discussing the tourist later in this book I will borrow as a key Jacques Derrida's concept of 'misdelivery'. Another famous concept in Derridean philosophy, *écriture* (writing), is placed in opposition to *parole* (speech), referring in general to a *relation in which the essence of things is essentially dependent upon the inessential*, taking as the example the warped interdependence in which writing derives from speech, and yet speech cannot stand on its own without writing. What I identify in 'Fukushima' and 'FUKUSHIMA' is this same warped relationship. Here, developing a tourist destination means developing *écriture*.

are based on immature illusions, once tour participants arrive in Chernobyl and understand how 'ordinary' it is, they naturally become interested in background information unrelated to the accident, because they come to consider the meaning of the accident within that richer context. This is the intended effect of my annual Chernobyl tour. I, too, was full of immature illusions when I first visited Chernobyl. Once people visit a place they had assumed to be 'extraordinary' and discover that it is actually ordinary, they can accept the gravity of the 'fate' that something 'extraordinary' occurred there by chance. This movement back and forth between ordinary and extraordinary is the key to dark tourism.

Is this simply a pie-in-the-sky ideal? Maybe, and maybe not. Either way, this was the level at which I sought to propose the necessity of a tourist destination in *Fukushima Nuclear Power Plant No. 1 Tourism Plan*. I saw it as a challenge that was both practical and theoretical, and philosophical as well as political.

But unfortunately it was not understood in this way and the conversation went nowhere. Reconstruction is a rough business, bound up with questions of profit. It is a world in which writers' careers are entangled. I am neither smart nor tough enough to deal with that kind of business, and as a result my suggestion for a tourist destination imploded without finding its proper readership. I am still painfully aware of the part played by my own shortcomings in this outcome.

But in any case, my suggestion was not related to the authorities or to capital. My suggestion regarding Fukushima was motivated purely by intellectual and ethical interests. This book contains the core of these interests. In that regard, this book is also a sequel to *Fukushima Nuclear Power Plant No. 1 Tourism Plan*.

2. Politics and Its Outside

1

In 2011 I published a book entitled *General Will 2.0*.[1] At its core is a rereading of the work of Jean-Jacques Rousseau.

Rousseau is widely known as the philosopher who laid the foundations of modern democracy. He is also known as the father of Romantic literature. In History of Philosophy it is commonly thought that there is a considerable gap between how humanity is conceived by Rousseau the philosopher, author of *Discourse on the Origin and Basis of Inequality Among Men* and *The Social Contract* and Rousseau the writer of literature who penned *Julie; or, The New Heloise, Emile, or On Education,* and the *Confessions.*

As a political philosopher, Rousseau is known as someone who took the near-totalitarian position that the individual should always follow the will of the community. The passage in *The Social Contract* that states that 'the general will is always in the right' (Part 2, Chapter 3) is well known. This passage has been interpreted as contending that the will of the community should supersede that of the individual; in fact, it is positively evaluated by conservative thinkers such as Carl Schmitt, whose work I will refer to below.[2] On the other hand, the literary Rousseau is remembered as a thoroughgoing individualist who valued solitude, scorned insincerity, and condemned the imposition of communal norms. Many see *Julie; or, The New Heloise* as the origin of the expression of love as a free outpouring of emotion unencumbered by custom or class, and *Confessions* shocked many readers with its raw descriptions of private sexual experiences and feelings of jealousy. Far from being a totalitarian, this Rousseau is viewed as a passionate existentialist comparable to Dostoevsky. Totalitarianism or

---

1.   H. Azuma, *General Will 2.0: Rousseau, Freud, Google*, tr. J. Person and N. Matsuyama (New York: Vertical, 2014).

2.   C. Schmitt, *Dictatorship*, tr. M. Hoelzl and G. Ward (Cambridge: Polity, 2014). See discussion beginning on page 100.

individualism? Society or existence? In other words, politics or literature? Ernst Cassirer called this split the 'question of Jean-Jacques Rousseau'.[3]

But is there really a split here? Are society and individual existence opposed to one another? I had my doubts about this, and in *General Will 2.0* I tried to show that a reinterpretation of *The Social Contract*, especially its famous concept of 'general will', could serve as the key to solving the puzzle of the supposed split. I invite you to read the book itself for the details, but my suggestion was that Rousseau's idea of 'general will' was developed precisely for those who by their nature don't like people—in more contemporary language, those who are socially withdrawn or suffer from communication disorders—as a paradoxical apparatus that serves to *generate a society without the mediation of sociality*.

Rousseau himself disliked people. He disliked society too. As he wrote in *Discourse on the Arts and Sciences* and *Discourse on the Origin and Basis of Inequality Among Men*, he believed that it was natural for humans to live separately in family units without building a society and thus without developing arts or sciences. And yet in spite of this fact, humans did build societies. Why? Rousseau needed to answer this question precisely because he did not believe that humans actually want to build societies. In other words, he needed to think of a mechanism through which 'literary' individualists come together to generate a totalitarian society. The concept of 'general will' was born of this need. Read from this perspective, we can understand *Julie; or, The New Heloise*, *Confessions*, and *The Social Contract* together without any contradiction arising.

I wrote *General Will 2.0* as I worked through these issues, but this led to the following question. There is no split in Rousseau; this is my interpretation. Why, then, have readers perceived a split in his work?

The main topic of the present work, the 'philosophy of the tourist', is deeply related to this question. On the face of it, this book is not an extension of *General Will 2.0*. It is neither an interpretation of Rousseau nor a treatment of social contract theory. But the 'tourist' that it focuses on is taken precisely as an example of a being who creates a society without having any intention of doing so. In that sense, this book is also a sequel to *General Will 2.0*.

---

3.   E. Cassirer, *The Question of Jean-Jacques Rousseau*, tr. P. Gay (Indianapolis: Indiana University Press, 1963).

People dislike people, and do not want to create societies, but nevertheless people do create societies. In other words, everyone has a public side to their character, even though no one wants to. It seems to me that it is decisively important to understand this paradox, and that it should lie at the foundation of all humanities disciplines.

In fact, as readers who have some knowledge of the history of social thought will know, this kind of understanding was widely shared among philosophers of Rousseau's era. For example, Adam Smith's *The Theory of Moral Sentiments*, published around the same time as *The Social Contract*, deals with the mechanism by which private and solitary individuals come to form a society, much like the work of Rousseau. Smith's exploration remains relevant today. Curiously, however, this paradox did not remain central to the deliberations of social thought in the humanities of the nineteenth century onward. Instead, an unnatural dogma came to take centre stage—one that holds that humans have always liked humans, and created societies or states through which to come together and elevate themselves—and that those who do not do so are unworthy of being called 'human'. I will discuss this issue, related to so-called Hegelianism and nationalism, in more detail below. For now, let us just say that from the nineteenth century onward, humans came to be simplistically divided between those who possess sociality and those who do not, those who possess a public character and those who do not, public people and private people, politicians and writers of literature, or, to use the words of the previous chapter, the 'serious' and the 'frivolous'. It is when we read it through the lens of this later division that Rousseau's thought appears to be split. And, as noted in Chapter 1, we lose sight of both tourists and terrorists when we try to grasp them through such a division. Twenty-first-century thought must render them visible again.

People dislike people. People don't want to create societies. Nevertheless, people create societies. Why?

This book seeks to find the clue to solving this puzzle not in a rereading of the general will, but in the tourist. At the same time, it raises an objection to the nineteenth-century political thinking that opposes a serious public sphere to a frivolous private realm.

In Chapter 2 we will establish a foundation for the philosophy of the tourist. But I would first like to consider two other philosophers, near-contemporaries of Rousseau, in order to build two stepping stones for thinking about the tourist. To clarify how we need to change thought itself in order to venture forth from those stepping stones, I will then move forward in time and consider three philosophers of the twentieth century.

As we shall see, the project of thinking about the tourist is closely related to the task of updating the modern normative view of the human and expressing a new view of the human, society, and politics.

2

The first philosopher we shall consider is Voltaire, a contemporary and critic of Rousseau.

Although I say that he was a critic of Rousseau, this is not saying much—Rousseau had a huge number of critics. He was working in mid-eighteenth-century Paris when the Enlightenment was at its height and socialite and salon culture was flourishing. But, as noted above, Rousseau was a misanthrope with poor social skills and something of a persecution complex. For that reason he had disagreements with many of his contemporaries, not only Voltaire. The most famous of these were with Denis Diderot and David Hume; the former is meticulously documented by Rousseau himself in his *Confessions*, while the latter has been published as an anthology of letters.[4] Both disagreements are so laughably stupid that those expecting a philosophical discussion can't help but groan, but on the other hand, we could also say that this stupidity served as a motivating force for Rousseau as he explored the aforementioned paradox (Why do people create societies even though they dislike other people?). With that said, this is a long story in itself, so I will leave it at that for now. In any case, Voltaire was a contemporary of Rousseau.

---

4.   On the dispute between Rousseau and Diderot, see the ninth volume of Rousseau's *Confessions*, which he wrote in his final years. On the dispute between Rousseau and Hume, Masakazu Yamazaki and Magoichi Kushida's *Akuma to uragirimono* [*Demons and Traitors*] (Tokyo: Chikuma Gakugei Bunko, 2014) is informative.[For discussion of the dispute in English, see D. Edmonds and J. Eidinow. *Rousseau's Dog: Two Great Thinkers at War in the Age of Enlightenment* (New York: Harper Perennial, 2006)—trans.]. Although, as I noted in the main text, the contents of the disputes themselves are so frivolous that one can only shake one's head, these 'debates' are essential reading along with the *Discourse on the Origin and Basis of Inequality Among Men* and *The Social Contract* in order to appreciate Rousseau's personality (and not just in the negative sense), and so as to understand what kind of people actually created the foundation of modern democracy.

Among Voltaire's works is a strange novel entitled *Candide*. It was published in 1759 (three years before *The Social Contract* and the same year as Smith's *The Theory of Moral Sentiments*), and is written in a very peculiar format which today we might describe as a slapstick adventure story interspersed with philosophical insights. Although it may be unfamiliar to readers today, it is highly regarded in literary history and inspired many later writers. For example, Dostoevsky, who I discuss below in Chapter 7, is known to have repeatedly said that he wished to write a Russian *Candide* as he planned what would become celebrated works such as *Crime and Punishment* and *The Brothers Karamazov*. In other words, these works are in some sense descendants of *Candide*. The Russian literary theorist Mikhail Bakhtin views it as a representative masterpiece of the Menippean genre (dialogical, carnivalesque literature), to which Socrates and Dostoevsky also belong.[5] Here it makes little sense to differentiate the latter two by saying that Socrates is a philosopher while Dostoevsky is a novelist. Socrates, Voltaire, and Dostoevsky were all masters of critiquing and relativising all forms of value through the power of laughter and satire.

What, then, did Voltaire critique? *Candide* is highly regarded in the history of philosophy as well. In that context, the importance of the work is held to lie in its criticism of Leibniz's 'optimism'.

Optimism is the thesis that 'this world is the best of all possible worlds, and that, although evil exists, it is purposive and can be affirmed as a means to realising a universal totality. In essence, this means that, since the world as a whole is running smoothly,'[6] there is no need to pay attention to any bad aspects that may lie in the details. The origin of this argument can be traced back to Plato and Aristotle (although we can see it at work everywhere in our daily lives), but the person who most systematically developed the philosophy of optimism was Leibniz, a philosopher who lived in the seventeenth and eighteenth centuries. In his *Theodicy* he argues that 'if there were not the best (*optimum*) among all possible worlds, God would not have produced any'.[7] God exists. God is the highest good. Thus, if God is the creator of this world, this world must also be

---

5. M. Bakhtin. *Problems of Dostoevsky's Poetics*, tr. E. Emerson (Minneapolis: University of Minnesota Press, 1984). See discussion beginning on page 109.
6. Entry for 'optimism' in W. Hiromatsu (ed.) *Iwanami tetsugaku, shisō jiten* [*Encyclopaedia of Philosophy and Ideology*] (Tokyo: Iwanami Shoten, 1998).
7. G.W. Leibniz, *Theodicy* (Chicago: Open Court, 1985), 128.

the highest good, the best possible world. The reason that it seems to us that there is evil in this world is because human knowledge is limited. Even if there are wars, disasters, accidents, even if people suffer, we can be sure that all of this is leading toward the highest good and salvation through God's immeasurable care. Such is Leibniz's world view.

Questions about the existence of God or whether the world is good might sound like issues unique to Christianity. Indeed, this is also a theology, and the decision as to whether one accepts or denies Leibniz's optimism is directly related to one's decision as to whether one accepts or denies the existence of God. Readers of Dostoevsky will likely recall a famous passage in *The Brothers Karamazov* in which one of the characters in the novel (Ivan) passionately declares to another (Alyosha) that, even if Christ were to return in the future and salvation were to become a reality, he cannot accept the existence of God so long as there is suffering and sadness here and now.[8] It is precisely Leibniz's optimism that is targeted here, and in this sense, Dostoevsky's dream of writing a Russian *Candide* is realised in this passage.

Yet, as we can see from the fact that its origins lie in Greek philosophy, optimism is a line of argument that can very well function outside of the Christian context. Even prior to the issue of the existence of God, the essence of optimism lies in one's attitude towards *this reality* that we are living right here and now, and its singularity and one-time nature. Advocates of optimism believe that there are no 'mistakes' in this reality, and that there is meaning in all suffering and sadness, while critics of optimism believe that there are people who are senselessly oppressed and killed. What is important here is this opposition.

It makes little sense to ask which side is 'correct'. We can only live in one reality in the first place, and since no one can compare this reality with another, how could we even decide whether there are 'mistakes' in it or not? So long as we are trapped in one reality, we cannot fundamentally evaluate the correctness of optimism.

---

8.   The end of Chapter 3 in part 2, book 5 'Pro and Contra'. There Ivan says: 'in the end, in the universal finale, at the moment universal harmony is achieved, something so magnificent will take place that it will satisfy every human heart, allay all indignation, pay for all human crimes, for all the blood shed by men, and enable everyone not only to forgive everything but also to justify everything that has happened to men. Well, that day may come; all this may come to pass—but I personally do not accept this world. I refuse to accept it! Even if I see the parallel lines meet myself, I'll look at them and say they have met, but I still won't accept it. That's the way I am, Alyosha, this is where I stand.' F. Dostoevsky, *The Brothers Karamazov*, tr. A.R. MacAndrew (New York: Bantam Books, 1981), 283.

This isn't a matter that can be solved by debate, then, but is rather a decision that must be deferred to individual faith and belief. No doubt there are those who think this world is afflicted by 'mistakes', and those who don't. We can only say that they are both correct. What is more important is the influence of this belief on people's actions. Leibniz thought that people would be happier if they believed that there were no 'mistakes', while Voltaire thought that people could not live with sincerity if they didn't believe that there were, and wrote *Candide* precisely to demonstrate this sincerity.

Now, the discussion thus far might lead some to believe that this question of optimism is ultimately a matter of faith, and therefore has nothing to do with knowledge and learning, especially that of the natural sciences. But that is a misunderstanding. Hiromitsu Yoshikawa has pointed out the optimistic character of the evolutionary theory that emerged in the mid-nineteenth century, referring to none other than Voltaire.[9] Darwin's *On the Origin of Species* was published exactly a century after *Candide*. Darwin's theory of evolution is typically understood as a completely scientific world view which did away with all (literary?) ideologies that assume that history has a particular goal or end, thus leaving no room for faith to intervene. But according to Yoshikawa, we can find optimism in Darwinism too. This is because evolutionary theory is primarily founded upon a very Leibnizian belief that *this* form of organism that we see now, in other words *this* reality, must be the 'best' form of organism to have been generated as a result of a long process. Organisms sometimes have flaws, if we are only paying attention to form. But the axiom of the evolutionary biologist is that even these 'mistakes' are remnants of a particular purpose in that long process—that is, they are not, in essence, mistakes. According to Yoshikawa, this issue continues to be debated in evolutionary biology. He argues that the essence of Stephen Jay Gould's critique of Richard Dawkins (the critique of selectionism) has not been properly understood by the academy, and that it lies precisely in a critique of his optimism.

Are there 'mistakes' in this world? Such a fundamental question cannot be decided through a discovery in the empirical sciences. But for that very reason, decisions on the matter can deeply infiltrate sciences that are supposed to be

9.   H. Yoshikawa, *Rifujin na shinka* (Tokyo: Asahi Shuppankai, 2014). See discussion starting on page 205.

supported only by evidence. On this point, Voltaire's critique of Leibniz continues to be important as it was two and a half centuries ago.

Voltaire claimed in *Candide* that the world is filled with 'mistakes'. But how exactly did he make this claim? What is interesting in the context of the present book is that, in doing so, he incorporated the motif of travel.

As noted in Chapter 1, during Voltaire's lifetime the Grand Tour was popular among upper-class British youth. This practice spread to the continent, and Rousseau, too, travelled to Italy in his youth. Given its popularity, novels written in that era sometimes featured travelling protagonists. However, the travels they depicted were not necessarily limited to the Grand Tour as such, that is to say a trip to Italy. For example, in Rousseau's *New Heloise*, the broken-hearted protagonist travels the world on a ship. Such devices reflected the fact that, during the age of Enlightenment, European humanistic knowledge was undergoing tremendous changes partly as a result of all sorts of 'marvels' brought from outside Europe. As Foucault showed in *The Order of Things*, intellectuals of that era were faced with the need to bring all disciplines of knowledge together in order to reconstruct from the ground up their definitions of the human, reason, and civilisation. Voltaire utilises this fictional device as well, and the eponymous protagonist of *Candide* travels to all sorts of places.

Candide is a simple and honest young man living in provincial Westphalia. He has been instructed by a tutor called Pangloss who taught him Leibnizian philosophy (optimism), and has fallen in love with Cunégonde, the beautiful daughter of a baron. Exiled from his home after he is caught with her, Candide sets out on his travels and enters into a rollercoaster series of life-changing events that include being pulled into a war in Bulgaria (said to be a reference to the war in Prussia), experiencing a major earthquake in Lisbon (an actual event in 1755), and acquiring precious gems in South America. His movements, beginning in Northern Europe then moving to the Ottoman Empire via the Mediterranean Sea, followed by a journey to Argentina and Paraguay in the New World, are global in their scope. Along the way Candide experiences indescribable suffering, witnesses the tragedy of wars and disasters, and comes to doubt the philosophy of optimism. Then in Holland he unexpectedly encounters Pangloss, who has also been exiled from his homeland and is now a beggar suffering from syphilis, and later in Lisbon rediscovers his former beloved, who has now lost her beauty and has become the servant of a Jewish merchant. Pangloss and Cunégonde have obviously suffered an unfair fate. And yet Pangloss still does not accept that the theory of optimism is mistaken, or admit that there are any 'mistakes' in the world. Even at the conclusion of the book when he is languishing in poverty, he continues to loudly affirm that there are no 'mistakes' in the world, maintaining that '[i]ndividual misfortunes contribute to the general good with the result that the more individual misfortunes there are, the more all is well'.[10] This absurdity is the key to *Candide*.

Voltaire needed to have his protagonist travel the globe in order to show his readers that there are indeed 'mistakes' in the world. It is here, I suggest, that we find the first philosophy to effectively make use of the motif of tourism.

Sociologically speaking, tourism was born in the nineteenth century. There was no tourism yet in Voltaire's time. In fact, if we read *Candide* literally, we see that the protagonist's travels are not at all those of a tourist, but more like those of a conscript, a refugee, or a victim of human trafficking.

I would nonetheless still call the travels depicted in *Candide* 'tourism' because they involve thoroughly hypothetical travel or, more precisely, fictive travel for the purposes of a *thought experiment* or to expand the powers of the imagination. As noted above, the modern tourism industry came into being alongside Cook's advocacy for social reform. The goal of tourism was the enlightenment of the tourist, that is, the expansion of their imagination. The travels presented in *Candide* share this goal. True, *Candide* features names of places from around the globe, but Voltaire himself never left Europe, and *Candide* is not an example of travel literature or a research report, but a satirical novel. Most of the stories in it are baseless tall tales which make full use of the stereotypes common to 'derivative works' as defined in the 'Supplement' above. There are cannibals in the Russian Sea of Azov, while in the depths of South America there lies a glittering utopia where even a pebble lying on the road is made of pure gold. In other words, in terms of the supplement preceding this chapter, everything that is depicted here is 'FUKUSHIMA' rather than 'Fukushima'. But Voltaire probably

---

10.   Voltaire, *Candide and Other Stories*, tr. R. Pearson (Oxford: Oxford World's Classics, 2006), 11–12. While this line does not appear at the end of the book, since Pangloss's philosophy remains constant to the end, it suffices to introduce his philosophy.

figured that this was all he needed for his purposes. Perhaps he even thought it was better this way. In critiquing the theory of optimism, instead of confronting his readers with real individual tragedies (since such examples are all too easily incorporated into the theory of optimism), by employing the thought experiment of world travel he tried to confront them with the general possibility that *there might always be* tragic realities in the world that go beyond our imagination. I see in this attempt a problematic similar to that of contemporary dark tourism. I will return to this issue of how tourism is inextricable from the expansion of imagination rather than the expansion of knowledge at the end of part 1.[11]

Another example of world travel as thought experiment is offered by Denis Diderot. This famous philosopher, a contemporary of Rousseau and Voltaire, is most remembered for his role as editor of the *Encyclopédie,* but in 1772 he wrote a short piece entitled *Supplement to Bougainville's 'Voyage'.*

Supplement to Bougainville's 'Voyage' was inspired by a firsthand account of world travel written by an actual adventurer named Louis Antoine de Bougainville. It is a strange book made up of two parts featuring two fictive dialogues written by Diderot, one between a European priest and a Tahitian, and another between two readers about that first dialogue. Reading such a text from the eighteenth century is a painful reminder of how rigid philosophy has become today, but in any case, there Diderot has the uncivilised 'Tahitian' (this in itself is Diderot's fantasy) say the following:

> Well, whether they burn or don't burn (for the crime of incest) in your country
> is nothing to me. But you cannot condemn the morals of Europe for not being
> those of Tahiti, nor our morals for not being those of Europe. You need a more
> dependable rule of judgment than that. And what shall it be?[12]

Europeans prohibit incest, but 'Tahitians' do not. As Voltaire did with *Candide,* through the device of hypothetical world travel Diderot is attempting to attain

11.   Although I will not explore this any further here, in considering the relationship between tourism and imagination, it is quite suggestive that Thomas Cook achieved the first circumnavigation of the globe in 1872, at precisely the same time that a French daily newspaper was serialising Jules Verne's *Around the World in Eighty Days.* See Hirukawa, *Tōmasu Kukku no shōzō,* 185.

12.   D. Diderot, 'Supplement to Bougainville's "Voyage"', in *Rameau's Nephew and Other Works,* tr. J. Barzun and R.H. Brown (Indianapolis: Hackett, 2001), 208.

a universal perspective on the essence of humanity and society unconstrained by European common sense. This might remind us of Claude Lévi-Strauss, the leading cultural anthropologist of the twentieth century. Lévi-Strauss was precisely the person who chopped down common-sense views of humanity and society held by Europeans (Eurocentrism) through detailed fieldwork and bold theories, and his anthropological perspective was a direct descendant of the thought experiments of the age of Rousseau and Voltaire.[13]

3

The second philosopher, Immanuel Kant, needs no introduction. He is the most influential philosopher of the past three centuries. Hegel emerged under the influence of Kant, Nietzsche and Heidegger's philosophies developed as rebellions against Kant, and analytical philosophy emerged as a return to Kant—he is a towering figure.

In 1795, about forty years after Voltaire's *Candide*, during the French Revolution, Kant published a small book entitled *Perpetual Peace: A Philosophical Sketch*. It is a short text written near the end of Kant's life (he died in 1804 at the age of seventy-nine) and did not garner much attention for a long time. However, in the twentieth century, the age in which the League of Nations and the United Nations were formed, it began to receive far more attention, and today it is one of Kant's most widely read books.

As its title suggests, the book is a consideration of the conditions for the realisation of 'perpetual peace'. While peace is typically nothing more than a momentary 'truce', Kant's book discusses the creation of a more powerful system for maintaining peace. Kant believed that the world would consist of many sovereign nation states for the foreseeable future, and that a unifying

---

13.   See C. Lévi-Strauss, 'Jean-Jacques Rousseau, Founder of the Sciences of Man', in T. O'Hagan (ed.), *Jean-Jacques Rousseau* (Aldershot: Ashgate, 2007). In this text, in reference to Rousseau, Lévi-Strauss declares that 'it can be affirmed that—a whole century before it made its appearance— he had conceived, willed, and announced this very ethnology which did not yet exist, placing it first among the already established natural and human sciences' (26). Although I was ultimately unable to discuss this in the present work, in this passage Lévi-Strauss also discusses the importance of 'compassion'. I will refer to Rousseau's 'compassion' together with Rorty's philosophy (pragmatism) below, in Chapter 4. The argument I make there is that the philosophy of the tourist is a philosophy of misdelivery, and thus a philosophy of compassion, but if we consider that Lévi-Strauss said that anthropology is the scientific discipline of compassion, perhaps what I am trying to say in this book can ultimately be summed up in the suggestion that *tourists must be small-scale anthropologists*.

government above them would not be created (an assumption that is still valid today, over two hundred years later). Given these conditions, Kant asked what could be done to maintain peace in a situation in which multiple sovereignties exist side by side.

Allow me to summarise Kant's argument. He wrote that there are three conditions for the construction of perpetual peace.

The first is that 'the civil constitution of every state should be republican' (first definitive article). This is a rule concerning the domestic system of each country. Countries that participate in the system of perpetual peace cannot be despotic. They must be countries in which the people govern themselves rather than blindly obeying a king.

Some readers may interpret this as meaning that they must be democratic societies. For example, the use of the word 'democracy' as a kind of useful catchphrase has become widespread in Japan. But Kant does not say this. Republicanism (a concept regarding the method of governance) and democracy (a concept about the number of people who govern) are fundamentally different concepts, and it is entirely possible for a society to be republican (with a separation between the executive and legislative powers) without being democratic (governed by the people). Kant placed importance on republicanism, but actually denied democracy.[14]

The second condition is that 'the law of nations shall be founded on a federation of free states' (second definitive article). This is a rule concerning the international system. First each state becomes a republic where the liberties of its people are guaranteed, and *following this* the states agree to build a higher-level federation. Kant believed that this order was extremely important. Later in the twentieth century this became the theoretical basis of the League of Nations and the United Nations (as well as the EU, now facing a crisis of disintegration). What is important here is the fact that, as noted earlier, Kant denies the possibility

---

14.   For example: 'Therefore, we can say: the smaller the personnel of the government (the smaller the number of rulers), the greater is their representation and the more nearly the constitution approaches to the possibility of republicanism; thus the constitution may be expected by gradual reform finally to raise itself to republicanism. For these reasons it is more difficult for an aristocracy than for a monarchy to achieve the one completely juridical constitution, and it is impossible for a democracy to do so except by revolution.' I. Kant, 'Perpetual Peace', in *Kant On History*, ed. L.W. Beck (Indianapolis: Bobbs-Merrill, 2001), 96–97.

of a world republic (unified government). He believed that it would be difficult to realise a world republic because sovereign states do not desire the creation of such a thing, nor is there any reason they should desire it in future. Thus he attempted to imagine instead a 'negative surrogate' that would realise peace *as its de facto outcome*, even if none of the sovereign states wished for peace.[15] This is the system of perpetual peace that he proposes—and it is an idea that has much in common with the philosophy of Rousseau, who searched for the reason why people build societies even though they dislike them.

Kant's final condition is that 'the law of world citizenship shall be limited to conditions of universal hospitality'. This one is difficult to explain, since the previous two had to do with the form of a state, while this one ventures into the domain of the form of societies and individuals.

What are the 'conditions of universal hospitality'? Kant says something quite intriguing here. He states that 'it is not a question of philanthropy but of right'. What Kant is exploring with this question of hospitality is a matter of right, not the issue of whether the people of each nation ought to love or respect one another. But what kind of guarantees constitute 'conditions of universal hospitality'? Here Kant writes about the 'right of temporary sojourn'. People from countries participating in the federated states must be able to freely visit the other countries. Kant argues that perpetual peace cannot exist without the guarantee of this 'right to associate, which all men have [...] by virtue of their common possession of the surface of the earth'.[16] According to Kant—and this is a crucial point—this means only a right to visit, and *does not* by any means include the right to be welcomed and treated as a guest. He writes definitively that 'it extends the right of hospitality, i.e., the privilege of foreign arrivals, no further than to conditions of the possibility of seeking to communicate with the prior inhabitants'.[17] Foreigners may 'seek' to communicate, but their success in doing so is not guaranteed, nor need it be guaranteed.

This rule of universal hospitality is concise but mysterious, and for that reason has been the subject of much attention from researchers. It seems as if Kant is saying that, even with the first two rules in place, perpetual peace cannot

---

15.   Ibid., 102.
16.   Ibid., 103.
17.   Ibid.

be established only by means of conditions applying to states—by each state becoming a republic and then working together to build a federation of states. It cannot be attained until a 'world citizens' law' is established allowing individuals to move freely beyond their national boundaries.

Now, what is interesting for our purposes here is that today, this rule of universal hospitality reads very much like a rule regarding the *right to tourism*.

There was no tourist industry yet in Kant's time. The masses who would become tourists did not exist yet either. So it would be bad scholarship to conclude that Kant is writing about tourists here. What he probably had in mind were diplomats and trade merchants. He probably had no way of imagining the mass tourism familiar to us today.

But I think we can more clearly grasp the essence of Kant's vision if we reread him in that way.

As noted above, the third condition is clearly different in character to the first and second. Although we could say that according to the internal logic of *Perpetual Peace* the first condition corresponds to domestic law, the second to international law, and the third to world citizen law, in comparison to domestic and international law this world citizen law itself is completely hypothetical and different in character. But then this suggests that the third condition was developed in order to compensate for certain shortcomings of conditions one and two. If so, what are those shortcomings, and how does it compensate for them?

The road to perpetual peace outlined by conditions one and two is actually quite linear. It is a narrative of maturity in which mature citizens associate and create a mature state (republic), and then mature states associate and create a mature international order (federation of states). But such a narrative is sure to invite dissent from voices arguing that immature (non-republican) states can, and indeed must, be excluded from the international order. Indeed, this is happening in reality today. Politicians on the world stage have used the expression 'rogue states' since the end of the Cold War, especially following the 9/11 terrorist attacks on the United States in 2001. This category refers precisely to states that must be excluded from the international order, and has been used to refer to countries including Iraq, Iran, and North Korea. Islamic State (IS), the subject of much discussion at the time of writing, is also understood through this schema.

But one cannot so easily eliminate something simply by accusing it of being 'rogue'. Far from it, rogues continue to increase in number. What serves as the oppositional axis of international politics today is no longer oppositions between states (although of course these still exist), but more so the opposition between the international order and its 'other'—that is, rogues. The rogue state refuses entry into the international order, it refuses maturity as a state. But the international order refuses that refusal itself. As a result, rogue states become angrier. We are currently in the midst of this kind of vicious cycle. Such an opposition represents a different phase from the opposition between national interests studied by traditional political science. It is related instead to the 'frivolity' of the terrorist discussed in Chapter 1.

The international community today has struggled to confront this vicious cycle. Not only have they not been able to confront it in reality, there is no theory that might serve as the basis for such a confrontation. As noted at the beginning of this book, late-twentieth-century humanities thinking actively called for tolerance of the Other. But the rise of rogue states extinguishes the persuasiveness of that ethic. Although tolerance towards others is indeed important, established theories of the Other cannot answer to the understandable rejoinder that it is difficult to become tolerant if the other is not mature to a certain degree. Indeed, one of the foremost liberals in the United States, the political philosopher John Rawls, agreed that 'outlaw states' should be eliminated,[18] and the German sociologist Jürgen Habermas, a leading leftist intellectual, supported the 1999 bombing of Kosovo. Both met with widespread disappointment on the part of readers, but presumably it was difficult for them to express any other attitude as responsible intellectuals representing developed nations. And the cause of this difficulty is to be found two centuries earlier, in the first and second conditions set out in *Perpetual Peace*. For so long as we maintain the historical view that mature citizens build mature states and mature states build a mature international order, the international community must eliminate those that are immature. And like a spectre, this eliminated immaturity returns again and again.

---

18.   J. Rawls, *The Law of Peoples* (Cambridge, MA: Harvard University Press, 2001). See discussion beginning on page 80. Although the first edition of this book was published in 1999, it is based on a lecture delivered in 1993.

But the third condition contains a hint as to how we might escape this dilemma, and suggests a different way of considering the path towards perpetual peace. My suggestion is that this hint becomes even clearer when we go beyond Kant's original intentions and read the right of hospitality, which he probably defined with only a small number of government officials such as diplomats in mind, as a right to tourism on the scale of the masses.

In my view, what Kant tried to show by adding this third condition was that *aside from* the path toward perpetual peace in which state and law are the motivating forces, there is another path toward perpetual peace in which individuals, 'interest', and 'the spirit of commerce' serve as the motivating force—and that perpetual peace cannot be realised unless these two paths come together.

In the 'First Supplement' to *Perpetual Peace*, Kant writes:

> Just as nature wisely separates nations, which the will of every state, sanctioned by the principles of international law, would gladly unite by artifice or force, nations which could not have secured themselves against violence and war by means of the law of world citizenship unite because of mutual interest. The spirit of commerce, which is incompatible with war, sooner or later gains the upper hand in every state. As the power of money is perhaps the most dependable of all the powers (means) included under the state power, states see themselves forced, without any moral urge, to promote honorable peace and by mediation to prevent war wherever it threatens to break out.[19]

Here Kant clearly states that state and law are an insufficient foundation for perpetual peace. People divided into multiple nations and subject to the wills of multiple states can only unite through 'interest'. It is precisely 'the spirit of commerce' that nudges each state toward establishing a federation of states. Perpetual peace is impossible without commerce. When we read this supplement together with the third condition, we can see that Kant's right to hospitality is inextricable from 'interest' and 'the spirit of commerce'.

Thus it seems that we can better determine the scope of this idea of the right to hospitality by imagining it in terms of commercial tourism rather than only the 'hospitality' of diplomats, which is tied to the will of the state. Tourism is

---

19.　Kant, 'Perpetual Peace', 114.

not related to the maturity of civil society. Nor is it related to the foreign policy will of the state. In other words, it is related neither to republicanism nor to the federation of states. In their visiting of other countries tourists are guided only by their own interests and by the commercial spirit of travel agencies. Despite this, the fact of their visit, the fact of tourism, becomes a condition for peace. Isn't this what Kant was trying to say?

This, too, is something that is happening in reality today in the twenty-first century. Just as the international community has identified the 'rogue states' that generate terrorists, the world is sending out a massive number of tourists, and these tourists aren't necessarily originating from 'republics'. We may not be able to call China, or Russia, or Middle Eastern countries 'mature states' according to the Western standard, so as states they may not be included in the federation of states for the purposes of establishing a perpetual peace.

However, citizens of these countries also travel around the world as tourists, and in that sense *they are contributing to peace independently of the state system of their home country*. For example, relations between Japan and China or Japan and Korea have always involved serious political issues, but the deterioration of the situation has been significantly limited by the massive number of tourists that travel between the countries.

This function of tourism was already imagined at the moment of its invention. In planning his first tour from England to Scotland, Cook hoped that it would lead to friendship between the two regions.[20] Even if Kant was unaware of the existence of mass tourism, could we not say that his third condition anticipated the political function of this movement of which the individual is the subject? Couldn't this be why he defined the right of hospitality, or tourism, as something that must be respected as the right of every world citizen, in other words regardless of the system in that individual's home country? Thus, even though we may have no choice but to exclude rogue states, we must not exclude tourists from rogue states. We must welcome tourists from China no matter how much relations with China deteriorate, and we must welcome tourists from Russia no matter how much relations with Russia deteriorate. This is not to say that we hold China or Russia in high regard as states, but that if such a right is not

---

20.   Hirukawa, *Tōmasu Kukku no shōzō*, 14.

universally guaranteed, although a federation could be built without China and Russia, the principle of perpetual peace behind such a federation would erode.

As noted above, Kant differentiates between the right to hospitality and the right to be a guest. The guarantee of the right to hospitality implies only the right to visit another country, not the right to be welcomed as a friend—truly, a rule written as if it were intended as a definition of the tourist. Travel agencies only guarantee their customers the right to visit another country, not the right to be welcomed as a friend. As long as tourism is tourism, the physical safety of the tourist is guaranteed, but nothing more. Upon arriving at their destination the tourist may in fact be confronted with rudeness from locals and may have unpleasant experiences. Friendship between nationals of different countries cannot exist without visits, or tourism, but this doesn't necessarily mean that visits, or tourism, will lead to friendship. When we detail the condition in this way, it becomes clear that Kant's right to hospitality is more easily understood if we take the tourist as its model rather than the diplomat. Indeed, contrary to Kant's rule, diplomats are in fact in most cases guaranteed the right to be a guest (the right to be welcomed).

To summarise, according to Kant, mature citizens create a mature state, mature states create a mature international order, ultimately leading to the achievement of world peace. But in addition to describing this linear history towards perpetual peace, Kant also suggested a different path involving 'interest' and 'the spirit of commerce'. It is there that the concept of hospitality, or tourism, plays a decisive role.

4

According to Voltaire, then, those who go on tours notice the 'mistakes' in the world. According to Kant, those who go on tours help to establish perpetual peace.

These two theses seem unrelated at first glance. But both contain an impetus for resisting linear history. Mature citizens create a mature state, mature states create a mature international order, and the happiness of all people is achieved—this is precisely the world according to the theory of optimism. Indeed, Kant uses expressions such as 'destiny' and 'providence' in *Perpetual Peace*: 'In [nature's] mechanical course we see that her aim is to produce a harmony among men, against their will and indeed through their discord. As a necessity working according to laws we do not know, we call it destiny. But considering its design in world history, we call it "providence."[21] This passage clearly expresses the belief that although states are involved in 'mistakes' such as wars, these mistakes, too, ultimately lead to the good of perpetual peace through the wisdom of nature. Voltaire wrote *Candide* precisely as an attack on such beliefs. And I suggest that Kant included his third condition in order to capture aspects of the process which this belief cannot (although he himself may not have been entirely conscious of this intention).

So what kind of philosophical discussion has there been regarding this political potential of the tourist, or perhaps more precisely, the *apolitical* potential for friendship created by an immature 'drifting being' that doesn't belong to the linear narrative that proceeds from the state to the federation of states?

As noted in Chapter 1, this is where we encounter a serious obstacle in philosophy. But now we have some philosophical terminology at our disposal. Let's try to clarify what this obstacle truly is.

In the twentieth century, about 140 years after Kant's *Perpetual Peace,* a jurist by the name of Carl Schmitt emerged in the same Germanic world. Although Schmitt was born in the nineteenth century, he can quite rightly be called a thinker of the twentieth century. As a scholar, he carries a great deal of baggage, having provided a theoretical pillar for the Nazi regime; after the war he was arrested as a war criminal. Yet he is known for his original theoretical constructions, and has been a major influence in postwar social theory upon conservatives and liberals alike. Today there are supporters of his views on the extreme Right as well as the extreme Left.

Among his works, the most famous and among the most important theoretically is *The Concept of the Political,* written in 1927 and published in 1932. In this work Schmitt made the bold claim that the only moment when the political functions as the political is when friend is distinguished from enemy. This is commonly known as the friend-enemy theory.

Allow me to briefly summarise the theory. As the title *The Concept of the Political* suggests, the topic of the book is the question 'What is politics?'

---

21.   Kant, 'Perpetual Peace', 106.

According to Schmitt, all abstract judgements rest upon specific dichotomous oppositions that serve as the basis for those judgements. For example, aesthetic judgements rest upon the dichotomous opposition between beauty and ugliness (whether something is beautiful), ethical judgements on good and evil (whether something is just), and economic judgements on the profitable and the unprofitable (whether something generates wealth). These oppositions are fundamentally independent of one another: there are plenty of things in this world that are beautiful yet unjust or just but unprofitable. We are able to make such judgements because aesthetics, ethics, and economics constitute independent categories of judgement, and this independence of judgement is guaranteed by the fact that each of them rests upon specific dichotomous oppositions.

If that is the case, what is the specific dichotomous opposition—separate from aesthetics, ethics, and economics—that makes politics political? Schmitt believed that it was the opposition between friend and enemy.

Politics is founded upon the dichotomous opposition between friend and enemy. What exactly is this opposition? Schmitt argued that 'the friend and enemy concepts are to be understood in their concrete and existential sense' and that they should 'not [be] mixed and weakened by economic, moral, and other conceptions'.[22] 'Concrete and existential sense' means essentially: to kill or be killed.

In extreme conditions such as war, one decides to destroy the enemy in order to protect the friend. This is what Schmitt considers to be the essence of politics. Other dichotomous oppositions such as beautiful and ugly, good and evil, and profitable and unprofitable must not be involved in making this judgement. If such a judgement is 'mixed and weakened by economic, moral, and other conceptions', the enemy's position is more justifiable. Or perhaps one makes the judgement that, for example, it is more profitable to collaborate with the enemy. But such judgements are fundamentally different from politics, and should not be related to political judgements. In other words, even if it is ethically unjust and economically unprofitable, if there is something one must do to protect the existence of a friend, then one must pursue that action, and this is precisely what constitutes the 'political' for Schmitt. This is the friend-enemy theory.

---

22.   C. Schmitt, *The Concept of the Political*, tr. G. Schwab (Chicago: University of Chicago Press, 1996), 27–28.

I'd like to note here that Schmitt's 'friend' and 'enemy' are unique concepts that differ from the common-sense meaning that one might usually associate with these words. The opposition is completely unrelated to private friendship or feelings of animosity.

The 'enemy' in Schmitt's sense of the term is a 'public enemy', in other words the enemy of the community. It does not refer to private enemies—individuals toward whom you or I might harbour feelings of animosity for personal reasons. And so it is possible for a certain person to be an enemy privately, but a friend publicly. Indeed, in times of war we fight against 'enemies' that we have never met, alongside fellow nationals who we might hate. Or we might fight against personal friends as public enemies. These kinds of situations are sometimes spoken of as the farce or tragedy of war, but according to Schmitt this is precisely the essence of politics—that is, war. The differentiation between friend and enemy is made by, and only by, the public.

Friends and enemies are public beings, not private beings. Moreover, there is no politics without the differentiation between friend and enemy. This means that Schmitt's thinking on the political takes as its basis the borders that separate communities.

Politics first divides the world between insider (friend) and outsider (enemy) and thus establishes its community (the space of friends). That differentiation need not have any basis outside of political reasons. This is because the drawing of such a border itself is what defines the political. In fact, Schmitt's explanation of the enemy is largely tautological:

> The political enemy need not be morally evil or aesthetically ugly; he need not appear as an economic competitor, and it may even be advantageous to engage with him in business transactions. But he is, nevertheless, the other, the stranger; and it is sufficient for his nature that he is, in a specially intense way, existentially something different and alien, so that in the extreme case conflicts with him are possible.[23]

---

23.   Ibid., 27.

Politics arbitrarily decides its enemy. Furthermore, politics privileges the continuity of the community above all else, to the exclusion of all other judgements where necessary. This is the argument of *The Concept of the Political*.

Although I will only mention it in passing here, this prioritisation of 'politics' and 'community' is consistent throughout Schmitt's thought. In another book entitled *Political Theology*, Schmitt argues that the sovereign (the subject of politics) is the one who decides on the 'state of exception', meaning a state in which all legal order is suspended and the continuation of the state is seen as being at stake.[24] Usually, everyday life can be controlled through the application of law, but politics becomes necessary in the state of exception. And politics prioritises the continuation of the state above all else, including ethics and economics, and is capable of making extralegal decisions. This is what Schmitt thought.

It goes without saying that these are extremely dangerous ideas. They affirm dictatorship and the annihilation of the enemy without leaving any room for disagreement. Indeed, as noted above, true to his own words, Schmitt supported the dictatorship of the Nazis and helped to move forward the policies of elimination against the Jewish people.

5

The friend-enemy theory may be dangerous, but we cannot simply reject it because it is dangerous. The theory itself was not a product of emotional prejudices, a hatred for Jews, or a desire to extol the greatness of the German state; rather, it was a theory logically deduced as a result of thinking through the essence of the state and the human.

Let me explain. Between Kant and Schmitt there stands Hegel, who had a tremendous influence upon modern legal systems and political theory.

Hegel believed that the state constituted the 'reason' of civil society. For example, we Japanese today live within a geographical boundary called the Japanese archipelago. We use the same language, exchange goods and money, and together form a society. However, Hegel believed that this alone does not constitute a state. The state, he argued, does not manifest itself until its people, in this case the Japanese, become self-conscious of constituting a people who

---

24. C. Schmitt, *Political Theology*, tr. G. Schwab (Chicago: University of Chicago Press, 2010), 6.

constitute a society living together on the same land and sharing the same history (in Hegel's words, the people 'thinks and knows itself and implements what it knows in so far as it knows').[25] In other words, the state is first and foremost a product of consciousness rather than a product of fact. This rule serves as the foundation of modern political thought.

Decisively important here is the fact that, in Hegel's philosophy, the passage from civil society to state is described not as a simple historical or sociological development, but as something that takes place in tandem with the spiritual ascent of humanity.

According to Hegel, humans first emerge as a 'natural ethical spirit' within the family. To put it flatly, they live as self-sufficient beings enwrapped within the love of family. But then they venture outside of the home, and enter into civil society. Civil society refers to the realm in which people interact with language and when language, not love, serves as the medium for their togetherness. Here people come to satisfy their desires through the desires of others. In Hegel's words, the 'selfish end in its actualization [is] conditioned in this way by universality',[26] meaning that people become beings split between subjectivity and objectivity, particular and universal, or, in other words, private and public. To put it flatly, people in civil society cannot return to being self-sufficient in love but must continually consider how they look to others and what part they must play within society.

Ultimately, the state emerges as the impetus for unifying precisely this split. According to Hegel, by belonging to a state and becoming a national citizen, one can internalise the public will of the state as personal private will, and thus experience universality within particularity. For Hegel, it is precisely this realisation of internalisation (the union of particularity and universality) that constitutes the existential significance of the state in the history of Spirit. For those who have read my book *General Will 2.0*, I will add that Hegel arrived at this supposition of the strange concept of 'state will' that unifies particularity and universality through his interpretation of Rousseau's 'general will'; in other words, this is Hegel's solution to the question of Rousseau (the split between individualism and totalitarianism).

---

25.   G.W.F. Hegel, *Elements of the Philosophy of Right*, tr. S.W. Dyde (Cambridge: Cambridge University Press, 2003), 275 [§257].
26.   Ibid., 221 [§183].

One attains spiritual maturity by leaving the family, entering civil society, and finally becoming a member of a nation. Hegel writes that 'individuals' [...] highest duty is to be members of the state'.[27]

People do not become spiritually mature unless they belong to a state. This seems like an extremely odd argument.

At the very least, such an idea seems quite outdated in the twenty-first century, when globalism has conquered the world and the circulation of goods and people crosses national borders every day. In fact, the idea that all borders, including those between nations, are illusory and will be dismantled one by one through the development of information technology has gained a certain amount of influence in the world of information society theory, as represented in concepts such as Jōichi Itō's 'emergent democracy' and Ken Suzuki's 'smooth society'.[28] As a line of thinking, these ideas are typically understood as a branch of 'libertarianism' and are chiefly supported by entrepreneurs and engineers.

However, philosophically speaking, Hegel's theory of the state possesses a far deeper perspective. This is because he describes the necessity of the state not simply in terms of the necessity of already existing states, but as an issue having to do with the progress of Spirit. Humans can only know things about themselves (they can only know particularity). But on the other hand, they cannot live on their own (they cannot live without universality). Then how do we come to terms with both of these two? It is precisely in answering this question that Hegel arrives at the necessity of becoming a member of a nation state.

As such, although he calls this a theory of the state, it is something that goes beyond political theory and social thought. It is a discussion that is inextricably tied to issues related to the human and especially human *maturity*. Hegel believed

---

27.   Hegel, *Philosophy of Right*, 275 (§258).

28.   J. Itō, 'Sōhatsu minshusei [Emergent Democracy]', tr. S. Kumon, *Kokusai Daigaku GLOCOM*, 2003, <https://www.glocom.ac.jp/wp-content/uploads/2020/10/75_02.pdf>; Suzuki, *Nameraka na shakai to sono teki*. All of the former and part of the latter are included in H. Azuma (ed.), *Hirakareru Kokka: Kadokawa intaanetto kōza* [*The Open State: Law and Politics in a Borderless Age*] (Tokyo: Kadokawa, 2015). While I introduce them critically here, I agree with both Itō and Suzuki that our society is bound by various barriers such as national borders, and that, as these lose their self-evidence, we must now imagine a new process of politics that isn't premised on such demarcating barriers. However, while Itō and Suzuki believe that the disassembly of barriers proceeds through technical means, I argue that an intervention from the perspective of the humanities is necessary. Philosophy of the tourist is the name I have given to this intervention.

that in order for humans to become proper humans, aside from being a member of a family (in itself) or interacting with others in civil society (out of itself), they must belong to a higher community (in and for itself).

Sharp readers will notice that we have returned to our discussion at the beginning of the chapter. There I asked: 'People dislike people and don't want to create societies. Nevertheless, people create societies. Why do they do this?' Hegel, a philosopher of the nineteenth century, answered this by saying that people can overcome the immature self that does not want to create a society by building a state and becoming a member of a nation.

Schmitt's friend-enemy theory arises when one pursues Hegel's view of humanity further.

For humans to be humans, they must unify universality and particularity by internalising some kind of state will. There is no humanity without this unifying function, so where there is no state, there is no humanity. In order for humans to be human, there must be a state to which one can belong on a level of judgement independent from aesthetics, ethics, and economics. Politics refers to a set of actions whose purpose is precisely to ensure the continued existence of the state. It is on the basis of this logic that Schmitt is able to argue for the necessity of politics as that which differentiates between friend and enemy and clarifies the contours of the state.

Thus, the friend-enemy theory isn't simply a dangerous thought or something that we can disregard as an obsolete theory. Instead, we might say that it is a line of thinking that will return again and again unless we overcome the Hegelian view of humanity.

We could also say that it is actually a line of thought whose return is becoming increasingly likely today. Reading *The Concept of the Political* in 2017, many passages seem surprisingly timely.

The Concept of the Political was written in opposition to the liberal and individualist thought that was gaining influence in Weimar Germany. In Germany at the time, people were already making arguments similar to those made for globalism today: national borders would soon disappear through the development of transportation and trade, states would vanish, and the world would become one. Schmitt's discussion is constructed in resistance to that line of thought, and for that reason *The Concept of the Political* is filled with examples and passages that can be tied to the critique of globalism today.

This is not at all surprising when we consider the matter from a historical perspective. The globalism of today is a revival of movements in liberalism and economic integration that began in the late nineteenth to early twentieth century only to enter a seventy-year hiatus owing to the two World Wars and the Cold War. Thus, it should come as no surprise that there are parallels between Schmitt's interests in the 1930s and ours in the 2010s. For that reason, there is a significant possibility that Schmitt's friend-enemy theory will return now that globalism is progressing. Moreover, that theory is far more philosophically sophisticated than the run-of-the-mill critiques of globalism we see today.

Then as now, there was no shortage of critics of globalism (i.e. the liberalism of the early twentieth century). Many of them argued that incorporating globalism would damage domestic industries or destroy domestic culture. But Schmitt does not enter into these discussions. For him, such a critique brings economic or aesthetic concerns (judgements as to whether globalism is unprofitable or ugly) into the realm of politics, and in doing so ultimately sullies the value of politics.

On the contrary, Schmitt denies globalism simply because it erases the differentiation between friend and enemy and thus erases politics itself. In *The Concept of the Political* he refers to a liberal intellectual who was active at the time and argues that in his line of thinking 'the political concept of battle in liberal thought becomes competition in the domain of economics and discussion in the intellectual realm'.[29] Liberalism reduces the necessity of the state to economics and morality. But friends are not differentiated from enemies because it is in the individual's interest to do so (i.e. it is economically profitable) or because it makes one feel good about oneself (i.e. it is ethically just). It is something that the structure of the human spirit requires, as long as humans pursue their own humanity. Liberals fundamentally misunderstand this point—and it is this ignorance that irritates Schmitt.

Thus Schmitt believes that globalism, which plots the demise of the state, must be resisted, whether or not it leads to economic profit or the expansion of domestic culture. If the state ceases to exist then politics will cease to exist.

---

29. Schmitt, *The Concept of the Political*, 71.

And if politics disappears, then humans will no longer be human. Schmitt denies globalism so that humans can be human. It is indeed a powerful critical logic. Schmitt describes the ideal of a borderless world in a depressed tone:

> As long as a state exists, there will always be in the world more than just one state. A world state which embraces the entire globe and all of humanity cannot exist. [...] If the different states, religions, classes, and other human groupings on earth should be so unified that a conflict among them is impossible and even inconceivable [...] [w]hat remains is neither politics nor state, but culture, civilization, economics, morality, law, art, entertainment, etc. If and when this condition will appear, I do not know.

> [...] Were a world state to embrace the entire globe and humanity, then it would be no political entity and could only be loosely called a state. If, in fact, all humanity and the entire world were to become a unified entity based exclusively on economics and on technically regulating traffic, then it still would not be more of a social entity than a social entity of tenants in a tenement house, customers purchasing gas from the same utility company, or passengers riding on the same bus.[30]

As long as humans are humans, they will build states, and make friends and enemies. As such, there must always be multiple states. Schmitt argues that if there were only one world state and public enemies were to cease to exist, philosophically speaking we would have to conclude that this would be a world without states, without politics, and thus without humans.

By internalising a universal will as a particular will, people are able to spiritually mature and become 'human'. The impetus for this can only be provided by the state, not the family or civil society. People cannot become human without becoming a member of a nation state. They cannot become human without differentiating between friend and enemy. It was while in search of a logic with which to attack globalism that Schmitt arrived at this theory.

---

30.   Ibid., 53–54, 57.

It goes without saying that this theory constitutes a tricky obstacle for the topic of the present book, a philosophy of the tourist.

If it is the case that no one can become human without going through the opposition of friend and enemy, then the 'tourist who is neither villager nor nomad' would have to be regarded as an immature subhuman being. A simple gathering of individuals amounts to nothing more than 'tenants in a tenement house, customers purchasing gas from the same utility company, or passengers riding on the same bus', and such individuals are not worthy of political consideration. In which case, groups of tourists who leave the system of their ancestral land and cross borders based on their own individual motives fundamentally cannot be the object of political thought. Although I said above that thinking about the philosophy of the tourist means thinking about the possibility for friendship created by an immature 'drifting being' that doesn't belong to the linear narrative leading from the state to the federation of states, as we now see, the friend-enemy theory and the Hegelian paradigm that serves as its basis tend to foreclose the possibility of any such kind of thinking. Modern humanist thought possesses a structure that makes it more difficult to seriously consider the tourist the more you seriously attempt to consider the human.

But obstacles are also possibilities. It seems likely that Hegel and Schmitt's paradigm which blocks the philosophy of the tourist also provides us, inversely, with an outline of what the philosophy of the tourist must be.

Modern thought held that humans do not mature unless they go through the opposition between friend and enemy. In which case, in building a philosophy of the tourist we must find a different mechanism for maturation that does not proceed through that opposition. In other words, we must think of a mechanism that brings the universal and particular together without the condition of belonging to a state. Moreover, modern thought imagined a linear history of the spirit that proceeded from the family to civil society, then to the state, and finally to a federation of states. If this is the case, then in order to disrupt that linear narrative, we must consider the possibility of a different political organisation that does not proceed to the state after having passed through the family and civil society.

Am I being too abstract? Perhaps the discussion so far reads that way. But what I am trying to say here is highly concrete. If people were to be able to obtain universality *instantly* instead of through the process of belonging to just one particular state and internalising its values for themselves—in other words, awakening to their self-identity as members of the nation and doing such things as reading the newspaper and participating in elections and demonstrations, and finally *after all of that* arrive at being world citizens—what would that look like? That is the possibility I would like to consider.[31]

6

We now have a firm grasp of the challenges that face the philosophy of the tourist.

Where, according to the framework of modern thought, things that fall outside of the linear narrative that proceeds from the family to the citizen to the nation and to the world citizen are understood fundamentally as falling outside of politics, I prefer to think that this is precisely where a new path for politics lies. The philosophy of the tourist articulates this possibility, and that is what this book seeks to obtain.

In the next chapter, then, we will finally grapple with this challenge. But before we do so, in the second half of this chapter I would like to add two new keywords that will help us grasp from multiple angles the opposition between the friend-enemy theory and the philosophy of the tourist by examining two philosophers who were contemporaries of Schmitt's. Here we shall see that the possibility of the philosophy of the tourist is intertwined with many different issues.

---

31.   Searching for a route through which an immature individual may directly connect to the universal without the mediation of self-consciousness as a member of a nation state (i.e. become a mature adult)—translated into the words of Japanese subculture criticism this is essentially the issue of 'sekai-kei' (world-type)'. 'Sekai-kei' is a general term referring to a narrative type that found some success in otaku content in Japan in the 2000s in which the small love interest harboured by the protagonist is linked to a massive event such as the destruction of the world, without any reference to a realistic setting such as the state or society. I once attempted a new type of literary criticism by extending the usage of this term in subculture and elevating it into a key concept. See my book *Sekai kara motto chikaku ni* [*Closer to the World: Problems of Literature Separated from Reality*] (Tokyo: Sōgensha, 2013). Part 2 of the present book is titled 'Philosophy of the Family', and it is deeply linked to my theoretical treatment in that previous work of Motoko Arai, a writer who explores the 'uncanny family'. The stuffed animals that she loves so much are precisely the uncanny [Arai is famous for owning over 4000 toy stuffed animals and treats them as a kind of 'spiritual lifeform.'—trans.]

The first keyword is 'animal'. In the supplement preceding this chapter, in introducing the concept of derivative works, I referred to my book *Otaku: Japan's Database Animals*. As the title suggests, the term 'animal' is a key term in that book.

I borrow this concept of animal from a French thinker named Alexandre Kojève. Kojève was about a generation younger than Schmitt, and had some interactions with him (Schmitt was born in 1888, Kojève in 1902). He was a philosopher who followed a unique trajectory, having been born in Moscow, sought refuge in Germany after the Russian Revolution, and served as a French diplomat after the war.

In a book entitled *Introduction to the Reading of Hegel*, a collection of transcripts of his lectures from the 1930s published in 1947, Kojève writes: 'the Hegelian-Marxist end of History was not yet to come, but was already a present [...]. Observing what was taking place around me and reflecting on what had taken place in the world since the Battle of Jena, I understood that Hegel was right to see in this battle the end of History.'[32] In other words, the 'History' in which humans live as humans essentially ended with the 1806 Battle of Jena (a turning point in the Napoleonic Wars), and the two World Wars of the twentieth century only confirmed that the present had already entered 'post-history' (the era after the end of history). Given that later, toward the end of the twentieth century, the American political scientist Francis Fukuyama employed this schema in developing his theory of the 'end of history' and his book of the same title became a global bestseller,[33] perhaps some readers will be familiar with the concept via that route. However, Fukuyama identifies the end of the Cold War as the moment that confirms the end of history.

It might sound outrageous to claim that human history has come to an end, but here too, just as with Schmitt's thought, Hegel's unique view of the human is in the background. For Hegel (as interpreted and summarised by Kojève), humans are spiritual beings who wager their existence on seeking the acceptance of others and continuously reforming their environments. 'Man's humanity "comes to light" only in risking his life to satisfy his human Desire—that is, his Desire

---

32. A. Kojève, *Introduction to the Reading of Hegel*, tr. J.H. Nichols, Jr. (Ithaca, NY: Cornell University Press, 1980), 160 [emphasis removed].

33. F. Fukuyama, *The End of History and the Last Man* (New York: Free Press, 1992).

directed towards another Desire. [...] Without this fight to the death for pure prestige, there would never have been human beings on earth.'[34] The flipside of this is that Kojève and Hegel believe that beings who have lost their pride, do not seek the recognition of others, and are self-sufficient in their received environments, cannot spiritually be called humans, even if they may be biologically human. If all of humanity become such self-sufficient beings, then, *human* history ends, even if the species homo sapiens continues to exist. Kojève called the world after the Second World War 'post-history' with this view of humanity in mind. Faced with the Cold War that followed the World Wars, he was trapped in the somewhat helpless feeling that humans had not invented any essentially new ideals since the Napoleonic Wars.

It is in passages concerning this 'post-history' that the word 'animal' appears in Kojève's work:

> Hence it would have to be admitted that, after the end of History, men would construct their edifices and works of art as birds build their nests and spiders spin their webs, would perform musical concerts after the fashion of frogs and cicadas, would play like young animals, and would indulge in love like adult beasts. But one cannot then say that all this 'makes Man happy.' One would have to say that *post-historical animals* of the species *Homo sapiens* (which will live amidst abundance and complete security) will be content as a result of their artistic, erotic and playful behavior, inasmuch as, by definition, they will be contented with it.[35]

Humans still conduct social activities in the post-historical world. They build cities and produce culture. But we can no longer call this 'human' activity; it is closer to the play of animals.

After this searing passage, Kojève sets up the American consumer as an example of the 'post-historical animal':

> The 'American way of life' [is] the type of life specific to the post-historical period, the actual presence of the United States in the World prefiguring the 'eternal

---

34. Kojève, *Introduction to the Reading of Hegel*, 7.
35. Ibid., 159. Emphasis in the passage mine, emphasis in the original removed.

present' future of all humanity. Thus, Man's return to animality appeared no longer as a possibility that was yet to come, but as a certainty that was already present.[36]

Those living in postwar America are nothing more than animalistic consumers who have lost their pride, don't need the recognition of others, are self-sufficient in their given environment, and simply buy commodities in search of pleasure. According to Kojève, there are no longer any 'humans' here, nor is there any history, but only the eternal present.

Kojève saw American consumers as 'animals', then, but it is worth noting that he also refers to postwar Japan in the same footnote and says that the Japanese cannot become animals for a specific reason. In *Otaku* I argue that his definitions of 'animal' and 'post-history' best describe the otaku of Japan from a specific period onward. On this basis I analyse the dynamic of derivative works referred to above, ultimately suggesting the unique concept of 'database animals', although I will not discuss that any further here. In any case, even readers unfamiliar with Hegel's paradigm will probably instinctively understand Kojève's point that American consumers who are surrounded by junk food and entertainment, without any need for politics or art, and who entrust their pleasures to the unending stream of new products, may seem like 'animals'. In that sense, although he might take it too far, what Kojève is saying here is not so outrageous.

What I would like to highlight here is the fact that Kojève formulated this view of history in the 1930s, during the same era that Schmitt published *The Concept of the Political*. As I noted earlier, *Introduction to the Reading of Hegel* is a book with a complicated make-up, consisting of lectures from the 1930s published in the 1940s, with footnotes then added in the 1960s; the passages I cited above are from one of these later footnotes. But while they may have been written in the 1960s, there is no disputing the fact that the framework of discussion around the 'human', 'history', and the 'animal' were created in the 1930s. Thus, Kojève's problematic deeply resonates with that of Schmitt's. If we compare Kojève's above passage on 'post-history' with Schmitt's passage concerning the 'world state' cited earlier, you will notice how they are constructed using

36. Ibid., 161.

surprisingly similar metaphors. Both Schmitt and Kojève posit the problem of the *loss of the human* in an age in which all that remains in the world is consumer activity, where competition to the death between humans is in the past, and where there are no longer wars between states over their ideals. Schmitt called this the loss of the political (the spread of liberalism), Kojève called it the end of history (animalisation).

Schmitt and Kojève both resisted globalism. As it spread beyond borders and covered the world with a homogeneous consumer society, globalism appeared to them as a serious challenge to the Hegelian view of humans. By connecting Schmitt's friend-enemy theory to Kojève's theory of post-history, we have been able to obtain the word 'animal' as a word describing the appearance of the human that globalism brings. Humans always possess friends and enemies. And there are always states. But animals have neither friends nor enemies, nor do they have states.

On this basis, we can say that tourists, who leave their state and their people, seek neither the recognition nor the welcome of others, and drift about guided only by their individual interests, are also 'animals'. And in fact, although I will not delve into details here, the history of tourism is closely connected to the history of globalism. When early globalism was derailed by the outbreak of the Second World War, the business that Thomas Cook had founded in the nineteenth century (Thomas Cook and Sons) also faced a major crisis. It was even nationalised at one point. It only really revived from the 1970s on, in a new era in which 'post-historical' animalisation became more ubiquitous, and the highly consumerist 'postmodern' society came into being. Tourism, then, is a product of the end of history. The exploration of the philosophical meaning of tourism is inseparable from the exploration of the post-historical animal.

7

The second keyword is 'consumption'. 'Labour' and 'anonymity' are related terms here as well. Here I would like to read Hannah Arendt.

Arendt, too, is a philosopher with a unique career. Born in 1906, she was roughly a contemporary of Kojève. She was a Jew born in Germany who sought refuge in the United States and wrote mostly in English after the war. The author of works such as *The Origins of Totalitarianism* and *Eichmann in Jerusalem*, she is commonly known as a political philosopher who delivered an acute analysis of the crimes of the Nazis; at the same time, the fact that in her youth she was a lover of Heidegger, a philosopher close to the Nazis, is a well-known piece of gossip. Although she has always been seen as a leading philosopher of the twentieth century, she has become even more appreciated over the past twenty or so years.

In 1958 Arendt published *The Human Condition*, a book which, like the works of Schmitt and Kojève, is concerned with the loss of the human. Arendt, too, believed that unique philosophical conditions applied to living as a 'human', aside from being biologically a member of the species *homo sapiens*. She also believed that people had now lost those conditions, and *The Human Condition* was written so that people could regain them.

Arendt divided the social activities that humans take part in into three types: action, work, and labour. She argued that while 'action' and 'work' give meaning to human life, 'labour' does not. The problem is that, despite this fact, labour is privileged in contemporary society.

In order to simplify the discussion, I will explain Arendt's argument with a focus on the opposition between 'action' and 'labour'.

For Arendt, the *polis* of ancient Greece provided one ideal for publicness. 'Action' is an ideal type, developed with the political action (of the *polis*) of Ancient Greek citizens serving as the model. More concretely, it refers to the linguistic and physical activity of appearing in a public space (the *agora*), giving a speech, and debating with others. Today, in the twenty-first century, we could understand it as referring to activities such as running for office and giving speeches at political meetings, participating in citizens' movements, or contributing to society through non-profit organisations.

'Labour', on the other hand, refers to 'the activity which corresponds to the biological process of the human body'.[37] This correspondence to biological

---

37. Arendt defines 'work', which I omitted here, as providing 'an "artificial" world of things, distinctly different from all natural surroundings.' H. Arendt, *The Human Condition* (Chicago: University of Chicago Press, 1998), 7. In other words, if 'labour' corresponds to working at a convenience store for money and 'action' corresponds to volunteering to serve society or political movements, then 'work' corresponds to making things in the context of a task or hobby. Although I could not easily place this third term within the broader argumentative structure of this book (the stratified structure of politics and the economy), this 'work' is actually crucial for thinking about contemporary society. We are living

process means that here only the power of the body is at issue. To put this in contemporary terms, we might think of wage labour performed at places such as convenience stores and fast-food restaurants, which is calculated according to the number of personnel and time, and is the same no matter who is performing the labour.

Importantly, Arendt makes this distinction by drawing our attention to *who* performs the action—that is, the proper noun attached to the actor and what is intrinsic to them—a person's face and name. According to Arendt, these proper characteristics of the actor are decisively important in the case of action. Indeed, what is important in a politician's speech is the question of *who* is making that speech, the politician's face, rather than the content of the speech itself. On the other hand, the face or name is completely unimportant in the case of labour. Factory labourers and store attendants are merely anonymous numbers. Indeed, few probably care who is working the register when they go to a convenience store to buy a piece of merchandise. They may not even care which branch of the store they are at. To borrow Arendt's words, in labour only faceless vital power, or '*vita activa*', is being bought and sold.

Arendt also associates this opposition with the question of whether or not there is an 'Other' or 'publicness'. According to Arendt, there is always an other at the site of action. There can be no speech without an audience, nor can there be any volunteer work without coming face to face with the entity you are serving. Since the essence of action lies in linguistic communication based on humans revealing their faces to one another and acknowledging one another's difference, action necessarily requires the existence of an other, which in turn also leads to a consciousness of the public realm.

In contrast, there is no Other at the site of labour. The essence of labour lies in humans losing their face and providing *vita activa* that is calculated according

---

in the era of otaku and engineers. We could call this an era of 'work'. In *The Human Condition* Arendt writes that action was replaced by work in modernity, but its victory was immediately overcome by labour. (*The Human Condition*, discussion beginning on page 294) The Industrial Revolution was a result of the victory of those who work, that is, makers and fabricators. From this perspective, we could say that the revolution in information technology that we will examine in Chapter 6 was a movement that attempted to resurrect work/makers, with the internet serving as the stage. According to certain idealists, this would also lead to the resurrection of action (the resurrection of politics). However, in reality it only led to the proliferation of labour, that is, a swarm of anonymous internet users yanked around by fake news and affiliate marketing.

to the number of personnel and time. Arendt believes that this leaves no opportunity for the other to appear. Perhaps some readers will disagree, saying that, for example, workers working the cash register face the other in the form of customers, and that this involves a human-to-human relationship.

However, Arendt would likely answer that the customer in that situation is merely a destination of *vita activa,* and does not necessarily appear there as an other. The relationship between store clerk and customer is more like the relationship between a machine and a human than a relationship between humans. Concretely speaking, cash register attendants can very well be replaced by robots and self-check-out kiosks; indeed, this will likely happen in the near future. There is no Other in labour, and labourers work only for a wage, meaning that labour is essentially a 'private' experience (undertaken for oneself) and does not connect to any public consciousness. People take on tasks in part-time jobs to receive an hourly wage; they don't necessarily work in order to improve the convenience store or society in general.

Based on the above, Arendt argued that humans only live as humans when they are engaged in action, whereas the conditions for being human are denied them at the site of labour.

This is the key argument in *The Human Condition,* where Arendt writes: 'The *animal laborans* [...] is imprisoned in the privacy of his own body, caught in the fulfilment of needs in which nobody can share and which nobody can fully communicate.' Labour is nothing more than an activity for satisfying one's animal desires (appetite, for example). For that reason, people cannot connect with one another through labour. My satisfaction (wage) is independent from your satisfaction. In contrast, '[a]ction, the only activity that goes on directly between men without the intermediary of things or matter, corresponds to the human condition of plurality, to the fact that men, not Man, live on the earth and inhabit the world.' While the desire for things only entraps people within their lonely satisfaction, action, or communication through language, has the ability to connect people. It is in action that, for the first time, people can 'show who they are, reveal actively their unique personal identities and thus make their appearance in the human world'.[38]

---

38.   Arendt, *The Human Condition,* 118–19, 7, 197.

Humans can finally become humans when they reveal themselves (give their names), deliberate with others, and attain a public consciousness. They cannot become human when they remain anonymous and exchange their *vita activa* for personal wages without any deliberation with others. This is the conceptual opposition that serves as the basis for *The Human Condition*. Only public beings who reveal themselves are worthy of the name 'human'. Anonymous, private beings are not worthy of that name. This being the case, borrowing Kojève's term, we should call the latter 'animals', and indeed, as we have seen, Arendt herself uses the expression *animal laborans*.

Arendt's schema can easily be understood without the need for any philosophical background. Perhaps many readers will agree with the notion that those working the register at convenience stores have been stripped of the human condition.

However, it is also known that this philosophy of Arendt's possesses a significant theoretical weak spot. For the ancient Greek city-states to which Arendt refers as a model were founded upon a system of slavery.

Perhaps revealed and public 'humans' and anonymous, private *animal laborans* were clearly differentiated in ancient Greece. Arendt suggests reviving this differentiation in the present. But in reality, that system possessed a simple but cruel infrastructure in which the action/politics/*polis* of revealed citizens were supported by the anonymous labour/domestic work/*oikos* conducted by the slaves that each of these citizens owned. And that being the case, is it really appropriate to choose to revive this differentiation in the present as is? Emphasising only the public value of political activity and volunteer work and arguing that humans cannot be human when they are engaged in labour risks excluding from the political realm the variety of lines of thought that the site of labour generates. To put it bluntly, could we not say that it is Arendt herself who fails to treat the cash register operator as human? The political scientist Jun'ichi Saito, while lauding Arendt's work as a whole, is quite critical of *The Human Condition*, arguing that it must be 'critiqued from the core' because it 'chases from public space all kinds of inquiries concerning life' and 'judges voices that speak about the needs and pains of the body as inappropriate and unsavoury'.[39]

---

39.   J. Saito, *Kōkyōsei* [*Publicness*] (Tokyo: Iwanami Shoten, 2000), 56–57.

Then how might we overcome this weakness? If we must consider the pub-licness generated by *animal laborans,* what kind of views of the human and of politics does this require? We will leave the answers to such questions to specialists; what is important in the present context is that we can say that this weak point of *The Human Condition* was born of the same origin that caused the weaknesses in Schmitt's friend-enemy theory and Kojève's theory of post-history.

I raised the example of Arendt here because as a thinker she is generally contrasted to Schmitt and Kojève, especially to Schmitt. Indeed, Schmitt, who collaborated with the Nazis and Arendt, who fled Nazi persecution, sit at polar opposites to one another in terms of politics. Arendt is a leftist, while Schmitt is a rightist. But when we strip away these ideological motifs, the ideas of the two thinkers possess strikingly similar structures.

Schmitt, Kojève, and Arendt were all thinkers who reconsidered the issue of the human in the context of the major social shifts of the nineteenth and twentieth centuries. Schmitt arrived at the answer that the human draws a line between friend and enemy and conducts politics on this basis, Kojève arrived at the answer that the human competes over the acceptance of the other, and Arendt arrived at the answer that the human deliberates in the town square and creates a public. On the surface, these answers look quite different, but a shared problematic emerges when we consider what they proposed as an object to contrast to the human. Schmitt constructed his friend-enemy theory in response to the emergence of humans (liberals) who pursue only economic profit without paying heed to the friend-enemy divide. Kojève argued that humans were precisely those who possess the spirit of competition and create history in response to the emergence of people who are self-sufficient in their pleasures (animalistic consumers) who need neither competition nor history. And Arendt wrote *The Human Condition* in response to the emergence of, to repeat, the *animal laborans* who 'is imprisoned in the privacy of his own body' and has no need for the other.

Kojève criticised animalistic consumers, while Arendt criticised *animal lab-orans.* But in modern mass society, labourers directly become consumers. Thus the issue of labour and the issue of consumption are two sides of the same coin.

In fact, Arendt critiques consumerism using the same logic employed in her critique of labour. For her, labour turns *vita activa* into money, while consumption simply satisfies animalistic desires using that money: 'the spare time of the *animal laborans* is never spent on anything but consumption, and the more time left to him, the greedier and more craving his appetites.' Thus, 'mankind altogether "liberated" from the shackles of pain and effort would be free to "consume" the whole world and to reproduce daily all things it wished to consume', but the only thing that this 'utopia' generates is a 'mass culture' that pursues 'happiness' and will not provide any meaning to the life of humans.[40] This passage features language that is strikingly similar to passages in Schmitt critiquing the ideal of the world state and Kojève's cynical words critiquing the life of the post-historical 'animal'.

Schmitt, Kojève, and Arendt all inhabit the same paradigm. They each attempt to revive the good old definition of the 'human' in order to critique the featureless mass consumer society motivated only by economic rationality, without politics and without friends or enemies. In other words, each of them *attempts to deploy the tradition of the humanities for the precise goal of denying the utopia of pleasure and happiness that globalism enables*.

It is precisely this unconscious desire that the present book attempts to overcome by thinking about the tourist. The humanities in the twentieth century understood the advent of mass society and the emergence of the animalistic consumer as the arrival of something not human. And they attempted to deny this arrival. But this kind of denial cannot be viable in a twenty-first century in which globalism continues to progress. And indeed, the influence of the humanities declined rapidly as we entered a new century. For this reason, we need to reform the humanities itself. A consciousness of this crisis lies at the basis of this book.

Allow me to add one more point in closing. Following Schmitt and Arendt, in the late twentieth century many schools of thought emerged which, at least on the surface, engaged in the analysis of mass society and consumer society. Examples would include semiotic analyses of consumer society such as those of Jean Baudrillard and Roland Barthes in the Francophone world, the faction of cultural sociology known as Cultural Studies in the Anglophone world, and Friedrich

---

40. Arendt, *The Human Condition*, 131–35.

Kittler and Norbert Bolz in Germany. What is often called postmodernism is usually some combination of these, and it is usually the development in these areas that is referenced in the industry of so-called 'contemporary thought'. For that reason, readers familiar with those authors might wonder what I'm talking about when I say that thought in the humanities has excluded mass society. In that industry, it is held as common knowledge that Hegel's view of society and humanity was overcome long ago.

But in actuality, it is precisely this half-baked understanding that is, the snare to be avoided. For, if we look at reality, it is clear that the social and cultural analysis of the postmodernists that I just listed—although they have produced some results in the interpretation of particular phenomena or works—have not been able to even begin to dismantle the dichotomous opposition that differentiates the public from its outside, the human from its outside, and politics from its outside, and have had barely any real influence in politics.

Postmodernists have indeed declared that they would 'deconstruct' politics and its outside, and this idea became popular in the academy and among some readers. But we could say that their argument itself has been pushed to the outside of politics as something apolitical (as a form of play). Such postmodernists are sometimes lumped together as 'cultural leftists', and this (cultural) nomination itself proves that their work is not seen as something political. Indeed, at the time of writing, in 2017, the figures of so-called 'contemporary thought' can only either settle for the label of cultural leftist and lecture on literary criticism and art theory in universities, or throw all theory out the window (in other words abandon their pride as a postmodernist and return to being a modernist) and accept the style of old 'politics' as they take to the streets to participate in demonstrations. Here we see the opposition between politics and its outside reproduced in striking fashion. Nothing has been deconstructed and nothing has changed. I see in this condition the defeat of thought. This is why I think we need to return to the very basics and rethink modern thought's view on the human and on politics from its very core, and not simply rely on surface-level reinterpretations of past texts.

Thinking the tourist is useful for these purposes. Tourists are the masses. They are labourers and they are consumers. The tourist is a private being and does not take on any public role. Tourists are anonymous, and they do not deliberate with locals at their destination. They do not participate in the history of their destination either, nor in its politics. Tourists simply use money. They ignore national boundaries as they fly across the surface of the planet. They don't make friends or enemies. They have nearly all of the characteristics that Schmitt, Kojève, and Arendt sought to eject outside of the realm of thought as 'something not human'. The tourist is none other than the enemy of twentieth-century thought in the humanities in its entirety. Thus, if we get to the bottom of this issue, we will surely be able to go beyond the limits of twentieth-century thought.

If Hegel was only able to define the human through the dialectic that leads from the family to the citizen and from there to the state, can there be a definition of the human that is built upon the tourist? It is this that I want to think about.

3. Stratified World

1

Thinking about the philosophy of the tourist means thinking about an alternative line of political thought. If people were able to obtain universality not by affiliating with a particular state and internalising its values, but through a different circuit, what kind of path would they need to take? What new possibilities might the tourist—who is anonymous, true to their animalistic desires, makes neither friends nor enemies, and drifts between states—open up for the public realm?

As I made clear in the previous chapter, these questions are *fundamentally* unanswerable so long as we take as our premise the linear history of the spirit that posits a progression from family to national citizen and finally to world citizen. This is because, according to that line of thinking, being a member of a nation is equivalent to being political and thinking about the state is equivalent to thinking about politics.

Today we are faced with a reality that must cast doubt upon that equivalence. The twenty-first-century world is significantly different in structure from the world in the era of Kant and Hegel. Although both eras are based on the nation state and on states gathering together to create an international society, the way in which this gathering and creation take place is completely different. We can no longer say that thinking about the state is equivalent to thinking about politics. In the contemporary world we are seeing the expansion of a realm of politics unmediated by the state and a politics uncontrollable by the state, on both macro and micro levels. Hence we need a new line of political thought.

In Chapter 1, I raised the example of contemporary terrorism as a realm of politics uncontrollable by the state. Why, then, do such realms develop in the first place?

In the first half of this chapter, I will clarify the structure of the contemporary world that necessarily leads to the development of such realms (which are political, but are not included in what we understand as politics); in the second half I would like to finally begin discussing the possibilities generated by such nonpolitical politics for the public and for the universal—in other words, the philosophy of the tourist.

First, let us consider the *image* of the state. What is the state anyway? Hegel understood the state as the 'self-consciousness' of civil society (he actually understood it somewhat differently if we are being precise, but this is how we will summarise his view here).

Many people make their home in a certain land, trade goods among themselves, and live together. Here we have a civil society, but this alone doesn't produce a state. These people are not conscious of what they are doing, and are simply trading their goods motivated by the needs they face. A state is born only when a consciousness of identity is generated as they reflect upon this reality and search for the *reason* why they have a relationship with those others that they live with. This is the key to Hegel's philosophy.

The state is the self-consciousness of civil society. While this simple definition already has significant implications, there is another definition to which we must pay close attention.

Kant's theory of the international system in *Perpetual Peace*, discussed in the previous chapter, incorporates an interesting rule. He writes that 'peoples who have grouped themselves into a nation state' can be seen as possessing 'personhood'.[1]

Of course, he provides no basis for such a claim; he merely states it. And yet it can be said that this assumption is no mere passing impression, but provides a key to Kant's thought. Kant discusses the formation of an international society through multiple states and the formation of civil society through multiple people in analogous terms, but this analogy makes no sense unless we assume an equivalence between the state and the human. And indeed this equivalence shows up in various passages of *Perpetual Peace*. For example, as noted in the

---

1.   Kant argues that 'Peoples who have grouped themselves into nation states may be judged in the same way as individual men living in a state of nature', and in another passage writes that states must be treated as a 'moral person' and cannot be easily divided or incorporated into another state (Kant, 'Perpetual Peace', 102, 86). Kant believed that just as each person must be respected, states, too must be equally respected regardless of size or power.

previous chapter, Kant argues that in building a federation of states with a view to perpetual peace, each of the participating states must be republican states. There are many studies on this rule (first definitive article), but what is important here is that, structurally speaking, the idea that a state will not be welcomed into the federation of states unless it becomes a republic takes exactly the same form as the typical exhortation to an individual to 'grow up'. Kant was a philosopher who believed that, just as humans create civil society when they mature, states, too, create perpetual peace when they mature.

Kant thought of states as persons. Hegel thought of the state as the self-consciousness of civil society. Bringing these two definitions together, we obtain the following image: just as humans possess a body and spirit, nation states possess a civil society and a state. The bodily aspect and spiritual aspect of the 'substance' we call a nation state—that is, its economic aspect and its political aspect—correspond respectively to civil society and state.

This image neatly captures the world view of the age of nationalism. Scholars are divided on the issue of when this age began, but here I will follow Masachi Ōsawa's exhaustive study *The Origins of Nationalism*.[2] According to Ōsawa, while the origins of nationalism can be traced back to the age of absolute monarchies, it was not in full swing until the late eighteenth to early nineteenth century, precisely the era in which Kant and Hegel were writing. It was during this period that political systems became organised according to the unit of the nation state, and the scope of economies and taxation, which had hitherto formed quasi-naturally, were redefined with the concept of the 'national economy'. Certain territories in which there lived people with a shared language and customs, controlled by the same law and police, with a transportation network maintained through a unified central authority, came to be understood not only as political units but also as independent economic units. And as Ernest Gellner points out, they later came to be seen as cultural units as well.

Kant and Hegel witnessed the birth of this nationalism. For that reason, their view of the state became the prototype world view in the age of nationalism that followed. According to this view, the new unit of the 'nation state', rather than the individual, family, or tribe, was to be the common basis of politics, economics, and culture.

2.   M. Ōsawa, *Nashonarizumu no yurai* [*The Origins of Nationalism*]. (Tokyo: Kōdansha, 2007). See page 106 and the discussion starting on page 220.

We no longer live in this simple age of nationalism.

Today we live in an age in which most of the commodities that we eat, wear, see, and hear circulate beyond national borders—as if nation states did not exist. Whether we are in Tokyo, New York, Paris, Beijing, or Dubai, we can eat hamburgers at McDonald's, buy clothes at Gap, and watch Hollywood movies at the mall. As long as the city through which we are strolling boasts a certain level of prosperity and safety, there will not be much difference in how people dress or the advertisements in the streets, and there will be very little need to be conscious of differences between nation states. To put it another way, at the point of consumption, human society is becoming more or less one society, just as Schmitt and Arendt feared. This shift has progressed dramatically in the past quarter century since the end of the Cold War. Moreover, this trend is set to continue. The nation state no longer serves as the common basis of economy or culture.

At issue here is the fact that, despite these developments, there are still national borders, nation states, and nationalism. Not only that, their significance is beginning to increase. I am writing this in 2017. Last year the backlash against globalism became visible around the world: the UK decided to leave the EU, and the United States elected Donald Trump as president. European popular sentiment is largely shifting toward expelling refugees. In Japan, too, people publicly express xenophobic sentiments.

It was once optimistically declared that the age of nationalism was ending, and that the age of globalism was afoot. As noted in the previous chapter, this optimism can still be found among some 'information society' theorists. But even if this 'shift' may be realised in the future, it no longer seems that it will come about so easily. In reality, over the past quarter century, as globalism has increased, so too has nationalism as a reactive response. And now the clash between the two has become a political issue. In other words, it looks as though the world is becoming more interconnected and is erasing its borders on the one hand, but on the other it seems to be dividing ever more, and borders are being rebuilt. We are living neither in the era of a federation of states (the age of nationalism) as Kant dreamed, nor in an era of the world state (the age of globalism), as science fiction writers and IT entrepreneurs dreamed, but in an era characterised by a *split* between these two ideals.

How did this split occur? Ōsawa's aforementioned work develops an extremely complicated logic in order to explain the split.[3] It is the main theme of his lengthy book. But it seems to me that in some sense it came about more simply as the logical outcome of a quite straightforward reality.

Let us once again consider the *meaning* of the world view of the age of nationalism, where state and civil society were thought of as the spirit and body of one and the same substance (the nation state).

Let us try superimposing the contrast between spirit and body onto the contrast between 'conscious' and 'unconscious' in the Freudian sense, or in more vulgar terms the contrast between 'upper body' and 'lower body', where the upper body is the site of thought, the lower body the site of desire. With that being the case, we could say that, for the citizen (nation), the state/politics is the site of thought, whereas civil society/the economy is the site of desire. Indeed, citizens are understood as those beings who employ their sense of reason in deliberating over policy at the site of politics, while they follow their needs and desires in freely buying things at the site of economy.

Let us pursue this analogy a bit further. Humans typically act based on the rational thought of the upper body. At least, that is what they assume. They only show their upper body face to others. But in reality, they are troubled by the irrational desires held by their lower bodies. Managing desires is vitally important in leading a healthy social life. As Freudian psychoanalysis teaches us, if you fail to do so, you are liable to become ill.

Could we not say the same about the nation state? Peoples (nation states) typically act based on rational political thinking. At least, that is what they assume. And they only show other countries their face, or personality, as Kant would put it, in the form of the state. But in reality they are troubled by the irrational desires that plague civil society (such as xenophobia and hate speech). As such, managing these desires becomes vitally important to building a healthy international order. As you can see, when explained in this way, if we reword the first definitive article of *Perpetual Peace* (the civil constitution of every state should be republican) in human terms, it actually says something simple—vulgar, even. Kant is telling states that *before they can think about joining the international community, they must first be able to control their lower bodies.*

---

3.   Ōsawa, *Nashonarizumu no yurai*, 561.

The nation state is made of two halves, the state and civil society, politics and the economy, upper and lower body, conscious and unconscious. Based on these premises, Kant and Hegel believed in an ideal image of human ethics in which the international order is to be formed by the state standing over civil society and political consciousness repressing the unconscious of the economy.

I have somewhat belaboured this metaphorical point because when we understand the world order of the age of nationalism in this way, we can more clearly understand today's world order by identifying how it differs.

In the age of nationalism, a substance/nation state was constituted through the combination of two halves: state and civil society, politics and economy, public and private. This is why the nation state could serve as the basis of all orders.

But in the world of the twenty-first century, this premise itself has broken down. What is important here is to understand that it isn't the nation state itself that has broken down, but the *integrity* of the nation state.

The nation state is still alive today. The affairs of politics are still based on the unit of the nation state. Politicians gain the trust of citizens and work for the nation. The sense of the nation state still maintains its authority in this respect. But the economy does not operate according to the unit of the nation state. Merchants sell their wares to consumers around the world and collect money from consumers from around the world. Today, not just massive corporations, but even surprisingly small enterprises and individuals conduct their business across borders. There is no sense of the nation state at work in this realm. While political debate is separated by units of nation states, the desires of citizens are connected across national borders. Such is the reality of the twenty-first century.

To put it another way, in this twenty-first century in which we live, state and civil society, politics and the economy, thought and desire, under the guidance of the two different principles of nationalism and globalism, have grown into two different orders *that do not integrate with one another*. In my view, this is the crux of the issue that troubled Ōsawa. Globalism didn't destroy nationalism. Nor did it overcome nationalism. It certainly didn't produce a new nationalism within the global. It simply retained the existing order of nationalism and overlaid it with a completely different type of order.

As you can see from the above, although we are certainly not living in the age of nationalism, that doesn't mean simply that we live in the age of globalism either. Today, the two principles of order, nationalism and globalism, are applied to the two domains of politics and economics respectively, and are overlaid one upon the another. This is what I would like to call *the era of the stratified world* [*nisō kōzō*, more literally 'dual-layered structure'].

Kant understood the nation state as a human or a personality. In fact, during the age of nationalism, depictions of international relations were often modelled on human relations. Readers may remember seeing in their history textbooks old European political cartoons from the era of the Sino-Japanese War or the Russo-Japanese War in which countries including Japan are anthropomorphised. I mean the type of cartoons in which the US is a bearded man wearing a star-spangled top hat, China is an opium addict, and Russia is depicted as a bear. We don't see those kinds of political cartoons any more. In the age of the stratified structure, it is difficult to represent a state as one personality, whether it is the US, China, or Russia. Indeed, just because Trump was elected president doesn't necessarily mean that the US straight away becomes a closed nation state that is protectionist and xenophobic. The US cannot halt its trade with China, nor with any other country.

What kind of image is appropriate for such a world? Since in the era of the stratified world the economy continues to be connected no matter the level of political strife, if we were to depict international relations in a political cartoon, rather than showing each country as an independent human, the countries would instead lose their independence from one another, and would share one 'body' (civil society) with many 'faces' (states). There is actually a famous image that satisfies these requirements to be found in the history of Japanese manga: the monster that Daijirō Morohoshi depicted in his 1974 work *Biological City* (Figure 4, overleaf).[4] A spaceship brings back some unknown 'thing' from another planet, which causes people's bodies to fuse with any organism or inanimate object they touch. But they do not lose their independent wills. What ultimately emerges is an amorphous monster that is neither organism nor machine, with countless independent 'faces'. It is this image that is most appropriate for depicting the order of the age of the stratified world.

---

4.   See D. Morohoshi, *Kanata yori* [*From the Other Side*] (Tokyo: Shūeisha Bunko, 2004), 30.

Figure 4. Daijiro Morohoshi, 'Seibutsu toshi [Biological City]', in *Kanata Yori* [*From the Other Side*] (Tokyo: Shueisha Bunko, 2004). Reproduced with permission.

An era in which the economy connects but politics remain unconnected. A world in which desires connect but thought remains unconnected. An era in which the lower halves of bodies are connected, but the upper bodies refuse to connect. While this is the order of the age of the stratified world, if we pursue this line of thinking further, although some may find it crass, we could say that relations between nations in this age tend to become something like people becoming physically intimate without ever declaring their love for one another.

Today, the economy/the body directly connects across national borders, faithful to its desires. But politics/the face is unable to catch up with that reality. Politics/the face believes that there are many unresolved issues between two countries and that they should refrain from entering into an economic/physical relationship, because a trusting relationship hasn't yet developed. But civil society/the body is already familiar with the pleasures of intimacy and cannot simply cut off relations—it will seek out this intimacy whenever it has the chance. Metaphorically speaking, this kind of situation is happening all over the world. Japan's relation to its neighbours is an example of this as well. What is at issue here is that the struggle between the notion that a loveless relationship should be ended and the reality that it cannot be ended only raises the level of stress within society...and such situations never end well.

Indeed, it is probably imprudent to deepen economic dependence without being able to build a relationship of political trust. It may even be impure. In that sense, the age of the stratified world is imprudent and impure to the core. But in the end, if the relationship cannot be ended then one has no choice but to steel oneself and nurture the love. Aren't international relations similar to human relations in this regard?

2

All of the above was something of a tangent. But in any case, we now live in a world with a stratified structure constituted by the dual layer of state and civil society, politics and economy, thought and desire, nationalism and globalism. That is our hypothesis here. We are now being faced with the need to rethink situations that we have no choice but to call political, even though they fundamentally do not fit the definition of 'politics' according to the paradigm of Kant and Hegel (the paradigm of the age of nationalism). And this is because the image of the world has undergone a major transformation.

Schmitt, Kojève, and Arendt all understood the advent of globalism as the arrival of 'the nonhuman'. They believed that the expansion of the economy would lead to the extinction of the human. Thus, we may call these two layers the layer of the human and the layer of 'the nonhuman', or in other words *the human layer and the animal layer.*

We might think of the twenty-first-century world as a world in which the layer of nationalism where humans live as humans and the layer of globalism in which humans can only live as animals run in parallel while remaining independent. The philosophy of the tourist envisaged in this book, defined according to this image of the world, is an attempt to explore the possibility of linking the layer of globalism with the layer of nationalism via a route *different* from that of Hegelian maturity; it asks whether there is *another* route for connecting to the public and the universal while citizens remain in civil society and individuals remain true to their own desires.

Here I would like to add one more line of thought from the history of philosophy. Up to this point, I have maintained that most thought in the humanities has barely considered the politics generated by the non-political realm, and that it has been fundamentally incapable of doing so. But if we turn our attention to the political thought of the Anglophone world in the late twentieth century, we find one exception in which this issue has in fact been considered (or at least an attempt has been made to consider it).

Libertarianism is a new line of thought that was born in the United States in the mid-twentieth century. To borrow Susumu Morimura's concise definition, it consists in 'an understanding of social ethics and political thought that advocates the maximising of individual freedoms and the minimising of government control'.[5]

Economic freedom is included in the freedoms respected by libertarians. Respecting economic freedom as much as possible essentially means taking a cautious stance on the issue of the redistribution of wealth by the state, and for this reason libertarians necessarily take a negative stance toward the welfare state (big government). Libertarianism is sharply opposed to liberalism on this point. Liberalism in the United States today takes the ideologically opposite position of supporting the welfare state in which the redistribution of wealth is emphasised and economic freedom is regulated, although it respects individual freedom of personal morals and behaviour. Although owing to their historical trajectories they have come to be referred to by words with similar etymologies, the two are not to be confused.

Because libertarianism holds the freedom of the individual in high esteem, at times it approaches anarchism. In fact, Robert Nozick's 1974 book, often said to be the theoretical starting point of libertarianism, is entitled *Anarchy, State, and Utopia*. In this book, Nozick develops a careful discussion of the extent to which the monopolisation of violence and the limitation of individual rights by the state can be justified through a step-by-step argument setting out from John Locke's supposition of the state of nature and the primitive property rights of

---

5.   S. Morimura (ed.), *Ribatarianizumu dokuhon* [*Libertarianism Reader*] (Tokyo: Keisō Shobō, 2005), iv.

the individual. He concludes that the state can only be morally justified when it is a minimal state (a state which protects its citizens from violence and crime and assists in the enforcement of contracts), and that anything more extensive cannot be justified.[6] Nozick accepted the existence of states even so, but there are those who reject the state altogether. Some, like Murry Rothbard and David Friedman, argue that all public (or at least what we assume to be public) services responsibility for which is currently shouldered by the state should be left to market principles, including the police and justice system, not to mention education and insurance. For this reason, libertarianism is highly compatible with economic thought, and has an especially deep relationship with a school of thought in economics called 'law and economics'. Law and economics approaches the issue of law through economic theory; in other words, it conducts a comparative analysis of the effects of law and nonlegal measures in terms of their respective costs.

In the context of the present work, what is notable in the libertarian theory of the state is that it is completely different in character to the theories of Hegel and those who followed him, discussed in the previous chapter.

In Nozick's minimal state the dialectical (spiritual historical) function that served as a first premise for Hegel and Schmitt is entirely absent. Nozick considers the state only as a minimum mechanism of adjustment that allows multiple individuals with different interests to live together. The minimal state does nothing to change the desires of individuals. It does not turn individuals into members of the nation. Instead, it is thought of as a value-neutral foundation upon which functions (such as education) for turning individuals into members of the nation may optionally be attached. Nozick called his minimal state 'a framework for utopias' (a meta-utopia).[7] In other words, the libertarian 'state' is

---

6.   R. Nozick, *Anarchy, State, and Utopia* (New York: Basic Books, 1974). On libertarianism in general, aside from the book cited in the previous footnote, see S. Morimura, *Jiyū wa dokomade kanō ka* [*To What Extent is Freedom Possible?*] (Tokyo: Kōdansha Gendai Shinsho, 2001).

7.   Nozick, *Anarchy, State, and Utopia*, 297. Although there is not space here to elaborate on this point, in this section Nozick discusses the very idea of optimism which served as the starting point of this book (although he does not refer to Leibniz). According to Nozick, the optimum among all possible worlds, in other words the theoretical framework of authority necessary for pursuing utopia, is the minimal state. We each build our own utopia upon the minimal state and live in our own best possible world.

understood not as a layer of politics/the human, but as a mechanism belonging to the thoroughly nonpolitical layer of the economy/the animal. Hence libertarians are able to discuss the state as if it were a private enterprise.

This then suggests the possibility that libertarian theory is constructed in a way that is free of the Hegelian paradigm that links together the state, politics, and the human as equivalents. And this is of decisive importance. Interpretations based on the ideological opposition between leftist liberalism and rightist libertarianism are largely irrelevant in the face of this important point. Since it is free from the Hegelian paradigm, libertarianism carries within it the seeds of a new political thinking.

In spite of this (or perhaps because of it), scholars in the humanities are typically lukewarm about such a prospect. It was not until the 2000s that the importance of libertarianism became widely known in Japan. Few have approached the important question of *the significance of libertarianism for the humanities*, even though it could serve as the seed for the philosophy of the tourist.

The attention of scholars in the humanities observing the contemporary Anglophone world has instead been focused on the 'liberal-communitarian debate'. This involves a political standpoint different from libertarianism called 'communitarianism'. In a word, this is a social-ethical standpoint that privileges the good of the community over universal justice. Like libertarianism, communitarianism is a new line of thought that emerged in the late twentieth century.

The birth of communitarianism is actually intimately linked to the birth of libertarianism: both emerged as critiques of liberalism. The classic theory of twentieth-century liberalism is said to have been presented in John Rawls's 1971 book *A Theory of Justice*. Nozick's *Anarchy, State, and Utopia* was actually written as a critique of *A Theory of Justice*, with this critique serving as the starting point for libertarianism. Communitarianism was also inaugurated by a book that was written as a critique of *A Theory of Justice*: a key book in its development was Michael Sandel's 1982 *Liberalism and the Limits of Justice*. There Sandel argues that, while Rawls's theory is premised on a universal subject that pursues universal justice (the unencumbered self), this is too powerful an assumption, and political theory can only be premised on a subject embedded in a particular

set of values belonging to a particular community (good, rather than justice).
Through the 1980s and the 1990s, Sandel's book sparked a lengthy debate in
the Anglophone world of political science between liberals and communitarians.[8]

The liberal-communitarian debate is understood to be an event of considerable importance in the world of political science. But in my view, the emergence
of libertarianism is a far more significant event, with great consequences for
the future.

The crux of the liberal-communitarian debate is quite simple: liberals believe
in universal justice while communitarians don't. That is all there is to it. And
theories that maintain the idea of universal justice emerged as the descendants
of Kant and Hegel, who believed in the linear narrative that proceeded from the
individual to civil society to the state, and finally to the world citizen.

Kant and those who followed him did not believe that the story ended with
individuals becoming members of a nation. They believed that belonging to a
particular state was merely one stage in the ascent toward a more universal subject. Unlike the closed-off nationalism of today, the nationalism of the nineteenth
century was linked to perpetual peace (Kant) and to the World Spirit (Hegel).
Liberals still believe in that developmental schema (dialectics). In contrast,
communitarians no longer believe in it. There lies the essence of the debate. In
other words, it is merely a phenomenon corresponding to the destruction of the
Hegelian paradigm. In contrast, as I noted earlier, the emergence of libertarianism
carries with it the possibility of a theory that goes beyond that paradigm.

Above I noted that globalism does not destroy nationalism, but preserves it
while overlaying it with a different, alien order. But this requires an addendum.

To be sure, globalism preserved nationalism. But this does not mean that it
did not change anything. In the past, nationalism was the first step in ascending
toward the World Spirit. But today that ascension does not exist, because the
World Spirit has been replaced by the world market. The nationalism of today
must eternally remain a nationalism—that is, it is doomed to remain a love for
a particular community, without ever attaining universality. The communitarian

8.   On this debate, see S. Mulhall and A. Swift, *Liberals and Communitarians* (Oxford: Blackwell, 1996).

critique of liberalism corresponds to precisely this dysfunction of contemporary nationalism.

Libertarianism is the philosophical expression of globalism, while communitarianism is the philosophical expression of contemporary nationalism. And liberalism is the philosophical expression of the nationalism of the past.

Liberalism believed in universal justice. It believed in tolerance toward the other. But this standpoint rapidly lost its influence in the late twentieth century, and today only libertarianism and communitarianism remain. Libertarians speak only for the pleasures of animals, while communitarians speak only for the good of the community. At this rate, no universal will appear, nor will the Other. This is the philosophical challenge that we now face.

3

Let us finally begin our engagement with the philosophy of the tourist. The term refers to a philosophy that would address the politics that is being established outside of politics; a philosophy concerning a public realm based on the animal and on desire, and a new philosophy of the other made possible by globalism. As such, how does it relate to the stratified world described above?

When introducing a new philosophy, it is usually difficult to gain the trust of others without referring to preexisting philosophies. So here I would like to suggest a path toward the philosophy of the tourist by reference to Michael Hardt and Antonio Negri's 'multitude', one of the most talked about concepts in recent political thought.

I do not necessarily want to say that the tourist *is* the multitude. That would make this book unoriginal. But I believe that, with appropriate changes, the concept of the multitude can be recast as the concept of the tourist called for in this book. And I believe that this will serve as the starting point for a new political thought and political subject for the twenty-first century era.

What is the multitude? In order to explain this, I must first explain the concept of Empire that Hardt and Negri proposed.

Hardt and Negri published their co-authored book *Empire* in 2000.[9] They called the globalising post-Cold War world 'Empire', and argued that it was generating an order completely different from the previous order, which was made

---

9.   M. Hardt and A. Negri, *Empire* (Cambridge, MA: Harvard University Press, 2000).

up of alliances between sovereign states. This suggestion garnered tremendous attention outside of the world of theory, and the book became a global bestseller.

This discussion of Empire actually has a great deal of affinity with the theory of the stratified world explored above. Hardt and Negri juxtapose the system of nation states with the system of Empire, writing that '[t]he declining sovereignty of nation states and their increasing inability to regulate economic and cultural exchanges is in fact one of the primary symptoms of the coming of Empire'.[10] In other words, Hardt and Negri believe that nation states can no longer sustain economic and cultural control on their own, and that this gives rise to a new order. This is precisely my understanding as well. 'Empire' refers to the new political order separate from the nation state that is created by states, enterprises, and citizens as they seek to make economic and cultural exchanges function more smoothly. In the terms of the present work, we can think of the system of nation states as corresponding to the layer of nationalism and the system of Empire as corresponding to the layer of globalism.

What is also important is the fact that, with the word 'Empire', Hardt and Negri attempt to capture the paradoxical set of issues raised by the politics created by the layer of the animal/globalism—that is to say, *the political order created by that which the humanities have traditionally excluded from political thinking.*

The Japanese translators of Hardt and Negri summarise their thinking as follows: 'Globalisation is typically understood as an economic phenomenon, and even when considered from a political perspective, it is usually understood simply as a threat to the politics based on the nation state and popular sovereignty. Against such common sense, Hardt and Negri suggest that what we are faced with in the vortex of globalisation is the formation of a new political order and a new form of sovereignty.'[11] The drift of Hardt and Negri's argument can be appreciated even with this short introduction: globalisation itself creates a new domain of politics, but this politics does not involve the nation state. This is the crux of their argument.

As I have meticulously laid out above, from the perspective of the traditional humanities, this argument contains a contradiction. This is precisely why the

---

10. Ibid., xii.
11. M. Hardt and A. Negri, <*Teikoku*>, tr. K. Mizushima et al. (Tokyo: Ibunsha, 2003), 514. The author of the passage cited above is Kazunori Mizushima.

questions that Hardt and Negri raise are so important. But it also means that we cannot understand their argument without understanding the importance of this paradox and the need for flexible thinking in grappling with it. To do otherwise would mean reading *Empire* as just another book in international politics that labels the behemoth United States as an 'empire' and analyses its mechanism. This kind of misreading is actually quite typical, and many suggested that *Empire*'s argument was already obsolete in the wake of the 9/11 terrorist attacks (the book was published in 2000) and that the world was now entering a 'post-Empire' age.[12] But such criticism has no relation to Hardt and Negri's argument, since what they call 'Empire' is the order that globalisation itself produces—an order that is likely to continue to expand for as long as humanity continues its economic activity, whether or not the United States is the 'hegemonic state', and indeed whether or not such a state exists at all.

Be that as it may, there are differences between *Empire* and the understanding put forward here. Hardt and Negri are addressing the 'shift' from the system of nation states to the system of Empire. In other words, they believe that the age of nation states is soon to end, and that the age of Empire will then arrive (or at least this is what their writing seems to suggest). In contrast, here we address the coexistence of the two systems.

However, I actually believe that the argumentation of Hardt and Negri, too, fits the co-existence/stratified structure model better than the shift model. I base this claim on their theory of power.

Empire makes the important argument that the system of nation states and the system of Empire differ as to their principal form of power. 'Disciplinary power' is privileged in the former, 'biopower' in the latter.

Disciplinary power and biopower are two categories employed in contemporary French theory. Broadly speaking, disciplinary power refers to a type of power in which those in authority control the object of their power by giving them commands and doling out punishments. Biopower, on the other hand, refers to power which, while respecting the free will of the objects of its power, in the

---

12.   For example E. Todd, *After the Empire: The Breakdown of the American Order* [2002], tr. C. Jon Delogu and M. Lind (New York: Columbia University Press, 2006). Although Todd does not refer to Hardt and Negri's book, it seems certain from the title that the author has *Empire* in mind.

end still succeeds in controlling them according to the aims of the authority by adjusting rules, prices, or the environment. It is called biopower in the sense that it intervenes in the social and bodily life of the people who are subjected to it.

The history of these two concepts is quite complex, and although it is generally thought that Foucault invented both, he actually never juxtaposed them in this way. Disciplinary power appeared in his 1975 book *Discipline and Punish*, while biopower appeared in the 1976 book *The Will to Knowledge* (volume 1 of *The History of Sexuality*), and these two books set out to analyse quite different phenomena. Later on, however, in 1990 (after Foucault's death) the philosopher Gilles Deleuze, a friend of Foucault, juxtaposed the two in a short essay and suggested a simple schema according to which the 'disciplinary society' was the model up until the nineteenth century, with disciplinary power predominating, but contemporary society is shifting to a 'society of control' in which biopower is dominant.[13] This schema of a shift from discipline to control soon became widely known because it was far easier to grasp than Foucault's original argument. Hardt and Negri, too, refer to Deleuze's schema. (As an aside, building upon Deleuze's discussion of card keys and GPS, in Japan, the issue of biopower/control—power that controls the environment—has been linked to theories of power in the information society under the heading of 'the power of architecture'.)[14]

13.   G. Deleuze, 'Postscript on the Societies of Control', *October* 59 (Winter 1992), 3–7.

14.   See H. Azuma, 'Jōhō jiyūron [On Information and Freedom]' [2002/2003], *Jōhō kankyōronshū Azuma Hiroki korekushon S*. [*Collected Essays on Information Environment, Hiroki Azuma Collection S*] (Tokyo: Kōdansha BOX, 2007); H. Azuma and S. Hamada (eds.), *ised: Jōhō shakai no rinri to sekkei—rinri-hen* [*ised: Ethics and Design of Information Society: Ethics*] (Tokyo: Kawada Shobō Shinsha, 2 vols, 2010). The two *ised* volumes are a record of a large-scale research conference that I led between 2004 and 2006 at the Center for Global Communications (GLOCOM), International University of Japan. The separate volumes on ethics and design correspond to the stratified structure that is the topic of this book. Indeed, at this conference I proposed a figure I called the 'Stratified Structure of the Postmodern', which became the starting point for the present book:

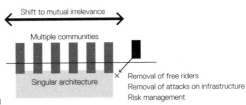

Freedom of social interiority (Subject) with coexistence of freedom of the subject and control of the body
Coexistence of diverse values; Realm in which disciplinary power is active; Logic of the market is dominant

Control of the body
Value-neutral infrastructure; Libertarian meta-utopia; Realm in which the power of environmental control is active; Logic of security is dominant

Shift to mutual irrelevance

Multiple communities

Singular architecture

Removal of free riders
Removal of attacks on infrastructure
Risk management

In any case, it is on the basis of this genealogy of the theory of power that Hardt and Negri develop their argument that the shift from a disciplinary society to a control society will be realised in political terms as a shift from nation states to Empire. This theory of power is one of the keys to *Empire*.

But how appropriate is this argument? I believe that the shift in the form of power upon which the argument is premised is itself suspect.

Why? Because the two forms of power, discipline and control, should not be thought of as mutually exclusive. Discipline and control can very well be activated at the same time. Deleuze's explanation of these two forms of power is inextricable from his own unique philosophical system. Although on the surface it may seem as if discipline and control are opposed to one another, this impression is a product of Deleuze's interpretation. In reality, the authority or controller can use multiple means to realise its goal. For example, if it wants to chase homeless people from a park, it can directly order them to leave, or nudge them toward leaving 'of their own accord' by changing the design of the benches and pedestrian paths or building a shelter nearby.

If we turn our attention to thought in the Anglophone world, the aforementioned 'law and economics' movement and the closely related field of behavioural economics take up as their field of study this kind of mutual adjustment between multiple forms of power.[15] Far from being mutually exclusive, discipline and order are complementary, and we can find an infinite number of examples of both at work in contemporary society.

The example that Deleuze provided for a control society is a 'city where one would be able to leave one's apartment, one's street, one's neighborhood, thanks to one's (dividual) electronic card that raises a barrier; but the card could just as easily be rejected on a given day or between certain hours.'[16] But the assigning of such a card does not mean that disciplinary commands and surveillance disappear. By coincidence I am in a hotel as I write this, and many hotels today control entry into rooms and movements between floors using precisely the

15. R. Thaler and C. Sunstein, *Nudge: Improving Decisions About Health, Wealth, and Happiness* (London: Penguin, 2009). One of the authors, Sunstein, is a constitutional scholar known in Japan for his work on information society. In this book, the relationship between architecture and law are discussed using none other than the language of economics. The title *Nudge* exemplifies how the authors' interest is on the soft manipulation of the will. It is precisely this manipulation that is the key to biopower/control.
16. Deleuze, 'Societies of Control', 7.

kind of card Deleuze imagined. Once I've checked out, I won't be able to return to this room using the same card, nor will I even be able to push a button in the elevator. But that doesn't mean that there isn't anyone staffing the lobby or that the various warning signs are removed. The cards exist more as insurance in case these kinds of commands and surveillance fall short (for example, when the customer does not speak the local language). In which case, shouldn't we say that disciplinary society and control society are overlaid one on top of the another, and that therefore nation state and Empire are similarly overlaid?

Or perhaps we could put it this way: earlier, I associated nationalism with the human and globalism with the animal. The nation state is a system that treats humans like humans. In fact, it is the nation state that makes humans human (through disciplinary training). That was Hegel's view.

Then what about Empire? If we pursue this opposition between the human and the animal further, we could say that Empire is a system that treats humans as animals. Empire does not call upon individuals for anything. It only wants them to be consumers. Here the individual is nothing more than an entry in the big data gathered from a planetary-scale global marketplace.

But this is not simply to reiterate humanistic, leftist accusations along the lines that 'Empire doesn't treat humans as humans!' As noted earlier, biopower is a concept that was employed in *The Will to Knowledge*, and what Foucault revealed in that book was how the path taken in nineteenth-century Germany and France—where the importance of public sanitation was discovered, statistics became important, the living environment of workers improved, and welfare systems were planned—was directly linked to the expansion of state power (in the form of biopower).[17] Amid intense competition, the nation states of the nineteenth century were faced with the need for a plan to increase the population of workers in order to raise productivity. The idea of public sanitation was born of such concerns. No doubt it raised the quality of living among workers. But its origin was no different from the notion of controlling the sanitation of livestock for the purpose of raising the productivity of a farm.

---

17.   M. Foucault, *The History of Sexuality, Vol. 1: An Introduction* (New York: Vintage, 1990), 137. On the relationship between the discipline of statistics and the development of the welfare state, see I. Hacking, *The Taming of Chance* (Cambridge: Cambridge University Press, 1990).

The workers who are the subject of public sanitation, then, are faceless. And equally, they are nameless. Each is simply one among millions of data points; in fact, public sanitation cannot be achieved without such large-scale analysis. For this reason, it is closely tied to progress in methods of statistical analysis. In this regard, biopower is in essence a power that controls humans as one would control animals. Indeed, some of the technologies of the control society that Deleuze employed as examples, such as those embedded in card keys and GPS, were in many cases first introduced for livestock.

Moreover, the treatment of humans as humans and as animals are by no means mutually exclusive. It is quite possible for the same individual to be treated as a human (as a being with a will and a face) in a particular site of communication and then elsewhere to be treated as an animal (as an anonymous sample), as a statistical object. In fact, contemporary society is full of such examples.

Take the issue of the declining birth rate as an example. As long as we treat each woman as a particular being with a face—that is, as a human—our society cannot command them to give birth to a child. That would be ethically wrong. On the other hand, to the extent that the totality of women is analysed as a faceless crowd, that is, as animals, it is possible to say that a particular number of women *must* give birth to children, and that for this to occur a particular kind of economic or technical environment ought to be put in place. This stance is not seen as ethically wrong. And in contemporary society (quite strangely!), these two moral judgments are not held to be contradictory. This agreement itself proves that our society judges discipline and biopower separately. While the nation state cannot encourage reproduction, Empire can. That is the contemporary ethic of reproduction.

While we live as humans, we also live as animals. We are individuals with a face while also living as one of an anonymous crowd. In this sense, all contemporary humans are ambiguous beings, and the stratified structure of the world that we have explored above necessarily proceeds from such ambiguity. And this is precisely why we need the tourist. I shall come back to this troublesome relation between the individual and statistics in the next chapter.

For now, let us return to the multitude. It is originally an abstract noun in English that means plurality. It also refers to a crowd or the masses, but not in a positive sense; in fact, it was once a negative word that suggested a foolish mob.[18] But Hardt and Negri, while referencing the ideas of thinkers such as Spinoza, reinterpret it as a word that broadly refers to a resistance movement (counter-Empire) against the system of Empire, but which is born from within Empire. Today it is one of the only concepts that remains pertinent in philosophically evaluating anti-establishment citizen movements.

Empire defines the multitude as an 'alternative' created by the system of Empire—the movement of a 'new proletariat' that demands 'global citizenship' and the 'reappropriation' of the means of production—and as 'biopolitical self-organization'.[19]

This is an extremely abstract definition, but if we read carefully we see that the book is not suggesting anything too complicated. While the multitude essentially refers to anti-establishment movements and citizen movements, in contrast to movements of the past it does not reject global capitalism. Instead, it makes use of the power of global capitalism. For example, it actively uses the internet in collecting information and mobilising people. It also collaborates with companies and the media. And it conspires to change the system from the inside. This is why the multitude is referred to as a resistance movement and alternative created by Empire itself. The bearers of this multitude are not a fixed party organisation as in communism, but a guerrilla solidarity (self-organisation) in the form of a transnational network made up of multiple citizens and NGOs. As successful examples of multitude, Hardt and Negri cite the 1999 anti-globalisation demonstration in Seattle (the demonstrations against the WTO Ministerial Conference) and the World Social Forum which had its first meeting in Porto Alegre, Brazil, in 2001.[20]

---

18. For example, in his *Reflections on the Revolution in France,* Edmund Burke uses the phrase 'swinish multitude' to refer to the chaos that erupted through the revolution. E. Burke, *Reflections on the Revolution in France and Other Writings* (New York: Knopf, 2015), 493.

19. Hardt and Negri, *Empire,* 393, 400, 406, 411.

20. M. Hardt and A. Negri, *Multitude: War and Democracy in the Age of Empire* (London: Penguin, 2004), 285–88; 294.

This concept of multitude was received feverishly by leftist activists whose movements had lost their direction after the Cold War structure collapsed and their ideology foundered. As mentioned above, *Empire* became a bestseller. In reality, Hardt and Negri's analysis was also prophetic. In late 2010, a decade after the publication of *Empire*, there was the so-called 'Arab Spring', featuring a chain of demonstrations and the collapse of regimes. The following autumn saw the 'Occupy Movement' (the movement to occupy Wall Street), which continued for several months. These seemed like new examples of success by the multitude, as people mobilised by social media played a major role, unlike in previous movements supported by official political organisations. In fact, Hardt and Negri quickly published a short book in a show of solidarity with these movements.[21] Their ideas have become important in Japan, too, in discussions about the series of events between the anti-nuclear power demonstrations since 2011 and the 2015 protests against security legislation in front of the National Diet.

Furthermore, the concept of the multitude is important in the context of this book because it is imagined as a movement that traverses the stratified structure, as a possible link for connecting the political layer to the economic layer.

I made critical reference to Arendt in Chapter 2. In fact, Hardt and Negri, too, when they explain the concept of the multitude, criticise Arendt's theoretical tendency to differentiate completely between that which is 'political' and that which is 'social', and to separate political liberation from movements based upon economic demands (class struggle). The wording here is slightly different since I refer to different texts by Arendt, but the gist of their criticism is entirely consistent with mine. Arendt's political theory was based on the principle of distinguishing between politics and economy (society), private and public, *polis* and *oikos*. Indeed, as I have been emphasising thus far, she believed these distinctions to be the condition of politics.

However, Hardt and Negri argue that the multitude is precisely the kind of movement that does not make these distinctions. The multitude begins its movement from its own life (*oikos*), from the site of labour and life. And this leads to the critique of Empire. The neologism 'biopolitics', which combines 'life' and 'politics' (although originally Foucault's word) is used again and again precisely in order to emphasise this dynamic. They declare that '(a)ny theoretical effort in this

21.   M. Hardt and A. Negri, *Declaration* (Independence, KS: Argo-Navis, 2012).

context [that of the multitude] to pose the autonomy of the political, separate from the social and the economic, no longer makes any sense'.[22]

A *poliš* that begins with *oikos*. A public politics with private life as its starting point. The issue of LGBT might be a good example for readers having trouble imagining what this might look like. It goes without saying that gender choice is a private matter. As such, it is not a matter that ought to be discussed politically, according to Arendt's definition of politics, and in fact for a long time it wasn't taken up by politics. It was thought that the hardships of LGBTQ people were a matter that should be solved in private without relying upon politics. Some conservatives still feel that way today.[23] But it is precisely this distinction that the multitude destroys.

Above I wrote that the philosophy of the tourist seeks a route that traverses the animal and human layers, that is, a route that links citizens to the public while allowing them to remain in civil society layer as citizens. As it is clear from the above discussion, Hardt and Negri's idea of the multitude in fact comes quite close to achieving that goal. While *Empire* is generally received as a book about international politics, it is actually a philosophical book that attempts to reform the definition of politics itself, and the image of the multitude is quite close to that of the tourist considered in this book.

Be that as it may, there is a fatal flaw to the concept of the multitude. For that reason, a certain revision must made to the philosophy of Hardt and Negri in order to build a philosophy of the tourist.

---

22. Hardt and Negri, *Multitude*, 78.
23. In July 2016, the American IT businessman and investor Peter Thiel reportedly said the following at the Republican National Convention. 'When I was a kid, the great debate was about how to defeat the Soviet Union. And we won. Now we are told that the great debate is about who gets to use which bathroom. This is a distraction from our real problems. Who cares?' (*Forbes Japan*, 22 July 2016, <http://forbesjapan.com/articles/detail/12973>). Although Thiel is a Trump supporter, this statement simply communicates the essence of political opposition today. Over the past several decades, liberals have proposed expanding the realm of politics and bringing many private issues, including sexuality, into the arena of public debate. Public issues (how to defeat the Soviets) are not differentiated from private issues (who uses which bathroom). The origin of this line of thinking can be traced back to the famous catchphrase of the 1960s, 'the personal is the political', and Hardt and Negri's theory of the multitude is an extension of this. Thiel feels aggravated by this tendency, and Trump's supporters were precisely people similarly aggrieved. 'America First' also meant 'politics first'.

Hardt and Negri are quite eloquent in their description of the emergence of the multitude. Indeed, as noted above, as we enter the twenty-first century, calls for an alternative to globalisation (another globalisation or alterglobalism) are growing louder throughout the world. Self-organising through networks (leaderless mobilisation) has become the norm as well.[24] In this sense, the presence of the multitude has clearly increased.

Then how does its power link itself to actual politics? How do demonstrations drive politics? In fact, Hardt and Negri's work lacks any strategic theory for this. It almost seems as if they are saying that the existence of demonstrations is itself already a politics.

Ōsawa summarises this fact and criticises it in the following way (his treatise on nationalism actually begins with this criticism): 'A mechanism for directly connecting the activity of the multitude to sovereignty is necessary. What [...] is this mechanism? They say "ether!" Ether refers to the system of communication ubiquitous in the globalised world. [...] The use of a mystical factor like ether as a premise is not an explanation of such mechanisms—it is an act of giving up any explanation.'[25] In other words, to put it bluntly, it seems as though Hardt and Negri are saying that, so long as the multitude congregates and raises its voices, the power of the internet *will do the rest*. At issue here is the power of belief. Or 'love'. In fact, the long discussion in *Empire* ends with the following passage that almost reads like a profession of faith:

> There is an ancient legend that might serve to illuminate the future life of communist militancy: that of Saint Francis of Assisi. [...] This is a revolution that no power will control—because biopower and communism, cooperation and revolution remain together, in love, simplicity, and also innocence. This is the irrepressible lightness and joy of being communist.[26]

---

24. Although I could not explore it here, Hardt and Negri also use the metaphor of an 'orchestra with no conductor' in discussing the self-organisation of the multitude (*Multitude*, 338). On the other hand, in his book *Surveillance Society* published around the same time as *Empire*, the sociologist David Lyon uses a similar metaphor in describing the system of the side that surveils (the side of Empire), calling it 'surveillance as social orchestration' (D. Lyon, *Surveillance Society: Monitoring Everyday Life* [Maidenhead: Open University Press, 2001], 56). In other words, the authorities self-organise and their opposition also self-organises. But does this really amount to saying anything?

25. Ōsawa, *Nashonarizumu no yurai*, 22.

26. Hardt and Negri, *Empire*, p. 413.

It is indeed a beautiful passage. But it does not give us any strategy.

The new movement needs no party, ideology, or leader. It need not even be anticapitalist. It only needs to believe in the power of the network. All it needs is love. Unfortunately, *Empire* and *Multitude* can be read in this way. In fact, the Japanese commentary on the latter features a very passionate passage by the translation project leader, in which we read: 'the project of the multitude is also a project of love, and the struggle of the multitude is also an experiment in love'.[27] Japanese readers, at the very least, have read this in Hardt and Negri's work.

To put it in somewhat vicious terms, maybe *Empire* became a global bestseller and continues to be referenced by activists today not in spite of this lack of theory in the movement of the multitude but *because* of it, rather than its popularity owing to the power of its analysis and the depth of its thought. As long as you believe in the internet and love, the self-organisation of biopolitics will do the rest—it is quite a convenient theory of the movement. Even if this is a misreading, people have felt themselves empowered by precisely this kind of misreading.

Hardt and Negri's definition of the multitude is too vague, and at times mystical. This attracts romanticist self-satisfaction. The philosophy of the tourist must avoid this weakness.

And in order to avoid this weakness, we must know where it comes from. How did the concept of the multitude come to harbour such a weakness? I believe there are probably two reasons for it.

The first is that Hardt and Negri's discussion is 'monistic'. In the world of *Empire* there is only Empire. Moreover, there is only one Empire. This singularity of Empire is crucial to their discussion. I will not get into the details, as it will distract us from the overall point, but this feature is inextricably tied to the philosophy of Spinoza. In any case, since according to their discussion only Empire exists in the world, the arising of the multitude must then be dependent upon Empire; resistance against Empire is necessarily dependent upon Empire. This self-circulating schema in which Empire itself generates the enemy of Empire and the struggle between them takes place within Empire is decisive in rendering the theory of the movement of the multitude ambiguous.

---

27.   M. Hardt and A. Negri, *Maruchichūdo (ge)*, tr. S. Ikushima (Tokyo: NHK Bukkusu, 2005), 275 [emphasis removed]. The author of the cited quote is Kazunori Mizushima.

In fact, Ōsawa, too, argues that the flaw in this theory of Empire lies in its attempt to create a monistic theory. The only way to fix this flaw is to think about the outside of Empire, that is, the nation state. Ōsawa begins his exploration of nationalism from this starting point. As I will discuss in the next chapter, I will explore this 'outside' in a way different from Ōsawa.

The other reason is that their concept of multitude is very much influenced by previous post-Marxist theories of movements, although this requires a complicated explanation.

While today the arguments put forward in *Empire* have become more well known, there were many attempts to explore a new theory of movement prior to its publication. One of the most influential among them is the theory of 'radical democracy' advanced by Ernesto Laclau and Chantal Mouffe.[28] Their interest lay in the question of how to build solidarity among various resistance movements in a world in which trust in the communist revolution has been lost or, in short, a world in which the 'grand narrative' of the Left has collapsed. 'Radical democracy' refers to the new image of solidarity they proposed.

What was the image of solidarity they offered? In order to simplify my explanation, I will here refer not to the text by Laclau and Mouffe, but to the summary offered by Slavoj Žižek in his 1989 book *The Sublime Object of Ideology* (Laclau and Mouffe's names are among those listed in the acknowledgements in the book). According to that book,

> here, we have an articulation of particular struggles (for peace, ecology, feminism, human rights, and so on), none of which pretends to be the 'Truth,' the last Signified, the 'true Meaning' of all the others; but the title 'radical democracy' itself indicates how *the very possibility of their articulation* implies the 'nodal' determining role of a certain struggle.[29]

Here Žižek is pointing out that what is important in Laclau and Mouffe's new image of solidarity isn't the contents of each resistance movement, but *the fact of solidarity itself*. In the past, communism functioned as the 'grand narrative',

---

28. E. Laclau and C. Mouffe, *Hegemony and Socialist Strategy: Towards a Radical Democratic Politics* (London: Verso, 2001).

29. S. Žižek, *The Sublime Object of Ideology* (London: Verso, 2009), 96 (emphasis mine).

providing meaning to these various resistance movements. And this gave them grounds for solidarity. But communism is no longer functional. That being the case, solidarity must be forged regardless of content. In the struggle over hegemony today, it is the sheer *fact* of solidarity that is effective. This is the argument of Laclau and Mouffe. And in fact, on this point, Hardt and Negri's multitude, too, has the same characteristic. They see the multitude as a body of movements that forms networks of solidarity which expand the dimensions of the struggle, regardless of the particular issues each of them faces:

> [T]he primary point is that their practices, strategies, and objectives, although different, are able to connect and combine with each other to form a plural, shared project. The singularity of each struggle fosters rather than hinders the creation of a common terrain.[30]

For now, let us shelve the specificity of individual struggles and simply focus on solidarity. Since the enemy is always power, let us build solidarity, whether it is with peace movements, ecological movements, or feminist movements.... Movements that lost their ideological pillars after the Cold War have stumbled toward such convoluted strategies, and it is clear to anyone that there are serious issues with this kind of formulation. While this kind of contentless solidarity (which in fact actively opts for such contentlessness) may lead to success in strengthening mobilisation and wresting away hegemony in the short term, it will certainly invite the weakening and hollowing out of each struggle in the long term. In fact, this has happened in many countries, including in Japan in the 2010s.

The solidarity of the multitude is an extension of the warped strategy of post-Marxism, and is founded on the nullification of the specificity of struggles. For that reason, its theory of movements cannot help but be vague.

---

30. Hardt and Negri, *Declaration*, 65. However, Hardt and Negri do not refer directly to the theory of radical democracy in proposing their concept of multitude. Furthermore, Laclau and Mouffe have been critical of Hardt and Negri's conception since the publication of *Empire*. But on the point discussed above, the commonalities between Laclau and Mouffe and Hardt and Negri are clear.

In fact, I referred to this radical democracy about twenty years ago in a book entitled *Ontological, Postal* (there, too, through the citation of Žižek), describing it as 'negative theology'.[31]

Negative theology originally refers to a current in Christian theology, and as the words suggest, refers to the attempt to prove the existence of God through negative expressions (God is not *x*). I borrowed this term in *Ontological, Postal* in an attempt to show that French thought of a particular period as a whole came to possess a negative-theological character, but that one philosopher among them (Jacques Derrida) attempted to resist it.

Although I won't go into any further detail here, in the context of that book, 'negative theology' is used as a term to broadly describe logics of proving existence that are mediated by negation, such as 'the Other exists by way of not existing' and 'the outside exists by way of not existing'. We can say that the logic of radical democracy is precisely a negative theology in this sense. A solidarity that has no shared ideology (communism), and thus cannot exist in the first place, must be built precisely through the mediation of the impossibility of solidarity. Solidarity exists by way of not existing. Žižek became interested in Laclau and Mouffe because this negative theological logic resembled the logic of Lacanian psychoanalysis. The ideas of Hardt and Negri, too, inherit this characteristic.

In other words, Hardt and Negri's multitude is a negative theological being, and that is why *Empire* could only have ended with a profession of faith.

---

31.   See the discussion beginning on page 138 in H. Azuma, *Sonzaironteki, yūbinteki* [*Ontological, Postal*] (Tokyo: Shinchōsha, 1998).

4. Toward a Postal Multitude

1

What we call 'liberalism' today is essentially a universalist programme, a programme of tolerance that calls for equal enjoyment of all rights for all people, and for the dignity of every person to be respected. We must respect everyone as we respect ourselves. This ethical principle originates in Kant's famous categorical imperative from *Critique of Practical Reason*: '[A]ct that the maxim of your will could always hold at the same time as a principle in a giving of universal law.'[1]

Today we are living in an age in which this universalist programme is collapsing. There were warning signs in the realm of philosophy. We could say that the rise of the critique of rationalism known as postmodernism was one example, as was the split of Anglophone liberalism into communitarianism and libertarianism. In any case, having been robbed of the universalist programme that sees us progressing from an individual to a member of a nation and finally to a world citizen, we are now entering an era in which our choices are limited to either living as a free yet solitary individual without pride (animal) or living as a member of a nation who has friends and pride, but who ultimately serves the state (human). For a world in which there is a coexistence of the system of Empire and the system of nation states, or the layer of globalism and the layer of nationalism, is in fact a world in which the path toward the universal global citizen has been blocked.

I wrote this book because I do not want to live in a world like that. In other words, with this book I would like to reopen the path towards the global citizen, but with a method different from the Hegelian dialectical ascension of the individual to the nation and to the world citizen. Namely, the path of the tourist.

What is the tourist? As already noted, it is first of all that which crosses over between the system of Empire and the system of the nation state and

---

1.   I. Kant, 'Critique of Practical Reason', in *Practical Philosophy*, tr. M. Gregor (Cambridge: Cambridge University Press, 1999), 164 (Part I, Book 1, Chapter 1, Section 7).

connects private lived sensations to public politics while remaining private. And it bears some similarity to the concept of the multitude as proposed by Hardt and Negri.

Multitude is one of the only remaining concepts in philosophy that can be used to positively discuss the possibility of anti-establishment movements after the fall of communism. For that reason, if we think that some such movement will still be necessary in the future, and if we wish to argue this case to a broader audience and not simply to seclude ourselves in our own self-satisfaction, we must inherit this concept in some way. The theory of the tourist presented here has been constructed within such a perspective.

But what cannot be forgotten at this juncture is that there are two fatal flaws to the concept of multitude. First, the multitude is believed to be a reaction that is generated from the principle of Empire itself, and from within Empire. Secondly, it is believed to be dependent upon a 'negative-theological' principle of solidarity in which a plurality of lives develop linkages between them while remaining plural and without points of commonality. In simple terms, the mechanism of the multitude's emergence remains unclear, and the logic governing its expansion after that emergence is also underdeveloped. For this reason, Hardt and Negri's theory of the movement harbours the risk of devolving into something literary and romantic that we might call faith.

The concept of the tourist must be built in such a way as to overcome these two weaknesses. More concretely, first, instead of its being imagined as a reaction born naturally from within Empire, it must be a concept that is accompanied by an explanation of its mechanism of generation. Secondly, it cannot rely upon a romanticist negative theological principle, but must build solidarity in a different way. So how are we to think such a concept, and what kind of tools should we use?

Here I would like once again refer to my book *Ontological, Postal*, published nearly twenty years ago. In addition to discussing the concept of negative theology, there I also oppose it to a different concept: the 'postal'.

What is the postal? As I noted in the previous chapter, 'negative theology' refers to the paradoxical rhetoric of saying that something that cannot exist exists by way of not existing. This is why we can call the solidarity of the multitude negative-theological: in the case of the multitude, solidarity is held to be something that exists by way of not existing, or the fact that solidarity cannot be built is inversely understood, on a meta-level, as that which produces solidarity.

In contrast, 'postal' is a word that refers to the realistic observation that, although that which cannot exist simply doesn't exist, it may *appear* to exist as a result of a myriad of failures in the actual world, and *to that extent may produce effects that make it seem as if it exists*. In this book I will refer to such failures as 'misdeliveries', just as I did in *Ontological, Postal*. Negative theology holds that God exists because it does not exist. But postal thought holds that, although we might assume that God does not exist, because of a myriad of failures in reality, God *appears to* exist, and to that extent produces effects in reality that make it seem as if it exists (we might say that it was precisely this dynamic that Voltaire and Dostoevsky attempted to expose). Since I do not have the space to explain this any further here, I refer readers who would like a more thorough discussion of the concepts of the postal and misdelivery to *Ontological, Postal*. In any case, in that book I used this opposition as an axis for arguing that contemporary thought should leave negative theology behind and be reborn as a postal thinking.

I was only a graduate student back then, and looking back on it now the book seems rather audacious. How could I, in my twenties, have hoped to lead the rebirth of contemporary thought in its entirety? Still, I have been able to effectively use this opposition between negative theology and the postal in many subsequent works. They are succinct terms that express two types of thinking that often manifest themselves when we begin to speak about something 'transcendental'.

And so, in this book, too, I would like to think about a *postal multitude* instead of a negative-theological multitude.

I would like to propose the following definition: the tourist is the postal multitude.

Latent in this definition is the possibility of philosophically broadening the trajectory of my preceding discussion of the tourist in one fell swoop. In Chapter 2, I explained how difficult it is to think about the tourist in the terms of contemporary social thought. By naming the tourist 'postal multitude', it now becomes possible to skip over this explanation by borrowing the words of philosophical works other than this one. This is because 'post', or '*écriture*' (although I will omit further discussion of this term in this book) are terms that refer generally to that which evades Hegelian dialectics. Understanding the tourist as a postal being means that we are understanding it as a being that evades Hegelian dialectics. The tourist exists outside of Hegelian thought. For that reason, its existence becomes important for our contemporary society, which is ordered in a way (stratified structure) that cannot be understood through Hegelian thought. This is the essential thought at the basis of this book.

Even on the level of everyday speech, it is not at all unnatural to call tourists a 'multitude', and one that is 'postal'. First of all, the fact that tourists are the 'multitude' is fairly self-evident. A billion tourists are dispatched around the world every year and indulge in consumption without regard for any ideology; there is no other figure that fits better the term 'multitude', with its connotations of the crowd and the mob.

What about 'postal'? Here, postal refers not to the system of actually delivering something somewhere, but to a situation that includes multiple possibilities of misdelivery—that is, failure in delivery or the occurrence of some kind of unforeseen communication (although those involved in the actual postal services may not appreciate this use of the term!) The tourist is certainly 'postal' in this sense. We encounter many different things as tourists. In some circumstances we may encounter things we probably wouldn't in our home countries. For example, even people with no interest in art might tour museums while visiting France or Italy.

And interestingly, these 'misdeliveries' are certainly not negative experiences. Dean MacCannell, whose work I referred to in Chapter 1, examines the fact that guidebooks published for a British audience at the time of the 1900 Paris Exposition listed sewers, morgues, and slaughterhouses as destinations. The readers of these guides would never go to such places in their home countries. But while in Paris, they did. And while they did so purely out of curiosity, MacCannell argues that it also functioned to suture the fragmented image of modern society: Such displays of work 'dramatize the enormous differentiation of the modern work force and, at the same time, reintegrate all classes of workers, from stock brokers to sewer cleaners, in a single system of representation.'[2] This demonstrates that the essence of tourism is the misdelivery of information, and that this

---

2.   MacCannell, *The Tourist*, 62.

misdelivery is linked to a type of enlightenment—an issue that is related to the dark tourism that would come much later. A novice who has never even touched an art book encounters the Mona Lisa at the Louvre, while an aristocrat who has never entered the kitchen visits a slaughterhouse in Paris. It goes without saying that such encounters are replete with misdeliveries. No one can expect tourists to properly understand the things they see on such a tour. But even so, it is precisely these misdeliveries that can lead to new understandings and communication. That's what makes tourism so attractive.

Hardt and Negri's multitude was nothing more than a negative-theological multitude. For that reason, they could only dream of a solidarity formed by not linking arms. But I would like to think the *postalisation* of the multitude through the concept of the tourist. In doing so, I hope to consider a form of solidarity that is built through an accumulation of the sorts of illusions that make it seem as if solidarity exists, illusions that are generated after the fact, following constant missed attempts at solidarity. People try to build solidarity with one another, but this doesn't go very well. And it is not going well everywhere. But in retrospect, it almost seems as if there is something resembling solidarity, and this illusion nudges forward the next attempt at solidarity (and its failure). This is the image of the solidarity of the tourist, or the postal multitude.

When the multitude is postalised, it becomes the tourist. When the tourist turns into a negative theology, it becomes the multitude. Is this too odd a definition? It only seems so if one is still fooled by the apparent disparity between the words 'multitude' and 'tourist', and has not noticed the proximity between the activities of the tourist and those of 'professional' civic activists of the twenty-first century who tout the ideals of solidarity, seek sites for demonstrations, gather information on the internet to travel the world, and also show up in places completely unrelated to the politics of their own country. I don't intend to disparage activists here. However, I do think that if we are going to celebrate such activists as the multitude, we should take tourists at least as seriously.

The solidarity of the negative-theological multitude was thought to exist by way of not existing. The solidarity of the postal multitude is imagined as the accumulation of illusions in which solidarity appears to exist, an accumulation that is generated, after the fact, as a result of countless failures in building solidarity.

Hardt and Negri dreamed of the solidarity of the multitude. Instead, I dream of the misdelivery of the tourist. Where the multitude go to demonstrations, the tourist goes on junkets. Where the former builds solidarity without communication, the latter communicates without solidarity. Where the former is a reaction born of Empire and calls for the politics of the nation state to intervene in private life, the latter is the noise born of the liminal space between Empire and the nation state, and will no doubt quietly change public spaces by way of private desires.

Above all else, unlike the negative-theological multitude, the communication of tourists or the postal multitude is open because of its connection to chance. Although the tourist doesn't deliberately build solidarity, they do exchange words with people they happen to meet. Whereas demonstrations always have an enemy, tours have no enemies. While demonstrations (radical democracy) fit within the friend-enemy theory, tourism lies outside of it.

The negative-theological multitude (demonstrations) was born of nothing and connected by nothing. The postal multitude (tourism) is born of misdelivery and is connected by misdelivery.

In order to prevent the concept of the multitude from slipping back into something mystical and romantic, I will close Part 1 by introducing a mathematical model that expresses (or may express) the mechanism of genesis of misdelivery and its dynamics.

2

What is the mathematical model that I am referring to? Here I would like to refer to network theory, which has seen rapid growth over the past quarter century.

Network theory doesn't necessarily study computer networks such as the internet: the concept of network is far broader. A great many phenomena—including relations between states, food chains in an ecosystem, proteins in cells, and brain cells—have the structure of a network in the broad sense, comprising multiple 'elements' and 'relations' linking these elements together. Network theory analyses the mathematical properties of these relationships regardless of the properties of the elements that make up the network. It is also known as graph theory.

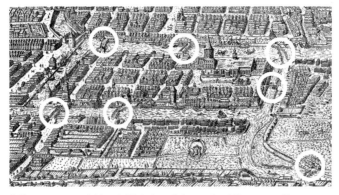

Figure 5. There were seven bridges in Königsberg. Euler wondered if it was possible to cross over each and every one of those seven bridges once and return to one's starting point, and how that question could be solved in general. Map by Joachim Bering, 1613. Image: Wikipedia Commons.

Network theory abstracts out the shape of a network and analyses it. In doing so, it represents elements as dots and the relations between elements as lines. For example, when interpreting relationships among friends as a network, people are represented by dots, while friend relations are represented by lines. Since network theory refers to these dots or elements as 'nodes' and lines or relations as 'links' or 'edges', I will use these terms here. While it seems that, depending on the researcher, edges are sometimes given weight or directionality, network theory is basically a theory that deals with the 'shapes' that nodes and edges create.

Network theory dates back to the eighteenth century and the work of mathematician Leonhard Euler. It is often said that his solution to the famous unicursal puzzle called the 'Seven Bridges of Königsberg' is the starting point for this theory (Figure 5). Unicursal refers to the act of circulating through the entire network, passing through each node and edge once and once only. An abstract theory concerning the relationships between nodes and edges is necessary to judge whether a unicursal circuit is possible in a particular diagram, and it was Euler who took that first step. Later, in the twentieth century, many of the tools of network theory started to become available, although it was not immediately applied to the modelling of relationships between actual things. But the theory saw rapid development in the 1990s when Duncan Watts and Steven Strogatz discovered the 'small-world network' and Albert-László Barabási and

Réka Albert discovered the 'scale-free network'. Network theory today can easily mathematically recreate and analyse complex real networks such as human relations and food chains.

Now, according to this new theory, 'complex networks', including human society, are said to possess three features: high clustering coefficients, a short average path, and scale-freedom.

Here I would like to briefly survey these three features. I would also like to preface this survey by saying that I have no specialised training in mathematics, so the explanations below are nothing more than summaries of introductory books published about a decade ago.[3] This is all we need for the purposes of this book, but those interested in more recent developments should refer to specialised literature in the field.

Let us begin with the first feature, which is also the most straightforward: a high clustering coefficient.

While the word 'cluster' refers to a crowd or a bundle, more recently it has also been used frequently as a piece of jargon referring to small groups. A clustering coefficient is a mathematical variable that designates how many neighbours exist within a network.

What are neighbours? Let us define 'being a neighbour' as a situation in which all members of a certain group are friends with one another. A is friends with both B and C, and B and C are also friends. Only in such a case can we say that A, B, and C are neighbours. In network theory, this kind of relationship is expressed by a situation in which three nodes are all connected by edges, that is, a situation in which the edges form a triangle. In network theory, a 'cluster' (a set of neighbours) refers to such a triangle.

Let us look at Figure 6 as an example. In this graph (network), nodes A, B, and C, and nodes D, E, and F each form a cluster, or a triangle. In other words, in this graph there are two clusters.

Next, we consider how many clusters could potentially be created within this same graph. A new cluster is born if we link node C with node E. In other

3.   My principal references here are N. Masuda and N. Konno, *'Fukuzatsu nettowāku' to wa nanika* [*What Are 'Complex Networks'?*] (Tokyo: Kōdansha burūbakkusu, 2006), and N. Masuda, *Watashitachi wa dō tsunagatte irunoka* [*How Are We Connected?*] (Tokyo: Chūkō shinso, 2007). Of course, I am responsible for any errors in explanation.

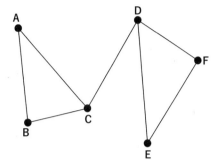

Figure 6. Simple Network.

117

words, the number of clusters in Figure 6 is not as high as it could possibly be. This is where the cluster coefficient comes from: it is an index of how many of the theoretically possible clusters have formed in reality. Mathematically, it is defined as the average of the probability that the two nodes connected to a given node are connected (the probability that the friend B of A and friend C of A are also friends). If the cluster coefficient is 1, this would mean that for each node, the two nodes connected to it are also connected by an edge.

Researchers have demonstrated that if we abstract into graphs all relationships in human society, such as human relations in a school or partnerships among businesses, the cluster coefficient becomes quite large. Human society is constituted through a high-density layering of triangles in which a friend and a friend are friends with each other. Even readers unfamiliar with the mathematical details can probably grasp this instinctively. Society is not at all a gathering of individuals. It is not that there is an individual, and then we suddenly advance to the world. There are many intermediate groups made up of the layering of triangular human relationships such as family, region, and workplace, and society is made up of a further layering of these. Twenty-first-century network science calls such a condition a 'high clustering coefficient'.

The second feature is a short average path. Put flatly, this refers to the feature in which, if one tracks a friend of a friend of a friend, and so on, one can surprisingly quickly cover the entirety of the membership of the network.

According to network theory, the minimum number of edges that can connect one node to another is called the 'path length' between the nodes. Returning to Figure 6, for example, we must travel through at least three edges to get from node A to node E. Thus, the 'path length' between A and E is 3. A short average path just means that the average of all possible path lengths between nodes is a low number. In such networks, one can (on average) go from one node to another by travelling through a small number of edges.

Human society does indeed exhibit this feature, and this was known prior to the development of network theory. In sociology there is the famous hypothesis of 'six degrees of separation'. According to this hypothesis, although there are currently around seven billion people in the world, we can go from one given person to another (for example a farmer living in a small African country to a reader reading this book in Japan) by passing through only six friend relationships. Stated another way, this is the hypothesis that the totality of human society of seven billion people fits within the parameter of 'your friend's friend's friend's friend's friend's friend'. Six is a surprisingly small number, but this was the figure arrived at through a social experiment by Stanley Milgram in 1967 using a physical letter (although the global population was far fewer than seven billion back then) and has been confirmed by additional experiments using the internet. While people often say that 'it's a small world', in this sense human society is indeed quite small.

So why is human society small? Actually, for a long time researchers struggled to create a mathematical model for this feature of human society. This is because it was believed that it stood in contradiction to its large clustering coefficient. There are many clusters in human society. Rather than making friends that are far away, all people prefer close relationships where their friends are also friends with one another. If that is the case, then shouldn't society be more fragmented, leading to a 'larger' world?

It was two researchers that produced a breakthrough here: the aforementioned Watts and Strogatz. They demonstrated mathematically that if there are a few 'short cuts' in a network, then the average path length dramatically decreases even if the clustering coefficient remains high.

What does this mean? Consider the three graphs in Figure 7. They are each made of the same number of nodes (22) and edges (44).

Figure 7a is a graph in which all of the nodes extend edges to nodes that are adjacent to the next adjacent nodes. This is called a one-dimensional lattice graph.

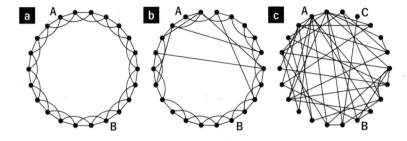

Figure 7. Based on Naoki Masuda and Norio Konno, *'Fukuzatsu nettowāku' to wa nanika?* [*What Are 'Complex Networks?'*], 78. The number of branches in c did not match the number of branches in a and b in the original, but has been modified in accordance with the explanation given there.

It contains many triangles, or clusters. It may seem as if there are no triangles because all of the nodes are located on a circle. But if you look closely, you can see that there are many assemblages where three nodes are connected by three edges. Moreover, none of the nodes have edges that reach beyond the node next to the closest adjacent node. In a sense, this graph represents an egalitarian and closed society in which each person has the same number of friends, and no one builds relations that go further than their neighbour's neighbour.

This graph gives a good illustration of one feature of human society: that it possesses a high clustering coefficient—that is, there are many neighbours. But under these conditions, the path length between two randomly selected nodes becomes quite long. Even though there are only 22 nodes, you need to travel through six edges to move from point A to point B, which are on opposite sides of the graph (this fact is expressed by saying that the diameter of the graph is 6). Moreover, that number grows in proportion to the number of nodes. Here, since the number of nodes is 22, the average length is just under 3, but with 100 nodes, the maximum length becomes 25 and the average length about 12.5, and if there are 1000 nodes, the maximum length becomes 250 and the average length about 125. It is therefore not an appropriate model for a human society of seven billion.

Then how about Figure 7c? It is close to something called a 'random graph', where nodes are connected mostly randomly.[4] This graph represents a completely open society in which friends are determined by something like a lottery.

4.   To be precise, the figure cited here is created by using the method of 'rewiring' explained in the passages below, taking edges from each of the nodes from Figure 7a and reconnecting them to another node according to a probability close to 1.

Since the connections between nodes are determined randomly, edges do not only connect nodes that are next to one another, but at times traverse the entire circle (the network). For that reason, the average path length becomes significantly shorter compared to Figure 7a. For example, the path length between point A and point B, which was 6 in the previous graph, now consists of just two edges. Thus, this graph represents the smallness of human society well. But in return, the clustering coefficient is now lower. Indeed, the number of triangles decreases in this graph compared to the previous one, but I think you might be able to instinctively grasp the reason for this too. In the world represented by this graph, all friendships are determined by lottery. As a result, while the path length between two given people becomes relatively shorter, in return the probability that two of your friends are also friends with one another (that they are neighbours) becomes lower. This graph, too, is not appropriate for creating a model of human society.

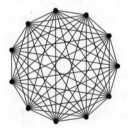

Figure 8. Example of a complete graph. The number of vertices is 11.

In this way, then, a high clustering coefficient and a short average path length seem to contradict one another. As an aside, although it is not introduced here, these two features can actually be balanced simply by increasing the number of edges. This is because, if all nodes are connected to all other nodes, the clustering coefficient becomes 1 (the highest possible number) and the average path length, too, becomes 1 (the lowest possible number). This shape is called a 'complete graph' (Figure 8). However, it is clear that this is not appropriate for creating a model of human society either. The complete graph represents a world in which all people are directly friends with all others. In reality, although there are variances, the number of friends that a given human can make is quite limited. Creating a model of human society using network theory requires that we achieve this balance between a high clustering coefficient (many neighbours) and a short average path length (a small world) while limiting the number of edges (the number of friendships).

Watts and Strogatz created a model that fulfilled these conditions. An example is shown in Figure 7b.

This graph was produced as a result of an intriguing operation in which Figure 7a, with a high clustering coefficient, is used as a starting point, and the edges connected to every node are 'rewired' with a given probability to a different, randomly chosen node. Since the operation is nothing more than a 'rewiring', there is no change in the total number of edges. Triangles are broken if edges are rewired (since one side of a triangle is removed), but if the rewired edges are few (if the probability of rewiring is low), there is not much change in the total number of triangles either. However, even if the rewired edges are few in number, many 'short cuts' are generated in the network as a result. Watts and Strogatz mathematically demonstrated that the existence of these short cuts brought about a dramatic shortening of the maximum path length and average path length without much change in the clustering coefficient. Figure 7b actually represents only a 15 percent rewiring of the edges in Figure 7a, and yet the path length between point A and B has shrunk from 6 to 3. They called this graph a 'small-world graph', and argued that it is appropriate for representing the network that humans create in reality.

Network theory calls the properties that result from the combination of a high clustering coefficient and a low average path length 'small-world properties' (a low average path length alone is sometimes called that as well). If we mathematically represent human society, it is neither a lattice graph, nor a random graph, nor a complete graph—it is a small-world graph.

3

It seems to me that this discovery by Watts and Strogatz provides a significant hint for thought in the humanities as well. If interpreted as a network of friendships, the lattice graph in Figure 7a expresses a closed set of human relations where everyone secludes themselves among neighbours. On the other hand, the random graph in Figure 7c expresses an absolutely open set of human relations where everyone is open to chance encounters.

In comparison, the small-world graph in Figure 7b shows a set of human relations in which everyone basically secludes themselves among friends, but once in a while (probabilistically) a stranger invades that closed set of relations (rewires it), and that new encounter (short cut) is precisely what all of a sudden makes the world small.

Here the words 'probability', 'rewire', and 'short cut' each have a strict mathematical definition.[5] But even without getting into these definitions, it isn't too difficult to grasp the importance of this model. At the beginning of this book, I wrote that the theory of the tourist was also a theory of the other. I also wrote above that universalism is now faced with a crisis. The social thought of the twentieth century, or universalism, which preached only openness to the other, has today lost its persuasiveness. What the discovery of Watts and Strogatz teaches us is that what provides human society with its dynamism is neither the absolute exclusion of the other nor perfect openness to the other, but a condition that is *in between* the two.

While we do not completely exclude the other, we aren't completely open to the other either. The extent to which we are constitutes the 'probability' of our openness to the other. This probability is always a value between 0 and 1. If the probability of rewiring in the lattice graph of Figure 7a is 0, nothing will ever change. In the opposite case, if the probability of rewiring is 1, it would turn into a random graph resembling Figure 7c, since all of the edges would be rewired. In other words, the small-world network is something that is generated when the probability of rewiring toward the other is neither 0 or 1, but somewhere in between. Readers of *Ontological, Postal* might recall my argument that to think about misdelivery is to think about probability.[6] The incorporation of probabilistic rewiring in order to create a model for human society may be

---

5.   On the definition of 'rewiring', see D. Watts, *Small Worlds: The Dynamics of Networks Between Order and Randomness* (Princeton, NJ: Princeton University Press, 1999), 67sq. On the definition of 'short cut', ibid., 70sq. Explained without the use of mathematical formulas, rewiring can be defined as the process of starting with a node, generating a random number, and, if that number is greater than a given number, rewiring an edge connected to that node to a different node, or otherwise doing nothing; this is then repeated for each edge of each node. A 'short cut' is defined as an edge connecting two nodes, where in the absence of that edge the distance between those nodes (called its 'range') would be greater than 2. If the range is 2, then that edge is one side of a triangle (if one side of the triangle is eliminated, the distance between the two nodes changes from 1 to 2).

6.   Azuma, *Sonzaironteki, yūbinteki*, 18sq.

interpreted philosophically as corresponding to the incorporation of misdelivered communication in our understanding of the basics of human society.

Let us return to the mathematics. The third feature discovered by network theory is the 'scale-free'. This expresses inequality in human society.

I once again refer you to the three graphs in Figure 7 (page 119). As noted earlier, the graph of Figure 7b was obtained by rewiring the edges of Figure 7a according to a particular probability. Since all of the nodes in Figure 7a were connected to the same number of edges, rewiring generates a deviation in the number of edges. In fact, point A in Figure 7b is connected to three edges, while point B is connected to four. This inequality increases in a random graph. Point A in Figure 7c is connected to eight edges, while point C is only connected to one. We could say that this expresses a situation in which one person has eight friends, while another only has one.

Network theory refers to the number of edges connected to a node as the 'degree' of that node. Deviation in the number of edges is expressed by saying that the degree distribution is not uniform. The degree distribution is never uniform in small-world graphs and random graphs.

The idea of the scale free refers to features related to this degree distribution. Unlike the other two features we've looked at thus far (small-world properties), it is not derived from the 'shape' of the network. Scale-freedom is a characteristic that becomes visible when statistical procedures are applied to the relationships between nodes and edges.

Barabási and Albert, who I mentioned above, were the two researchers who discovered the property of scale-freedom. It was first discovered in reality rather than in theory.

Scale-freedom refers to the characteristic of being indifferent to scale—that is, it refers to a network in which the degree distribution exhibits the same shape regardless of scale. In scale-free networks, for example, the decline in numbers from the total number of nodes with ten edges to the total number of nodes with a hundred edges is the same as the decline in numbers from the total number of nodes with a hundred edges to the total number of nodes with a thousand edges. For that reason, no matter how high the number of edges is on the node you begin with, the possibility of finding a node with even more edges never reaches zero. To put it plainly, although they are few, there are always nodes where a massive number of nodes are concentrated. This is the basic characteristic of scale-free networks. Thus, they are also sometimes known as 'unequal' networks.

In the late 1990s, Barabási and Albert conducted a wide-scale structural analysis of the internet (more precisely the world wide web, the aggregate of pages written in HTML) and found that the web at the time exhibited precisely this characteristic. If we understand web pages as nodes and hyperlinks as edges, the links that lead to a page are degrees, and these degrees were seen to follow a scale-free distribution. That is to say, while a massive number of links were concentrated on a very small number of powerful pages (called hubs), there were barely any links to the vast majority of pages. If we think about this from another angle, in practical terms it means that the vast majority of pages were barely ever given any opportunity to be read. This discovery created shockwaves, because it was believed that the birth of the internet would provide all people with the opportunity to broadcast information (indeed there are still those who believe in this ideal). It simultaneously posed a significant theoretical problem, since the generation of such biases could not be adequately explained using existing theories.

Barabási and Albert tackled this mystery. What came after this is difficult to summarise because it involves the science of complex systems, but in a word, they incorporated the two concepts of 'growth' and 'preferential selection' into Watts and Strogatz's model.

Here, growth refers to the addition of new nodes in a network, and preferential selection refers to the condition in which these new nodes tend to select nodes with high degrees as destinations when attaching edges to preexisting nodes (there is a high probability of selecting high-degree nodes). If we interpret the incorporation of these two concepts philosophically, it implies that Barabási and Albert incorporated the concepts of time and subject (directionality) into network theory. The Watts and Strogatz model was static and mechanical. The increase in nodes was not considered and the rewiring of edges, too, was merely a temporary operation for the purpose of generating a small-world graph. By incorporating time into it, Barabási and Albert built a model for what was happening every day as new nodes entered the system and edges were rewired.

As a result, although the edges in the Watts and Strogatz model did not possess directionality, the edges in the Barabási and Albert model came to possess directionality. This is because in the latter model, the new nodes 'select' destinations for linking among the old nodes, but the opposite does not happen.

The small-world graph seems to express a happy set of relations in which all the members are blessed with friends and don't grow too far apart from one another. According to Watts and Strogatz, this is the mathematical expression of human society. But what if new participants joined from time to time and they all basically chose preferentially as friends those who already had many friends? Put in sociological terms, this is the kind of question that Barabási and Albert were raising. This hypothesis has some purchase in reality, too, since people do in fact often choose their friends that way, and new web pages, too, probably tend to select powerful pages to link to. And Barabási and Albert found that the scale-free property appeared in many models when simulations were run with the inclusion of the presuppositions of growth and preferential selection.

Now, this scale-freedom is a characteristic that appears in a probability distribution which in statistics is known as the 'power law distribution'. The power law distribution follows a mathematical formula called the 'power law'—an equation such as $1/k^r$ where r is the constant particular to distribution and k is the variable. When we say that the degree distribution of a network is scale-free, we are saying that it has the mathematical characteristic that the probability that a node with degree k appears, $p(k)$, is equal to $1/k^r$.

The main characteristic of the power law is that the value of $p(k)$ rapidly declines at first, but never quite gets to zero, even when k becomes greater (see Figure 9, overleaf). So $p(k)$ is inversely proportional to k^r. When we consider a power law distribution where the constant r is 3, when k is 2, $p(k)$ is $1/2^3$ or $1/8$; when k is 3, it is $1/3^3$ or $1/27$. It looks as if it would become zero very quickly, but even when k is 100, $p(k)$ is $1/100^3$ or $1/1$ million. Since this means that the event to which it refers occurs once every million times or to one person in every million, we cannot call the probability zero.

This characteristic means that the power law is useful in explaining the distribution in phenomena where there are a small number of values that are extreme outliers in a given sample. As noted earlier, it effectively explains the

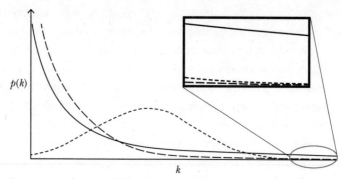

Figure 9. Comparison of power law (———), exponential law (— — — —) and normal distribution (-----). The curves in the figure are images representing the characteristics of the distributions and are not mathematically precise. Based on Naoki Masuda and Norio Konno, 'Fukuzatsu nettowā-ku' to wa nanika [What Are 'Complex Networks'?], 99.

distribution of the number of links to web pages; in a perhaps more relatable example, it is well known that the distribution of income and assets also follows this law. As is often pointed out, 'average income' doesn't necessarily refer to the income of the majority of people. This is because there are people who receive an income far exceeding the average, and this pulls the average higher. While the average income of the Japanese today is said to be around 4.2 million yen (according to 2015 figures given by the National Tax Agency), it is not rare for people to make a hundred times that (400 million yen). There are also a few who make 1,000 times that figure (4 billion yen). There may even be those who make 10,000 times the average (40 billion yen). The power law is adept at explaining these kinds of distributions where a few examples of extreme values continue to exist. This characteristic is sometimes called 'long tail', after the shape of the graph, as shown in Figure 9. Scale-freedom and the long tail point to the same characteristic probability distribution.

There are other mathematical models of probability distribution, but they cannot explain this long tail. For example, it is well known that human physical characteristics such as height and weight mostly follow a 'normal distribution'. In a normal distribution, the number of samples of an average value are the most numerous, and the numbers rapidly decrease as they deviate from the average. I will not introduce the formula here, since the discussion would get somewhat cumbersome, but samples that are extremely distant from the average cannot exist in a normal distribution. Indeed, in the human population we never run into anyone who is a hundred times or a thousand times the average height.

There is also another formula similar to the power law, the exponential law $1/r^k$. The distribution that follows this formula (exponential distribution) resembles the power law distribution at first glance, but ultimately exhibits different characteristics. If we say that $p(k)$ with variable 3 follows not the power law but the exponential law, in other words $1/3^k$ instead of $1/k^3$, when k is 100, the denominator of the probability becomes 3^{100} instead of 100^3 (1 million). This is an extremely small number (1 in a number that is 5 with 47 zeros) and is basically zero. In other words, the power law distribution can explain the emergence of the instance of $k = 100$, but the exponential distribution cannot.

Above, I wrote that Barabási and Albert succeeded in recreating this power law distribution (scale-freedom) by incorporating the suppositions of growth and preferential selection. If we turn this statement around, it also means that they explained the generative mechanism of the power law distribution with only two suppositions. This is actually what is most shocking about their work.

This is because it is known that, far from being limited to the number of links to web pages or the distribution of income, this power law distribution appears in a range of statistical data. Moreover, it appears not only in social phenomena, but also natural phenomena. For example, it is known that the relation between city size and the number of cities, the number of citations of an academic article and the total number of articles, the size of wars and the number of wars, the print run of books and the total number of books published, the size of financial crises and the total number of such crises, the magnitude of earthquakes and their frequency, the number of extinct species in a mass extinction and their frequency, all share this scale-free characteristic.

In other words, the income distribution of humans and the distribution of earthquake frequencies have almost the same shape, and moreover we can now easily recreate them through simulations using network theory models. Then couldn't Barabási and Albert's theory breach the boundary between natural and social sciences, and become a unified language that explains all phenomena? Excitement over this kind of idea, which spread around the world in the years following publication of their work, is well communicated in science writer Mark

Buchanan's 2000 book *Ubiquity*, and Barabási's own 2002 book *Linked,* which was aimed at a lay audience. For example, Buchanan writes the following on the power law distribution:

> Researchers in the past few years have found its mathematical fingerprints in the workings of all the upheavals I've mentioned so far, as well as in the spreading of epidemics, the flaring of traffic jams, the patterns by which instructions trickle down from managers to workers in an office, and in many other things. At the heart of our story, then, lies the discovery that networks of things of all kinds—atoms, molecules, species, people, and even ideas—have a marked tendency to organize themselves along similar lines. [...] So there can be a mathematics for people. It cannot tell you, of course, what any one person will do, and yet it may be able to say what kinds of patterns are likely to emerge out of the millions.[7]

The final chapter of Buchanan's book, entitled 'History Matters', addresses the possibility of a 'historical physics'. The concept refers to a form of physics that would analyse the mechanism of historical events using network theory, although the book does not fully address the feasibility of such a new materialism. In any case, Barabási and Albert's discovery that human society can be modelled using network theory and that in doing so we find the scale-free property certainly served to revive the possibility of a discourse that explains the structure of human society as if it were a natural phenomenon, following in the footsteps of nineteenth-century historical materialism (communism) and twentieth-century structuralism.

Above I wrote that scale-free networks are unequal networks. However, this 'inequality' cannot be understood in an anthropocentric manner. The fact that powerful nodes are preferentially selected among old nodes certainly does mean that the rich get richer, those with many friends attract even more friends, the highly valued rise in value, and the poor become poorer. And indeed, the capitalist value-economic society in which we live is built that way.

However, this is not necessarily because the rich 'exploit' the poor. From the perspective of mathematics, there is barely any differentiation between

---

7.　M. Buchanan, *Ubiquity: The Science of History... Or Why the World is Simpler Than We Think* (New York: Crown, 2000), 21 and 170.

rich and poor in the first place. Network theory only addresses the degrees
of distribution of the whole and does not concern itself with the individuality
of any given node. Just as there is a particular probability that an earthquake
(the concentration of energy along a fault) will occur, so there is a particular
probability of the occurrence of a concentration in wealth. While theory can
predict deviations in wealth, it cannot predict who will become wealthy and
who will become poor. Deviations in wealth are not created by a small segment
of the wealthy; rather, the selections made by each of the participants in the
network creates it *naturally*, and moreover *based on chance*. That is what the
discovery of Barabási and Albert suggests.

4

Let us now return to philosophy. What does the above contribute to our theory
of the tourist?

Network theory is mathematics, not philosophy. Mathematics uses not
only concepts, but also equations. Even words that seem understandable in an
everyday sense such as 'rewiring', 'shortcut', 'growth', and 'preferential selection'
actually all have strict definitions, making it possible to work with them using
mathematical operations. That is the particularity of mathematics, and its
method of thought is completely different from philosophy, at least the style of
philosophy pursued in this book.

It is therefore dangerous for a writer like myself to cite developments in mathematics based on the attractiveness of its concepts. Contemporary thought has
already lost trust through its use of mathematics. Some readers may remember
that contemporary French thought was harshly criticised as a pseudo-science
that babbles absurdities by interpreting mathematics in an uninformed way.[8] To
readers who hold such opinions, this entire book might seem absurd.

Despite that risk, I would like to propose using the above findings of network
theory as a type of grounding for the theory of the stratified world discussed
in the previous chapters. If 'grounding' is too strong an expression, I could
instead say that I would like to redefine the theory of the stratified world as
an interpretation of such mathematical findings from the perspective of the

---

8.   A. Sokal and J. Bricmont, *Fashionable Nonsense: Postmodern Intellectuals' Abuse of Science*
(New York: Picador, 1999).

humanities. It is by doing so that the theory of the tourist presented in this book finally gains substance.

In the previous chapter I noted that the stratified structure of Empire and nation state is an 'image'. In the era of nationalism, it was 'imagined' that each nation state was an independent human and that they created an international society by congregating together. Today the nation state has lost its independence, and we can 'imagine' it instead as a series of faces/politics attempting to reconstruct national borders on a shared, massive, transborder body/economy. The fact that these are images doesn't make them meaningless. Humans are ultimately driven by images, and differences in images lead to differences in reality. But if the bifurcation of Empire and nation state itself is nothing more than an image, then this book's proposal of a tourist/postal multitude that traverses them can also only be an image, and this entire discussion regarding the multitude will surely revert to mystical, romantic self-satisfaction (let's all live as tourists!).

That is precisely what I want to avoid, which is why I take the risk of bringing in mathematics. In order to demonstrate that Empire is substantive, that the nation state is also substantive, that the postal multitude is also substantive, and that it is possible to productively deliberate upon them, I want to touch upon the possibility that there is an intersection between social thought and network theory.

This book is certainly not the first instance in social thought to focus on the shape of networks. On this point I am following in the footsteps of previous generations.

About thirty years ago the opposition between 'tree' and 'rhizome' became popular in contemporary thought, having been proposed in Gilles Deleuze and Félix Guattari's 1980 book *A Thousand Plateaus* (the original article 'Rhizome' was published in 1976). What was demonstrated there was, to put it in the terms of the 2010s, the possibility of conceiving two different ways if thinking the social based on two different shapes of networks.

If we focus on the image of the tree and rhizome themselves, it is not mathematically accurate to oppose them to one another. In the network theory of the twenty-first century, it is the tree and the lattice that are juxtaposed. The decisive difference between the tree and the lattice is that one cannot move along a branch of a tree and end up at the same node from which one started, whereas this is possible in a lattice. The ends of branches on a tree do not connect to other ends. In lattices, they do. And in this respect, the rhizome is just like a tree. Although Deleuze and Guattari write that 'any point of a rhizome can be connected to anything other, and must be', if that were the case, they probably should have called it a lattice rather than a rhizome.[9]

Accurate or not, what is more important here is the fact that thirty years ago, philosophers were already attempting to create the language for a new social analysis based on a new network model. The tree—in other words, a network model with a trunk and branches with unidirectional splits, featuring one starting point and multiple ends, has a high degree of affinity with modern social organisations such as militaries, political parties, and large companies, which have one person at the top whose orders *descend* the chain of command step by step down to the local site of activity. For that reason, postmodernists took the opposite direction in attempting to think about a network with a shape different from the tree form. It is in this context that the word 'rhizome' emerged. The juxtaposition between tree and rhizome also appears in the arguments of Hardt and Negri discussed in the previous chapter. *Empire* contains a passage in which the concept of the rhizome is compared to the network structure of the internet (a nonhierarchical and noncentred network structure).[10] In their theory, the nation state system is considered through the model of the tree, the system of Empire through the rhizome.

Postmodernists believed that modern society and postmodern society differed as to the very shape in which power forms human relationships, and that the form of resistance, too, is different. This instinct is probably not mistaken. The forms of human relationships differed considerably between the nineteenth and twenty-first centuries, and this generated political differences as well. For example, there were of course no social media services in the nineteenth century, nor were there mobilisations using social media.

But Deleuze and Guattari possessed only extremely vague ideas about the rhizome. They didn't have the means to analyse the differences between tree and rhizome through measurable characteristics, nor did they know that this

9. G. Deleuze and F. Guattari, *A Thousand Plateaus: Capitalism and Schizophrenia*, tr. B. Massumi (Minneapolis: University of Minnesota Press, 1987), 7.

10. Hardt and Negri, *Empire*, 299.

was possible. Their theories operated on the level of images. For that reason, their stipulations about the rhizome were exceedingly literary expressions, such as: 'A rhizome has no beginning or end: it is always in the middle, between things, interbeing, intermezzo.'[11] On the basis of such a premise, even if one were to argue that the nation state is a tree and Empire or multitude is a rhizome, in the end this is nothing more than an impression, an image. Hardt and Negri's vagueness can be traced back to the vagueness of Deleuze and Guattari. Moreover, as I noted in the previous chapter, what is important today is not the shift from nation state to Empire, but the layering of the two (stratification); the concepts of tree and rhizome, however, are not made for layering. This, too, is a symptom of the vagueness of the concepts.

We now have powerful mathematical theories about networks that were unimaginable for Deleuze and Guattari. So shouldn't we rid ourselves of this vagueness by incorporating the findings of network theory and reviving the arguments of thinkers such as Deleuze and Negri as something scientifically and politically viable?

If so, then, concretely speaking, how should we incorporate them? We have been given the new concepts of small-worldness and scale-freedom rather than tree and rhizome. Tree and rhizome were words referring to the different shapes of different networks. That is why they couldn't be layered one on top of the other. Small-world and scale-free are words that refer to characteristics on different planes within the same network. Thus, they can be layered one on top of the other.

That being the case, could we not renew Hardt and Negri's arguments about the difference in system between nation state and Empire using the properties of small-worldness and scale-freedom as our axis instead of tree and rhizome?

At this point I can give only a rough sketch of such a mathematical renewal of postmodern social thought. With that in mind, my current proposal is something like the following.

Human societies exhibit the properties of small-worldness and scale-freedom. On the one hand there is the cramped world made of many clusters, and on the

---

11.   Deleuze and Guattari, *A Thousand Plateaus*, 25.

other, there is the unequal world produced by the power law degree distribution. What we have so far are mathematical truths.

However, if this is the case, could we interpret this as meaning that, *faced with the same society, there are times when we as humans sense the property of small-worldness and other times when we sense the property of scale-freedom*?

Mathematically speaking, each of us is a node within a network. And according to the properties of small-worldness and scale-freedom, the relationship between nodes can be interpreted either as that of two equal nodes linked together by an edge or as that of unequal nodes with a massive difference in the number of linked edges. The former is the interpretation made when we focus on the shape of the network, while the latter is the interpretation made when we focus on the degree distribution. In fact, as if in correlation with this, when we humans are faced with another human (the other), sometimes we feel that we are facing another human one-on-one, while at other times we are overwhelmed by the massive disparity in our wealth or power. Arendt, and many other twentieth-century thinkers in the tradition of the humanities, believed the former relationship to be the true way of being human, and insisted that in the latter the 'human condition' has been torn away. But in reality, we should think of these as two expressions of the same relation, which can be sensed simultaneously. This simultaneity or two-sidedness can be easily understood if we relate it to social media today: consider the instance in which a relatively unknown user with about a hundred followers sends a reply to a famous person with a million followers and just happens to receive a response. This response is a one-on-one communication, but at the same time is only one among countless responses. Both interpretations are correct. This apparent contradiction is a mathematical consequence of the structure of complex networks.

As we face the same society/network, we are always simultaneously experiencing the small-world form and the scale-free degree distribution. But then couldn't we consider that two systems—two systems of power—are generated from these two experiences? Couldn't we say that 'the human condition' and its outside, politics and its outside, the nation state and Empire, disciplinary training and biopower, the normal distribution and the power law distribution, the realm of communitarian communication where each human is treated as human and the realm of libertarian statistical processing where humans are counted only as a herd of animals, are simultaneously generated as two interpretations of power within one and the same social substance?

If we look at each node, we can see the order of the small-world. If we look at the degree distribution among all nodes, we can see the order of the scale-free. The nation state and Empire as presented by Hardt and Negri are most likely names given to two specific systems created by the accumulation of forms of power that evolved in correspondence to these mathematical orders. The disciplinary training of the nation state moves through the triangle clusters, working upon each node—that is, each individual human. In contrast, the biopower of Empire attempts to statistically manage the degree distribution of all nodes directly—that is, the entirety of society's members as a herd.

If this is the case, then the bifurcation of nation state and Empire into two layers is a structure underwritten by mathematical necessity. As long as human society is a network, there will always be, side by side, a system based on the order of small-worldness and a system based on the order of scale-freedom. While we can no longer return to the age of nationalism, we cannot completely shift to the age of globalism either. Although it is possible that the order of small-worldness will come to be based upon something other than the nation state, as long as humans are humans, the world will likely never be completely taken over by the scale-free order.

In order for the entire world to be covered by one network and for both the scale-free and the small-world order to become visible—that is, in order for the statistical truth of degree distribution to become visible in addition to the shapes of connections— transportation and information technology must reach a certain stage. Perhaps the Hegelian paradigm that for two centuries continued to reject the truth of the 'animals', pushing it to the outside of political and philosophical thinking, was nothing more than the social thought of an age when technology had not yet reached that stage—when as yet most people could only see the small-world order.

The above is a hypothesis, and a rather bold one at that. In reality, a far longer preparatory work, perhaps the length of an additional book, would be necessary to link the discourse in the humanities covered so far in this book with the mathematics of the network. I can hardly expect to persuade my readers with

the kind of rough sketch given above. This proposal must be developed further
on another occasion.

The reason why I nonetheless present the idea in this unpolished state is because I think that this kind of rereading of the tree and rhizome models through the concepts of small-worldness and scale-freedom provides insights that will help me to avoid falling into mysticism in thinking about the mechanism of development and strategy of the tourist/postal multitude.

Hardt and Negri understood the system of Empire as a rhizomic order. But they did not possess a clear concept of the rhizome. Thus there was no further elaboration on the development of the multitude other than to say that it should emerge from within the Empire/rhizome as a reaction.

However, this book's suggestion that we reinterpret the system of Empire as an order generated by scale-freedom and consider its coexistence with the order of small-worldness makes possible an entirely different explanation for the development of the multitude. Moreover, it also provides concrete guidelines for the strategy of the multitude which amount to more than a mere declaration of faith. It is precisely these guidelines that provide the core insights that will support the philosophy of the tourist that this book aims to develop, and its conclusions.

The new multitude is not a magical word referring to a mysterious, self-referential negative function that will destroy from within the order of the rhizome/Empire that gave birth to it in the first place. Thinking in the humanities is filled with such magical words, and I started writing this book because I was sick of this situation. The tourist, or postal multitude, that I propose in this book will become the practitioner of the memory of resistance, who has seized and retained the operation of rewiring or misdelivery that makes a small world a small world, *prior* to the moment when it is reappropriated by the scale-free order.

What does this mean? I will conclude Part 1 by touching upon the logic leading to that insight, and the new philosophical challenges that lie beyond it.

5

Watts and Strogatz discovered rewiring and shortcuts by thinking about the property of small-worldness, and Barabási and Albert discovered growth and preferential selection by thinking about the property of scale-freedom. This path taken by network theory also resembles a new 'mythology' concerning the origins of society, of the type that attracted European philosophers such as Hobbes, Locke, and Rousseau centuries ago.

To speak of mythologies is not to critique their discoveries. Indeed, I see them as truly philosophically profound. Here, 'mythology' refers to a narrative-like descriptive form that recomposes the logical process of some insight as if it were a historical process. Philosophers often favour such descriptions. For example, Nietzsche's *The Birth of Tragedy* is a book that describes a 'mythology' of Greek tragedy. The path taken by network theory boasts the principal features of mythology in that sense. First there was the fixed lattice graph, followed by the birth of the small-world graph, and finally the property of scale-freedom emerged. This process can be read as if it were itself the origin of society.

Humans find neighbours/triangles. As they add many neighbours, they create a community. But that alone does not make for a society.

In order for a society to be born, many triangles must be linked over short distances. Otherwise, the world of humans cannot become organised as one society, but splinters into a sea of neighbours/triangles separated from one another.

Then what is it that links neighbours/triangles together? Rewiring links them together. The shortcuts generated by rewiring bring people from close triangles to far away triangles and invite them to encounter the other.

In the terms of social theory, this corresponds to the process of the shift from family to civil society. If triangles represent the family or its expansion into tribal communities or village communities, the accumulation of triangles linked through rewiring can be thought of as civil society, the gathering of anonymous citizens. Watts and Strogatz described this shift from community to civil society in mathematical terms. The sociological term for what rewiring generates is *mobility*, while in Derrida's terms, it is misdelivery. Through the incorporation of rewiring, the lattice graph turns into a small-world graph. In other words, a community becomes a civil society by incorporating misdelivery.

But there is a hidden trap in this process. Rewiring is originally a matter of probability. In other words, it entrusts the selection of its new destination to chance. This is precisely why it fulfilled the function of shortening the distance between triangles, allowing people to encounter the other, and changing a community into a society.

But once the complexity of society reaches a certain point and new nodes join the network frequently, relinking itself changes in character, so that most relinkings are no longer left to chance. Barabási and Albert called the new form of rewiring that emerged at this moment 'preferential selection'.

The emergence of preferential selection greatly alters the character of the network. There was no directionality to linkages in the age of small-worldness. Two nodes were simply linked by one edge, and there was no directionality in the sense of one *wanting* to connect to the other.

But in the age of preferential selection, edges possess directionality. Or, nodes possess a will. New nodes select the most powerful nodes from among the old nodes. The opposite process does not exist. In the age of small-worldness, edges represented the equal (mutually beneficial) exchange relation between humans who were friends. In the age of preferential selection, edges have become the expression of the unidirectional relocation of wealth from anonymous consumers concentrated on famous producers or the unidirectional preference that unknown newcomers direct at established celebrities. If we express this phenomenon using the language of social theory, it corresponds to the birth of capitalism. Or, if we take an example closer to home, it corresponds to the shifts in friendships brought about by the emergence of social media. In the past, friendships expressed a one-on-one human relationship. Facebook, Twitter, and Instagram changed this, making friendship pass through a medium that promotes preferential selection. What was generated as a result was the property of scale-freedom and the power law degree distribution. In the process, the society of humans comes to be filled with staggering inequality.

The primitive lattice graph changes into a small-world graph through the rewiring of edges based on probability. The community becomes a civil society. But the misdelivery, or probability, that turned society into a society quickly changes into preferential selection (capital), bringing staggering inequality to the world.

I repeat, this is a mythology. It is a narrative that somewhat forcedly turns the logical process of network theory into a historical narrative. Just as *The Birth of Tragedy* lacked evidence for its hypothesis, I do not believe that the above process occurred in reality.

Yet it is also true that, when we recompose synchronic logic as diachronic history, it becomes easier to talk about what is missing in the structure of the world before our eyes. It becomes far easier to understand and manipulate logic when it is spoken in the form of a narrative. The reason why philosophers often speak in mythologies knowing full well that they are impossible to prove is that they are quite familiar with this characteristic of humans (perhaps excluding mathematicians and logicians). Hobbes, Locke, and Rousseau didn't necessarily naively believe their own mythology of the 'state of nature' as fact.

What, then, does this network mythology teach us? As I have repeated many times, we live in the age of the stratified world—an era in which politics and economy, human and animal, citizen and consumer, disciplinary training and biopower, nation state and Empire, nationalism and globalism, communitarianism and libertarianism all argue for differing principles while shaping different orders. Said another way, we now live in two orders simultaneously. Hence we are invited to consume like animals while being human, and simultaneously forced to speak about politics like humans while being animals. We are living neither in the age of nationalism nor that of globalism, but in both at the same time.

So where is the place of criticism and resistance in this age of the stratified world? Where is the place where we can express our unease with this world we are now facing, as Voltaire once did with his *Candide*? Ultimately, this place is what I am looking for in this book through the use of tourism and the tourist.

Schmitt, Kojève, and Arendt believed that the world of the nation state/ human would serve as the basis for resisting the emergence of the world of Empire/animal. Put flatly, they believed that they had no choice but to resist globalism with nationalism. In contrast, Hardt and Negri believed that from this point on, resistance would emerge from within the world of Empire/animal— that the multitude would appear from within globalism. In the 2010s, these two arguments went beyond the names of individual thinkers such as Schmitt and Negri, becoming the archetype of the choice available to 'critical intellectuals'. In resisting the violence of globalism, you can either seek your roots in nationalism, which sits outside of it (become a nationalist), or you can entrust your dreams to a multitude that will supposedly emerge from within it (commit to a movement that is exceedingly close to a form of faith)—these are the only options.

However, it seems to me that the mythology outlined above precisely gives us a hint that there may be a third choice—the possibility of another form of resistance that involves neither becoming a cynical nationalist nor waiting for the blind multitude.

Let us reread that mythology once more. Unlike Schmitt and Negri, we neither believe that the nation state system continues to thrive independently, nor the opposite, that it has been replaced by another system. It is *overlaid* by the system of Empire and continues to exist as a part of the world order.

According to the hypothesis of this book, the nation state is a system generated by the small-world order and Empire is a system generated by the scale-free order. Thus, unlike the tree and the rhizome, they can coexist without any contradiction. Now, what our mythology teaches us is that the system of Empire isn't something that clashes with the system of the nation state at all; rather, it is generated as a result when the impetus for the generation of the nation state—that is, the rewiring/misdelivery that made small-worldness possible, altering its form—loses its contingency and becomes organised. The nation state and Empire are both generated by the same misdelivery. Although without misdelivery there are no encounters with the Other, there are no disparities either.

If that is the case, couldn't we locate the new site of resistance against globalism neither inside nor outside Empire, but *in between* Empire and its outside—in other words, within the space of misdelivery that simultaneously generates small-worldness and scale-freedom? Wrenching misdelivery from the scale-free order—couldn't we think of this as the basis for resistance? This is my final proposal. It is a framework that neither Deleuze nor Negri could have reached, one made possible by the hypothesis of replacing the tree and the rhizome with small-worldness and scale-freedom.

The new resistance of the twenty-first century will be born in the crevice between Empire and nation state. It aims neither to critique Empire from without nor to deconstruct it from within, but rather to *reperform* misdelivery. Its members aim to meet people they were never meant to meet, go to places they were never meant to go, think thoughts they were never meant to think; they seek to infuse contingency back into the system of Empire, to rewire concentrated edges once again, and to revert from preferential selection back to misdelivery. And through the accumulation of these practices, they aim to continuously remind people that there is no necessary mathematical basis to the concentration of wealth and power in particular nodes, but that this is always something that can be disassembled, subverted, and restarted—that this reality is not the best possible world. It seems to me that this tactic of *remisdelivery* is the necessary condition that must be put in place as the basis of all realistic and sustainable resistance in this age of bifurcation between nation state and Empire. In the twenty-first-century order, rhizomic mobilisation without misdelivery can only resemble the biopower of Empire.

All resistance must begin with the reperformance of misdelivery. I will call this the *principle of the tourist*. The new solidarity of the twenty-first century begins there.

This fourth chapter, and indeed most of the book thus far, consists of abstract discussion. Although this is stating the obvious, as this is a book of philosophy, some readers may find that this kind of discussion alone does not allow them to really understand what this new solidarity might entail.

At the beginning of this chapter, I wrote that where the negative-theological multitude goes to demonstrations, the tourist goes on junkets, and where the negative-theological multitude builds solidarity without communication, the tourist communicates without solidarity. But if that is the case, does this mean that we are practicing resistance against Empire if we skip the demonstrations and simply go on tourist trips and say hi to everyone we meet? Of course not. The tourist of this book is a slightly more complex being than that.

What kind of guidelines for action does this principle of the tourist give us, then? Unfortunately, answering this question head on is beyond the scope of this book. Moreover, I wonder whether it is even a question that should be answered in the first place. As for myself, I feel that I have been answering this query in the form of action through the publication of the triannual magazine of criticism *Genron*, which the original Japanese version of this book was published as a preparatory volume of, and by holding the annual tour of Chernobyl mentioned in the supplement above. I do not participate in demonstrations. Instead, I organise tours, including intellectual tourism in the form of publishing. The question of whether these are successful tactics of misdelivery should be answered according to individual instances rather than theory. We cannot demonstrate that such and such kind of action constitutes an example of misdelivery or tourism in the same way we might simply say that participating in an election is politics, or giving a press conference is politics, or going to a demonstration is politics.

Despite all of this, in the hope that it will provide guidance to some readers, I will close (and I am really closing this time) by briefly introducing the thought of Richard Rorty, a philosopher who thinks about the possibility of solidarity from the standpoint of a world view quite close to that put forward in this book.

The standpoint of Rorty—an important thinker and a leading philosopher in the United States between the 1980s and 2000s—is that of 'pragmatism'. In a word, it is a position that holds that philosophical words like 'truth' and 'justice' don't actually refer to anything profound, but rather are nothing more than pragmatic labels that can be effectively used in everyday life.

In his 1989 book *Contingency, Irony, and Solidarity*, Rorty develops a political standpoint which he calls that of the 'liberal ironist'. At the basis of this standpoint is the split between public behaviour and private belief.

According to Rorty, this is an age that requires that 'we drop the demand for a theory which unifies the public and private'.[12] This is because in contemporary Western developed societies (the book was written in the 1980s), people are for example free to *privately* believe in a particular philosophy or religion, but any attempt to force it upon others as a public belief and force conversion is strictly forbidden. But since philosophy and religion are inherently activities that strive towards universality, there is actually a contradiction here: a religion that is simply private—something that one might believe in as a mere hobby—is no longer a religion or anything resembling one. But this is all that is allowed in contemporary society, and Rorty believes that this is a good thing. Hence he imagines a standpoint from which one can actively welcome this contradiction, the standpoint of the liberal ironist—'ironist' because it involves an attitude of living with contradiction.

Rorty's standpoint is also deeply related to another word that appears in the title of his book: contingency. Accepting the split between public matters and

---

12.   Rorty, *Contingency, Irony, and Solidarity*, xv.

private matters also means acknowledging that one's own private values are nothing more than a product of contingent conditions. It means acknowledging that I just happen to hold these beliefs because I happen to be Japanese and happen to be a man and happen to have been born in the twentieth century, and that I would likely believe something else had I been born under different conditions:

> [T]he liberal societies of our century have produced more and more people who are able to recognize the contingency of the vocabulary in which they state their highest hopes—the contingency of their own consciences—and yet have remained faithful to those consciences.[13]

These thoughts of Rorty's dovetail neatly with the theory of the stratified world put forward in this book. Rorty argues that contemporary people must accept the split between public behaviour and private belief. I have been expressing my observation that contemporary people have been split between the nation state system and the Empire system. As I wrote in Chapter 3, in the 1970s liberalism split into communitarianism and libertarianism, and this corresponds to the bifurcation of the world into layers. Communitarianism is a political thought that argues that all beliefs are ultimately prescribed by the contingency of the community (nation state) to which the subject belongs, while in contrast libertarianism is a political thought that argues that the foundation for society (meta-utopia) must be designed without any relation to any kind of belief. In other words, the former corresponds to the basis of private beliefs, while the latter corresponds to the basis of public behaviour. We live in an age where these two modes of thought exist side by side. We can probably interpret Rorty's proposal as an attempt to suture this split through 'irony' and, paradoxically, to rebuild liberalism on this basis.

But what is important here is that, as the title of his book announces, Rorty was also thinking about 'solidarity' in addition to contingency and irony. Rorty says that private belief cannot become public. Stated another way, he denies the existence of universal values. Then how should we build relations with the Other

---

13.   Ibid., 46.

without the help of universal values? This was Rorty's question, and it is the same question that we have been asking in many different forms throughout this book.

What was Rorty's answer? He employs words such as 'sense' and 'imagination' in making his case:

> I have been urging in this book that we try *not* to want something which stands beyond history and institutions. [...] my sketch of the liberal ironist was of someone for whom [the sense of human solidarity] was a matter of imaginative identification with the details of others' lives, rather than a recognition of something antecedently shared.[14]

In other words, Rorty argues that solidarity spreads through the power of empathy.

Rorty doesn't believe in universal ideals. So he cannot use words or logic as the basis of solidarity. As a pragmatist, he can only rely on concrete experience. Thus, we could say that it was inevitable that he would reach such a conclusion.

Many were dissatisfied with this conclusion, however. It was subjected to harsh criticism, on the grounds that a solidarity based on the possibility of empathy ultimately only meant the exclusion of the alien Other, and that this couldn't be called true solidarity. In fact, in a later book published in 1998, entitled *Achieving Our Country*, Rorty writes, mostly positively, about the function of 'pride' in relation to the state or tradition. Read retrospectively from that point, Rorty's writing on solidarity in *Contingency, Irony, and Solidarity* might be read as an early sign of a return to nationalism.

But I think that what Rorty attempted to show, at least in the earlier work, could instead be reread as something resembling the possibility that I have termed 'misdelivery'. I say this because, as demonstrated in the quote above, what Rorty tried to put in place as the basis of solidarity was not the widespread empathy generated by large groups of belonging such as ethnicity, religion, or culture, but only the extremely concrete and contingent empathy toward 'details' at the individual level. The sense of 'us' is actually generated *after* this empathy for the details of others' lives—after the fact and retrospectively. In the final page of *Contingency, Irony, and Solidarity*, Rorty writes that what generates

---

14. Ibid., 189–90. Emphasis removed.

this solidarity is not the question 'Do you believe and desire what we believe and desire?', in other words the acknowledgment of a shared belief or desire, but simply the question 'Are you suffering?'[15]

There happens to be a suffering human before us. We cannot help but approach them. We empathise. For Rorty, this is the basis of solidarity, the basis of 'us', and the basis of society. Isn't this precisely the operation of misdelivery where rewirings create a small-world graph?

Rorty rarely refers to Rousseau. But as I wrote in *General Will 2.0*, I also think of Rousseau when I read this passage.[16] As discussed above in Chapter 2, Rousseau didn't like people. He thought that there was no way that humans could like humans. He thought there was no way that humans would want to build societies.

Nevertheless, in reality humans build societies. Why? The answer Rousseau arrived at in his *Discourse on the Origins of Inequality* was compassion. Compassion 'hurries us without reflection to the relief of those who are in distress' and 'moderat[es] the violence of love of self in each individual, contributes to the preservation of the whole species'.[17] Rousseau writes that humanity would have likely perished long ago without compassion. It is precisely compassion that creates society, and society creates inequality. And compassion closely resembles misdelivery, as well as rewiring.

We might say that Rousseau and Rorty were both philosophers of misdelivery. It was precisely misdelivery that Hegel failed to observe and that we must now recover. The philosophy of the tourist is the philosophy of misdelivery. It is also the philosophy of solidarity and compassion. Without misdelivery, we cannot even create a society in the first place.

---

15. Ibid, 198.
16. Azuma, *General Will 2.0*, 172.
17. J.-J. Rousseau, *On the Origin of Inequality*, tr. G.D.H. Cole (New York: Cosimo Classics, 2005), 53.

PART TWO

PHILOSOPHY OF
THE FAMILY
(AN INTRODUCTION)

5. The Family

1

We now begin the second part of the book. In the first part, I argued that the twenty-first century can be understood as a stratified structure, bifurcated between the political layer and the economic layer, the nationalism layer and the globalism layer, the nation state layer and the Empire layer. I suggested that in such an era, the existence of the 'tourist' or the 'postal multitude' which connects these layers and increases the possibility of misdelivery will become important as a new starting point for politics. I believe that the first part therefore achieved the principal goal of this book, namely to develop a framework for a new philosophy on the basis of the figure of the tourist.

In the second part I offer two studies that consider the concepts of the uncanny and the child as an extension of the ideas developed in the first part. These will be the topics of Chapters 6 and 7.

However, these are preliminary sketches, and do not constitute the kind of organised discussion featured in Part 1. There are leaps in logic, and corners will be cut. Above all, these chapters are written in a form closer to literary criticism or essayistic writing than to academic philosophy. Readers who have followed the discussion closely thus far may feel put off by this, but I have included these studies because I believe that the framework of the book could not be brought to a satisfactory close without them, incomplete as they are.

The two sketches deal with themes that may on the surface seem unrelated. Chapter 6 discusses the new subject of the information society, taking as a hint the word 'cyberspace' that appeared in the 1980s. On the other hand, Chapter 7 explores the possibility of a subject that goes beyond the terrorist through a reading of the work of Fyodor Dostoevsky, written in the mid-nineteenth century. Both the object of inquiry and the historical era concerned are vastly different.

However, the two studies are related to the same question, which emerges from the discussion in Part 1: the question of identity.

In the era of the stratified world, personal identities are also largely split in two. Libertarian businessmen who live within globalism and develop their enterprises across national borders live with the individual as their sole anchor. They seek animalistic pleasure (in the Kojèvian sense) through money without belonging to any country or history. In contrast, communitarian citizens who live within nationalism and live and die by the 'politics' that go on within national borders continue to live with the nation state as their anchor. They belong to a particular history of a particular country, and seek the life of a human (in Arendt's sense), with an appreciation for the weight of previous generations. Individual or state? These are the only two identities that function in twenty-first-century secularised society, and this dichotomy, too, corresponds to the stratified structure of the world. This being the case, what anchors the 'tourist' who traverses these two layers? This is the question posed in Part 2.

Where one seeks one's identity largely determines the character of one's political thought. Taking the individual as a starting point means affirming capitalism (globalism), while taking the community as a starting point means supporting statism (nationalism).

Some time ago, communism promoted the concept of *class* as a third identity that was neither individual nor state. Indeed, perhaps what was revolutionary about communism was the very invention of this identity. It was precisely because communism was based on this third identity that it was able to simultaneously critique the freedom of the individual (capitalism) while denying the bourgeois nation state. However, communism lost its influence with the collapse of the Cold War structure. This leaves us today with no secure footing on the basis of which to criticise both individual and state at the same time. It is essentially owing to this lack that people today are constantly forced to choose between the two options of globalism or nationalism, empire or nation state.

In order to escape this situation, then, we need to invent or discover a fourth identity that is neither individual, state, or class. This is the question to which the framework of the philosophy of the tourist leads us.

I am actually not alone in thinking this way; others have put forward similar arguments. For example, the Russian conservative thinker Aleksandr Dugin has called for a 'fourth political theory'.[1] According to Dugin, each political theory has a key ideal. For liberalism it is the ideal of the individual, for totalitarianism the ideal of the state, and for communism the ideal of revolution. Although each has its strengths and weaknesses, none are suited to the contemporary world, he argues, and this is why we need a 'fourth political theory'.

Dugin is known as a far-right ideologue with close relations to the Putin administration, and this argument is deeply related to Russian geopolitical expansionism (Eurasianism). Heidegger's 'Dasein', which Dugin invokes as a candidate for a new ideal, has a history of entanglement with totalitarianism, and so in this respect, also, it must be said that it is a dangerous concept. I do not necessarily agree with Dugin's arguments themselves, then. But I must agree with his understanding that in the current era we need a new theory, one that is neither liberalism, totalitarianism (statism), nor communism, and a new ideal to support it. We cannot critique both nationalism and globalism without forging such a theory and discovering such an ideal. While Dugin is a rightist, we could say that the Left, too, has been engaged in a similar struggle in search of a new political theory since the end of the Cold War. The theory of the multitude we explored in Part 1 was a theory discovered by that search. However, as we saw, the multitude is an ideal with an exceedingly 'negative-theological' character. In other words, it lacked sufficient substance to be adopted as an identity.

For that reason, the multitude has only been able to generate 'carnivalesque' short-term mobilisations. The season of demonstrations/mobilisations arrived suddenly in Japan after 2011, and many leftists worked themselves up into a frenzy. But barely any traces of this remain today in 2017. It is everyday life, not carnivals, that moves politics forward. Put another way, it is identity, not mobilisation. The ideal of solidarity was defeated by a lack of identity.

Thus, I decided that I must add to this book a discussion, no matter how incomplete, of the identity sought by the philosophy of the tourist. Without such an attempt, this book will likely be received as mere wordplay that attaches Derrida's concept of the 'postal' to the newfangled concept of multitude.

---

1.   A. Dugin, *The Fourth Political Theory*, tr. M. Sleboda and M. Millerman (Budapest: Arktos, 2012), Chapter 2.

What, then, is the new identity to which the tourist must anchor themselves? One candidate I would like to consider is the *family*. I wonder whether it might be possible to reconstruct or deconstruct the concept of the family and forge it into a concept that expresses the new solidarity of the tourist. In so doing, we would finally be able to obtain the fourth ideal that can serve as the starting point for critiquing both the principle of order that commences with the individual (globalism) and the principle of order that commences with the state (nationalism). Postal solidarity is familial solidarity; the philosophy of the family is what comes after the philosophy of the tourist.

What? The family? Many readers may be disheartened by this suggestion. In fact, this word is rather unpopular, particularly among Japanese intellectuals.

There are several reasons for this. First and foremost, the word 'family' in Japan today has become a uniquely political term that in and of itself implies values linked to conservativism (and a brand of conservatism that leans heavily towards patriotism and xenophobia at that). Recently in Japan, conservatives have been clamouring for the recovery of the 'traditional family', as can be seen in their draft for constitutional revision released in 2012. The unpopularity of the concept is a result of these circumstances.

But the concept of the family is originally politically neutral. Both conservatives and liberals usually have a family, after all. And in truth, the fact that, in spite of this, simply uttering the word 'family' makes it seem like one subscribes to a certain ideology points to a far deeper problem. This warped situation is symbolic of the quandary in which liberals find themselves today. Japanese liberals ought to wrest this word back from conservatives, but there is no sign of that happening. At present, it is common sense among leftists today, and among intellectuals too, that anyone touting the importance of the family must be up to no good. There are probably more than a few readers of this book who harbour similar suspicions.

Furthermore, there is a history of arguments that point to the many forms of violence involved in the 'family', theoretically or ethically. A representative example is the research conducted by Marxist feminists such as Chizuko Ueno, who argue that paternalism (the family) is nothing more than an apparatus of violence complicit with capitalism in exploiting the domestic and reproductive labour of women. According to Ueno's definition, the family is 'the social realm that controls sexuality and reproduction'.[2] Discourses such as family love are nothing more than cosmetic niceties that cover up the essence of this 'control'. And indeed, Japan has a legacy of mobilising the metaphor of the 'family' or *ie*,[3] to legitimise the totalitarian state, as represented by the prewar discourse of 'one sovereign and his people [*ikkun banmin*]'. Equating the nation to members of a family can at times become an unbearable violence for the individual.

Moreover, today, in 2017, it is difficult to naively and affirmatively use this word without running into problems of 'political correctness'. Feelings toward the family vary from person to person, of course. There are good families and there are bad families—child abuse is something that does happen. The composition of families varies a great deal, too. While one might say that all humans have a father and mother, although this may be true biologically speaking, the situation is more complicated in a family composed through same-sex marriage, for instance. Without considering these individual examples, speaking about the concept of 'the Family' with a capital F is a dangerous act that risks inadvertently causing offence.

I completely sympathise with these worries and feelings of unease. If we are to adopt the concept of the family as the basis for political solidarity, all kinds of theoretical operations will be necessary in order to neutralise its violent nature, and this will pose considerable difficulties.

The reason why I nevertheless propose the family as a promising candidate is because I do not see any other usable concept that could serve as the core for an identity that is neither individual nor nation state.

First of all, class is unusable. It is too deeply entwined with communist theory, and the historical mission of this theory has ended. Homeland cannot be used either. Now that anyone can connect with the entire world through the internet, it is impractical to seek to anchor the subject in any particular geographical territory. Blood and genes cannot be used either; that leads only to racism.

---

2.   C. Ueno, *Kafuchōsei to shihonsei* [*Patriarchy and Capitalism*] (Tokyo: Iwanami Gendai Bunko, 2009), 296.

3.   [The Japanese word *ie* means 'household', and can refer either to the house as building or to a family lineage and estate—generally assumed to be patriarchal. It was the central concept in the Meiji government's civil code and ideology in the late nineteenth to early twentieth century. See C. Ueno, *The Modern Family in Japan: Its Rise and Fall* (Victoria: Trans Pacific Press, 2009), Chapter 3—trans.]

Gender is too broad; it only differentiates humans into several categories. Organisations based on philosophy or faith and communities based on hobbies and interests cannot become the core of identity; one can change one's affiliation at will, and any solidarity based on free will can easily be dissolved through free will. That is the weakness of the multitude. When we go through all of the possibilities like this, there isn't really anything other than family (or variants such as tribe or *ie*) that offers a concept equivalent to neither individual nor state, which cannot be changed according to free will, and is expansive enough that it can serve as a basis for political solidarity.

It is instructive here to recall the work of Emmanuel Todd. Prior to his work, scholars in the humanities looking to account for national social structures had been fixated on the contents of law and ideology alone. But with his work in the 1980s, Todd sent shockwaves through the academy by showing how the social structures of countries around the world were determined not by the so-called superstructure of law and ideology, but more simply by family structure.

For example, it is generally thought that communism spread because of the attractiveness of its (revolutionary) ideology. But if we study family structures, we find that the ex-Soviet bloc—that is, the group of regions that adopted communism—largely overlaps with those regions that tend to feature the form of family that Todd calls the 'exogamous communitarian family type' (a family structure where sons continue to live with their parents after entering adulthood and marriage, and the inheritance is divided equally between them). Why was this the case? Todd hypothesises that it was because the ethics implied by communism (which he describes as authoritarianism with an egalitarian tendency) were a good fit with the ethics implied by the exogamous communitarian family. In other words, the adoption of communism was determined not by its content, but by a compatibility between the form of communication it implied and the predominant family types of each region (Todd provides other similar examples).[4]

Incidentally, it has been suggested that this analysis of Todd's applies to individualist countries as well. On the surface, individualism (liberalism) appears to deny the importance of the family. The order of Empire develops by absolutising

---

4.   See E. Todd, *Lineages of Modernity: A History of Humanity from the Stone Age to Homo Americanus*, tr. A. Brown (Cambridge: Polity Press, 2019), Chapter 18, 'Communitarian Societies: Russia and China' [The author's reference is the Japanese translation of Todd's *La Diversité du monde: Famille et modernité* (Paris: Seuil, 1999), *Sekai no tayōsei*, tr. F. Ogino (Tokyo: Fujiwara Shoten, 2008), 75–76—trans.]

the individual. But Todd argues that this concept of the absolute individual is in fact the product of a family type called the 'absolute nuclear family' (a family type in which children build their own independent household in adulthood, and there are no particular set rules regarding inheritance), which developed in a certain region of Europe and later expanded to the United States. Indeed, as evident in the content of Hollywood films, while American society respects individual liberty, it also places great importance on a close-knit nuclear family. Milton Friedman, a representative libertarian, states matter-of-factly that '[a]s liberals, we take freedom of the individual, or perhaps the family, as our ultimate goal'.[5] If that is the case, then perhaps family form not only determines the order of the nation state, but also that of Empire to some degree. I think that a new perspective could emerge if we were to connect Todd's work with the theory of the stratified world elaborated above.

Either way, Todd's analysis shows that, even in the contemporary world where class has disappeared and apparently only the individual and the state remain, family (the family form) stubbornly persists as a core of identity. These research trends inform my argument that what is called for today is a recon-struction/deconstruction of the concept of family.

However, since unlike Todd I am neither a historian nor an anthropologist, I do not think that our conclusion should be simply to reduce the diversity of the world to the diversity of family types. Instead, if the diversity of the world is determined by the diversity of family types, I ask how we should act upon this factor, the family. To put it another way, I ask how we might build a new solidarity by using the attachment to 'the familial' that is in each one of us. This is what I hope to map out through the deconstruction of the family.

Allow me to add one more note. In Part 1, I referred to the Hegelian philosophy according to which humans undergo spiritual growth by progressing from family to civil society and then to the state. In other words, this philosophy holds that people mature by leaving the family and becoming individuals, and subsequently identifying with the nation state. If we take this schema as our premise, my suggestion that we once again consider the importance of the concept of the

5.   M. Friedman, *Capitalism and Freedom, 40th Anniversary Edition* (Chicago: University of Chicago Press, 2002), 12.

familial *after* the individual and the state might seem like a clumsy backwards step, in terms of Hegelian Spirit (*Geist*).

Such an interpretation would be mistaken. Some readers might think of the work of Kōjin Karatani here. Since his 2001 book *Transcritique*, Karatani has consistently advocated a theory that differentiates between three modes of exchange and three social formations which can be used to analyse contemporary society. The three modes of exchange are 'gifting', 'plunder and redistribution', and 'commodity exchange', and the three social formations are 'nation', 'state', and 'capital'—which in the terms used here correspond to 'family', 'state', and 'civil society'. It may sound odd to hear that 'nation' corresponds to 'family', but this interpretation makes sense given that, for Karatani, the 'nation is the imagined restoration of the community that was undermined by the commodity-exchange economy'.[6] The family is established through gifting, the state through plunder and redistribution, and civil society through exchange. And contemporary society is established through the intertwining of these three, in a complex system that Karatani calls 'Capital-Nation-State'.

On this basis, Karatani argues that the critique of contemporary society requires the invention of a new social formation, which in turn requires the rediscovery of a fourth mode of exchange. While Karatani calls this social formation 'association', it closely corresponds to Negri and Hardt's multitude. What is interesting for our purposes is that Karatani argues that the fourth mode of exchange that supports this association/multitude will be the restoration of gifting in a 'higher dimension'.[7] It may seem as though the world of gifting disappeared with the emergence of the market and state. But in fact it never disappeared, and is restored *in another form*. That was Karatani's argument, and he made the case that it was precisely there that we could find hope.

Karatani's discussion only provides vague stipulations concerning the important matter of this fourth mode of exchange, and it would be difficult to conclude

---

6. K. Karatani, *The Structure of World History: From Modes of Production to Modes of Exchange*, tr. M.K. Bourdaghs (Durham, NC: Duke University Press, 2014), 216. To be more precise about this correspondence, since Karatani uses the term state (*kokka*) to refer to the state institution, there is a misalignment in meaning with state (*kokka*) as used in this book. In the present book (adopting Hegel's terminology), state (*kokka*) is used to refer to a higher-stage existence that subsumes the opposition between family and civil society, and what corresponds to this in Karatani's work is actually 'Capital-Nation-State'. However, I have simplified this correspondence in the text.

7. Ibid., 8.

that it has succeeded, in theory or in practice. We do not get much of a sense of how gifting restored at a 'higher dimension' differs from gifting in its original form. The New Associationist Movement (NAM), which Karatani launched around the same time as *Transcritique* was published, quickly fell apart. But his intuition that the linkage between the nation state and capitalism (Capital-Nation-State) is the source of contemporary power, and that therefore in order to disassemble it, we must return to a *previous* structure—to concepts prior to the state and market—seems correct.

My suggestion that we rethink the family is actually also proposed as a renewal of Karatani's attempt as summarised above (recall my suggestion, at the opening of Chapter 1, that the theory of the tourist is a renewal of Karatani's theory of the Other). Just as Karatani sees a return to gifting after the state and capital, I see a return to the family after the nation state and the individual. Just as Karatani explored a new association supported by gifting, I explore a new multitude supported by familial solidarity. In other words, what I want to consider here is not the family itself but, to borrow Karatani's words, its restoration in a 'higher dimension'.

Thinking about the family is not at all a regression in thought. If upon reading the words 'the philosophy of the family' some readers imagined a tedious moralistic discussion about respecting one's parents, having more children, or being kind to one's siblings, that was nothing more than a simple misunderstanding.

2

The philosophy of the tourist must be supplemented by the philosophy of the family. The strategy of the postal multitude that travels to and fro between nation state and Empire, spreading misdelivery and compassion, must be supported by a new familial solidarity. This is why I have written this second part of the book.

But as I noted above, I have not yet adequately thought through the philosophy of the family. My explanation thus far is a rough sketch, and the two chapters that follow are nothing more than drafts for a future argument. I would like you to think of this part as an introduction to a book on the philosophy of the family that will someday be written. My discussion regarding the philosophy of the tourist itself ends with Part 1. In a sense, what follows is a lengthy supplement.

Bearing that in mind, I would like to introduce a few issues that may become points of interest in the deconstruction or restoration, in a 'higher dimension', of the concept of the family. These may or may not prove helpful in reading the two provisional chapters that follow. Either way, there are many interesting issues regarding the concept of the family that stimulate philosophical thinking, and contemporary thought would do well to apply more creative thinking to the question of what constitutes the family.

The first issue that I would like to focus on is the *coerciveness* of the family. The family is a group that can hardly be joined or left based on sheer free will, while simultaneously it is a group held together by strong 'emotion'. The familial possesses a coerciveness that goes beyond rational judgment.

I have touched upon the relationship between political movements and free will on a number of occasions. The post-Cold-War Left has invested its hopes in a new solidarity (radical democracy) created through the free will of fragmented individuals. However, as I have repeatedly stated, such forms of solidarity quickly collapse, and generally for the same reasons: groups that one has joined of one's own free will can just as easily be left. This makes them no different from hobby groups that meet on weekends—which is no adequate foundation for politics.

Family ties are not so simple. At the very least, family relations other than marriage are different from such temporary bonds. Most people become members of a particular family the moment they are born. There is no free will involved. And it is quite difficult to escape from that situation. While this coerciveness is generally understood negatively (and in fact, must be rejected in situations such as child abuse), the flipside of this is that it is precisely because of this coerciveness that the family can be considered as a candidate for political identity. Similarly, state and class were able to become identities that supported political thought precisely because they were (or were understood to be) coercive in nature.

We could also put this in the following way: People are prepared to die for individual or private reasons. They will also die for the state or for their class. Similarly, they are prepared to die for their family. Thus, the family can become the basis for a new politics. On the other hand, people are not prepared to die for their hobby groups. In *The Social Contract,* Rousseau wrote that people must be prepared to give their life for the general will.[8] Although this is an infamous passage that is often read as an advocacy of totalitarianism, it does sharply pinpoint the essence of politics. Rousseau was able to think the concept of the general will as the basis of politics because he thought it as something that people would die for. Where there is no possibility of death, there is no politics. Leftists today have forgotten this.

The second aspect of family that I would like to focus on is its *contingency*. In illustrating the collapse of a family, Dostoevsky once used the phrase 'an accidental family'.[9] While in this case the phrase simply refers to a family that comes together as a family without necessity, in truth all families are accidental families.

Let me explain. Firstly, everyone has a family. At the very least, they possess biological parents. While there are numerous cases in which parents die after birth or go missing, or social ties with the parents are broken off, at the point of birth (conception) humans necessarily possess two parents who have provided their genes and one parent who provided their womb (while this is a rather cumbersome way to put it, it is unavoidable given the presence today of phenomena such as surrogacy). Even more specifically, in cases such as artificial insemination, it is quite possible that, at the point of conception, one of the parents is no longer alive. Yet even in these cases, parents exist at the moment of providing their sperm or egg. More recently, there are complex cases where the nucleus of the egg and egg cells originate from two different mothers through fertility treatment. Still, unless they are a clone, everyone necessarily has at least two parents.

---

8. 'Now, the Citizen is no longer judge of the danger the law wills him to risk, and when the Prince has said to him, it is expedient to the State that you die, he ought to die.' J.-J. Rousseau, *The Social Contract and Other Later Political Writings*, ed. V. Gourevitch (Cambridge: Cambridge University Press, 1997), 64.

9. This phrase appears in the final scene (the letter) of *The Adolescent* (F. Dostoevsky, *The Adolescent*, tr. R. Pevear and L. Volokhonsky [New York: Vintage, 2003], 563). It also appears in *A Writer's Diary*, written around the same period: 'I (in *The Adolescent*) took a soul that was sinless yet already tainted by the awful possibility of vice, by a premature hatred for its own insignificance and "accidental" nature [...] All such are miscarriages of society, the "accidental" members of "accidental" families' (F. Dostoevsky, *A Writer's Diary*, tr. K. Lantz [Evanston, IL: Northwestern University Press, 2009], 84). [In the original Japanese text, the word 'accidental' in this sentence and the word 'contingency' in the previous sentence are both the same, *gūzen*, which I have glossed as 'contingency' and 'chance' in different passages in the book—trans.]

We could even say that this is an absolute necessity. Although people may choose not to have children of their own, they cannot forgo having parents.

But this necessity brings with it a troublesome characteristic. People cannot forgo having parents. I am me because I was born from my father and mother. This is an absolute necessity. Nevertheless, from the perspective of my parents who made me, there is no necessity to the fact that I was born. If they had engaged in intercourse on a different day, or even if, on the same day, a different sperm had combined with the egg, someone other than myself would have been born. From my parents' perspective, it is a contingent fact that the child that was born was me. Although people often say that 'children can't choose their parents', this is philosophically incorrect. Although a child certainly cannot choose his or her parents, the very idea of doing so is meaningless because you would no longer be you if you chose different parents. Those who 'cannot choose' in the true sense, in other words those who abandon themselves to chance, are actually the parents. We all go through a gigantic ontological lottery when we are born. There is no one among us who is a necessary being, born because they were meant to be born. The fact that a certain child is born of certain parents actually has no necessity to it at all. From the perspective of the parent, it is entirely contingent. In this respect, all families are essentially accidental families. In other words, the family is a strikingly precarious group whose basis is the contingency of the child.

Therein lies another very important philosophical issue. Earlier I wrote that there is no politics where there is no possibility for death. I also mentioned that Dugin's 'fourth political theory' references Heidegger.

As is well known, death plays a significant role in Heidegger's philosophy. Everyone dies. Moreover, they each die their own death alone. In other words, death is an absolute necessity. Heidegger took this as his starting point in building his philosophy. In doing so, he emphasised the absolute nature of death and the necessity of fate to such an extent that he ended up finding common ground with Nazism.

But as we have seen, when we grasp the human from the point of view of birth rather than death, the human condition appears to us in a completely different way. We see contingency, and we see the family. As such, could we not flip Heidegger's attempt on its head and imagine another ontological philosophy that starts not with 'everyone dies alone', but with 'no one can be born alone'? Although I was not able to go into this in any depth in *Ontological, Postal*, I actually believe that this is precisely the possibility latent in the philosophy of what Derrida calls 'dissemination'.[10] Dissemination refers to the discharge of sperm. The massive number of sperm creates our contingent nature. A new philosophy born out of the relativity of birth and the contingency of the family, a philosophy that could be counterposed to Heideggerian philosophy born out of the absoluteness of death and the necessity of fate....

The concept of the family is rich in possibilities for such re-readings. As I mentioned earlier when referencing the example of the discourse of 'one sovereign and his people [*ikkun banmin*]', in suggesting a political thought founded upon the concept of the family, I may be giving the impression of something like statism or totalitarianism. But what those ideologies imagine is what we might call a '*necessary* family'. In contrast, I consider the *contingent* family. The schema of this book, which examines the human from the perspective of the contingency of birth rather than the necessity of death, will surely harbour completely different political implications.

The third characteristic I would like to focus on is the *expandability* of the family.

Today in Japan the representative image of the family has become the nuclear family. But this is strictly a postwar phenomenon; Japan has not always been a country of nuclear families. According to Todd's classification, Japan is a region where the dominant model is the 'hierarchical family' (in which only one son continues to live with the parents into adulthood and after marriage, and that son also receives the inheritance), as it is in Germany and on the Korean peninsula.

---

10.   See *Sonzaironteki, yūbinteki*, 167n26, where I write: 'Unintended pregnancy and the child born as a result are *precisely* used as allegories for misdelivered—that is, mistakenly "sent"—letters (*émissions*) and their return. For the father, the origin of the child (ghost) is no longer clear, but it relentlessly demands "responsibility." As Derrida himself states, "dissemination," which served as his central theoretical concept in the 1970s, was itself a metaphor with strong reproductive connotations [...] Thus, it seems to me that for him sexuality was always related to a series of issues having to do with reproduction and pregnancy (communication) rather than the series of issues relating to sexual desire (formation of the subject) in the Foucauldian sense.'

Historically, the Japanese *ie* has been imagined to be something quite different from the nuclear family. It is said that the *ie* is centred on economic community rather than blood relations, and is an organisation that can expand relatively flexibly through adoption. It is precisely for this reason that Japanese society was able to smoothly adapt to modernisation by reinterpreting private enterprises as *ie*. Kunio Yanagita's *About Our Ancestors* (1946) and Yasusuke Murakami et al.'s *Ie Society as a Pattern of Civilisation* (1979) are instructive on this point. The latter study in particular was based on Tadao Umesawa's *Ecological View of Civilisation*, and in hindsight has points in common with Dugin's geopolitical ideas and Todd's anthropological research.[11]

_____

11.   Y. Murakami, S. Kumon, S. Satō, *Bunmei toshite no ie shakai* (Tokyo: Chūō Kōron sha, 1979). According to this work, the Japanese *ie* was a group based on neither blood relations nor territorial relations, but a principle of group formation particular to Japan which emerged in Tōgoku (a sparsely populated frontier settled by warrior groups) during the Kamakura period. Japanese society prior to the *ie* operated under the principle of the *uji* kin group, that is, the principle of primitive blood relations. The *ie* features the four characteristics of a flexible (super-consanguineous) principle of extension, premised upon long-term continuity (genealogical character), possession of a clear order of ranks and statuses among members (functional system of class), and a high degree of economic and political autonomy from the outside (independence) (Chapter 7). By the Muromachi era this principle of *ie* put to its own use the principle of *uji* (imperial authority), and in the Edo era it dominated the governance of the Tokugawa system. Although it faded somewhat during the modernisation of the Meiji era, it continued to wield considerable influence in the postwar era as the archetype of 'Japanese-style management'. Such is the historical understanding presented in this 1979 book. Now, from the perspective of the present work, what I would like to focus on is the fact that, as the title of their book suggests, this theory of Murakami and his co-authors is imagined in the context of a theory of civilisation on a global scale, and not simply as an explanatory principle for a phenomenon specific to Japanese history. Their concept of *ie* possesses a potential for universal extension. According to their thinking (see discussion starting on page 24), humans possess both a 'tendency towards individuality' (the tendency to desire to be an individual) and a 'tendency towards gathering' (the tendency to be together with everyone else), and human societies can be differentiated as 'separation-type societies' and 'permeation-type societies' depending on whether these two tendencies are upheld separately or are unified in some way. For example, ancient Greece, which differentiated between *polis* and *oikos*, was a separation-type society, while the nation state whose early buds can be identified in mediaeval Europe is a permeation-type society. Similarly, Imperial China, which differentiated between kinship and the system of bureaucracy, was a separation-type society, while the *ie* society which developed on its periphery in Japan in the mediaeval period was a permeation-type society. From this perspective, the theory of the stratified world set out thus far in this book could be interpreted as an argument that twenty-first-century human society is returning to a *separation-type society on a global scale* in which the place of Empire associated with the 'tendency toward gathering' (biopower) and the place of the nation state associated with the 'tendency toward individuality' (disciplinary training) are distinct. Perhaps the 'era of nationalism' is nothing more than a name for the short period of time during which a particular form of permeation-type society (the nation state) became dominant and took centre stage in human history. It is precisely for this reason that Japan, which

The same thing can be said about countries other than Japan. Although I cited the work of Chizuko Ueno earlier, in reality the family cannot be defined by sex and reproduction alone. It is closely related to concentrated habitation and economic cooperation, regardless of region. This is precisely why Todd focused on modes of habitation and inheritance in developing his classification system. To flip this around, it also means that any group that lives together and 'eats out of the same pot' can be understood as a family, regardless of sex or reproduction—such a dynamism has existed around the world and continues to exist today.

Also important is the fact that the concept of the family is inextricable from the feeling of intimacy (though Uno might argue that familial love is an illusion, the very fact that we continue to harbour such illusions proves that there is an inextricable relationship between the two concepts). At times, the question of who is and who is not a member of the family is dictated by private feelings of love. On this point familial membership differs significantly in character from membership of the state. Of course, the family cannot always expand based on private feelings of love alone, but at times love overcomes any set rules and processes. Adoptions, too, were not necessarily always conducted for the purpose of continuing the *ie*. While there are strict legal limitations in place today, things were originally a lot looser. As depicted in many stories—perhaps today in 2017, the director Sunao Katabuchi's anime film *In This Corner of the World* might be a good example—it was not at all uncommon in early postwar Japan for people to meet an orphan by chance and to adopt them out of pity.

This flexibility opens up the family to the Rousseauian, or Rortyian, 'compassion' discussed at the end of Chapter 4. Since the family is a contingent existence in the first place, it can be expanded through chance.

Beyond sex and reproduction and beyond dwellings and assets, the contours of the family can be determined by private feelings of love as well. While this characteristic gives rise to the expandability of the family, at the same time it blurs

features another form of permeation-type society (*ie* society) was able to become part of that dominance. But those conditions are changing rapidly today. So what is the significance of thinking about the family or *ie* in the era of this new separation-type society? Does the solidarity of the tourist/postal multitude signify a resistance to the separation-type order through the reincorporation of the principle of permeation-type society (*ie*)? Are we capable of forging *ie*, which was invented in Japan, into a universal organisational concept? Either way, I believe that a future 'philosophy of the family' must also be considered within the perspective of this kind of civilisational theory.

its boundaries. This is especially the case in today's Japan, where the traditional family form has declined. Of course there are still blood relations that we can identify on a broad basis, and these also imply financial relations. But today it is difficult to determine precisely where the family begins and ends. Let's say that I view my uncle as family, and my uncle sees his uncle (my great uncle) as family; that doesn't necessarily mean that I see my great-uncle as family. Private feelings of love do not extend in such a linear way. Contemporary people might be more inclined to see their pet dog as part of their family than a great-uncle they have never met.

The fact that the boundaries of the family are difficult to determine can also be articulated by saying that the commonality that defines a family is difficult to draw out with any exactness. I am like my uncle. My uncle is also like his uncle. But this doesn't mean that I am like my great uncle.

This, too, is related to a philosophically important issue. In *Philosophical Investigations,* Wittgenstein raised this kind of example in proposing the concept of 'family resemblance'. He writes: 'I can think of no better expression to characterize these similarities than "family resemblance"; for the various resemblances between members of a family: build, features, colour of eyes, gait, temperament, etc. etc. overlap and criss-cross in the same way. –And I shall say: "games" form a family.'[12] Let's say that there is a group of people. There is no particular commonality shared by all the group members. However, if you look at them individually, you see that they have different points in common. Thus, they establish a vague sense of cohesion as a group. Wittgenstein's argument is that the family, or the game (he understood all communication in terms of 'language games'), is precisely that which possesses this characteristic.

It is important to note that Wittgenstein's intention here was *not* to develop thoughts on the family as such. Rather, he was thinking about human communication in general, and arrived at the conclusion that its essence can be explained in terms of 'family resemblance'. Yet this only goes to show that a reconsideration of the family is absolutely necessary in the realm of contemporary thought, and in a sense different from that addressed by Todd. Above, I referred to dogs as

---

12.   L. Wittgenstein, *Philosophical Investigations*, tr. G. E. M. Anscombe (London: Macmillan, 1953), §67.

family members. Before concluding this chapter, I'd like to take a short detour on this point.

In Japan the word 'family' has actually been used with far more flexibility than has been suggested thus far. I say this because lately it has become common for pets such as dogs and cats to be considered as 'family'. Of course, they are not legally family. They are probably not family sociologically or anthropologically speaking either. But it is an incontrovertible fact that in our society an increasing number of people call their pets 'family'. There is even health insurance for pets.

The expandability of the concept of the family appears here in an extreme form. Because membership in a family can be supported solely with private feelings of love, at times it can even overcome species boundaries—a misdelivery brought on by compassion. Moreover, what is interesting here is the fact that, when we take the sensation of 'the familial' as our basis, sometimes even our impression of 'resemblance' can go beyond species boundaries. Do we not at times feel that an owner's face begins to resemble their pet's? But in such cases, what is alike? What is the 'face' of an animal in the first place? Do animals even have a face? There is a great deal that is of philosophical interest here.

What is important in the present context is that this expandability that the concept of family possesses is completely different from expandability based upon rational thinking. This is why membership of a state is something completely different from membership of a family. While the expansion of a nation requires a principle (rules), there is no set principle to the expansion of a family. This was precisely Wittgenstein's point.

Furthermore, this non-rational expandability is deeply related to the philosophy of birth. Let us take another example regarding animals.

The Australian ethicist Peter Singer is a thoroughgoing utilitarian, and is known for his arguments in favour of animal rights. Singer caused a stir when, in his 1979 book *Practical Ethics*, he argued that certain rights should be extended to apes. Singer didn't necessarily make this argument based on his fondness for animals (although he may well like animals), but because he figured that when we pursue the principle of utilitarianism (the greatest happiness for the greatest number) we must logically conclude that if discrimination among humans is unacceptable, then discrimination between species must be unacceptable as well.[13]

---

13.   P. Singer, *Practical Ethics* (Cambridge: Cambridge University Press, 1993), 55.

However, this conclusion does not mean that all animals and all life are uncon-ditionally equal. Singer's argument is based on utilitarianism, meaning that it is based on a principle of equality. He proposes that human rights should be extended to some animals because he believes that those animals fulfil the conditions for being subject to this principle. This also means that his theory of animal rights requires a process for determining whether a certain animal possesses the sensitivity that would make this principle applicable to it (i.e. how close it is to humans).[14] To put it flatly, it means that Singer introduces a hierarchy into animal life. And this implies introducing a hierarchy into human life as well. Singer's deliberation is thoroughly logical, and he avoids drawing conclusions based on vague common-sense notions. As a result, he has been harshly criticised for arriving at the conclusion that mature orangutans and chimpanzees possess a far more advanced 'personhood' than human foetuses and infants, and should therefore be legally protected.

Today, Singer's problematisation has become basic knowledge in the field of applied ethics. I will not get into what kind of ethical conclusions his logic suggests in thinking about other issues, nor what they might mean for the critique of contemporary society.[15]

14.   This logic in fact has exactly the same logical structure as Kant's argument in *Perpetual Peace* that all countries should be republics. The logic of liberalism always requires *credentials in order to participate* in happiness.

15.   From the perspective of utilitarianism, Singer grasps even the differences between humans and animals as continuous. It is unthinkable that such a thinker would affirm nationalism, which differentiates between nationals (friends) and everyone else (enemies). Indeed, in his 2002 book *One World: The Ethics of Globalization* (a book that was also written in response to the anti-globalisation movement in Seattle praised by Hardt and Negri), Singer argues for the necessity of a governing structure on a global level. Furthermore, he does not accept redistribution at the level of nation states (the welfare state). Singer criticises Rawls's *A Theory of Justice* and *The Law of Peoples* and declares that 'when subjected to the test of impartial assessment, there are few strong grounds for giving preference to the interests of one's fellow citizens' (P. Singer, *One World: The Ethics of Globalization* [New Haven, CT: Yale University Press, 2002], 180). Also worthy of attention is the fact that he provides strikingly concrete guidelines rather than simply abstractly arguing for the necessity of governance and redistribution on the global level. In a 2009 book entitled *The Life You Can Save*, Singer argued that residents of industrialised nations have an ethical 'obligation' to donate a portion of their income for famine relief in impoverished countries. More concretely, he argues that, for example, American taxpayers who are among the top 10% in income but not the top 5% (those who earn between $105,001 and $148,000) should donate 5% of their annual income. Wealthier people are of course assigned a higher amount that they are obligated to donate. Singer provides a strikingly detailed explanation of the basis of these numbers and their efficacy, and has even built a website which shares the name of his book to facilitate donations (<https://www.thelifeyoucansave.org>).

But the one thing I would like to point out is that, in Singer's hierarchical logic, it is unlikely that personhood would be granted to pets such as dogs and cats, much less hamsters and chameleons. Hamsters and chameleons are too distant from the human to extend the principle of utilitarianism to them. And yet in reality there are countless pet owners who count such animals as 'family'. That's what it means to be human. Singer's deliberation is so faithful to its principle that it can barely consider the expansiveness of compassion/misdelivery that makes it possible to accept an animal one has met by chance, regardless of its intelligence or ability, as a family member. The feeling of finding your pet hamster cute has no real place in Singer's theory of animals. But does it really mean anything to construct a theory of animals without considering such feelings?

While I am struck by the power of Singer's philosophy, at the same time I must point out that, when viewed through the lens of the arguments of this book, it shares the weaknesses discussed above. There is no compassion/misdelivery in Singer's arguments—only utility. For that reason, even with regard to donations to impoverished countries, he can only produce an argument centred on numerical guidelines based on 'the greatest happiness of the greatest number'. From Singer's philosophical perspective, loving a particular person and treating all people impartially are always opposed to one another. On the family, he states the following: 'For that reason the conflict [...] between being an ideal parent and acting on the idea that all human life is of equal value, is real and irresolvable. The two will always be in tension. No principle of obligation is going to be widely accepted unless it recognizes that parents will and should love their own children more than the children of strangers, and, for that reason, will meet the basic needs of their children before they meet the needs of strangers. But this doesn't mean that parents are justified in providing luxuries for their children ahead of the basic needs of others' (P. Singer, *The Life You Can Save: Acting Now to End World Poverty* [New York: Random House, 2009], 139). Love towards 'those we meet through chance' is always opposed to impartiality and ethics in Singer's philosophy. But in reality, is it not the case that both impartiality and ethics are only born of misdelivery? Is it not the case that the act of donating that Singer supports is itself actually not possible without a type of misdelivery—that is to say, without producing those who happen to receive a donation and those who do not? Is it not the case that it is precisely because people feel that they want to help those that they meet through chance that they make donations and support them, and that, were they to give a portion of their income for the anonymous collective happiness and interest of humanity as a whole, it would no longer constitute a donation and would instead just be a tax? In other words, could we not say that in insisting on the necessity of donation, Singer ends up nullifying its essence? In the terms employed in Chapter 4 above, it seems as if Singer is attempting to take the donations that were an expression of misdelivery in the small-world order and functionally maximising them in the scale-free order. I would like to repeat one more time in closing that there is something striking about the power of Singer's logic and its consistency with his own actions (it is said that he himself has given away 10% of his income in donations since his graduate student days). In his work the unethical nature of being a nationalist in the age of globalism is sharply criticised. My own critique has been constructed through deep consideration of Singer's line of questioning.

And when we think along these lines, the fact that Singer had to place the personhood of foetuses and infants below that of apes seems to become all the more significant. It starkly reveals the limits of rationalist thinking. We handle newborn children with care—this is the basis of human society. But maybe this care cannot be well justified in utilitarian terms, since newborns do not yet fully possess personhood. After all, they are simply a being that can be made again if they die—no different from a hamster that you can buy for five dollars. But then, if this is the case, would it not mean that we actually love a newborn in the same way that we love a hamster? Newborns do not possess personhood, but we love them nonetheless. *And that is precisely what allows personhood to emerge in children.* It is not that, first of all, there is love toward the human person, a love which then, sometimes, in exceptional circumstances, is extended beyond species boundaries. Rather, we are able to build families precisely because compassion/misdelivery *already* transcends species boundaries.

6. The Uncanny

This chapter outlines a thesis concerning the information society. To date, I have attempted several philosophical interpretations of the information society. Each one of these projects was abandoned, left unfinished.

There is a reason for this. On each occasion I became tormented by a sense of doubt—by the fear that the revolutionary nature of the information society itself may lie in the fact that within it, philosophy loses all meaning, so that the work I was producing on the matter, too, would be meaningless. This sense of doubt resembles the sense of doubt toward the philosophy of the tourist discussed in Part 1. The tourist, too, is an existence that nullifies the schema of philosophy itself. We have entered an era in which we must reconsider, one by one, the myriad ideas that traditional thought in the humanities tossed aside as being unworthy of philosophical deliberation.

In this chapter, then, I would like to use the concepts of this book to reorganise the issues I was trying to address in theorising the information society The postal multitude is a multitude made possible by the network. Thus, we must explore the relationship between the information society and the touristic, or familial, subject. The brief sketch given in this chapter is intended to serve as preparatory work to this end.

1

Around twenty years ago I wrote a long article entitled 'Why Is Cyberspace Called Cyberspace [*Saibāsupēsu wa naze sō yobareru ka*]?' (hereafter referred to as 'theory of cyberspace').[1] Although it was serialised in a magazine devoted to media theory, it was originally planned as a part of a larger book that would

---

1.   H. Azuma, *Saibāsupēsu wa naze sō yobareruka+* (Tokyo: Kawade Bunko, 2011). The article was serialised between 1997 and 2000 in the magazine *InterCommunication*.

incorporate the articles 'The Overvisibles [*Kashiteki na monotachi*]', then being serialised in a different magazine, and 'On Information and Freedom [*Jōhō jiyūron*]', which I would serialise in an opinion magazine a few years later.

The working title for this projected book was *The Cultural Logic of the Postmodern*. Part 1 would deal with theory, while Part 2 would combine my theory of cyberspace with 'On Information and Freedom' through a discussion of technology, and Part 3 would feature 'The Overvisibles', constituting a section on what we might call aesthetics. Mobilising a completely new theory of the postmodern, the plan was to explore how the subject of cyberspace links to information technology and, in 'On Information and Freedom', to discuss the relation between this subject and politics, and finally to consider cultural changes in 'The Overvisibles'. However, this plan was never realised, and my attempt to build a grand theory of postmodern society based on a philosophical interpretation of information technology ultimately never saw the light of day. In fact, the book that has now been published as *Otaku: Japan's Database Animals* was produced by revising 'The Overvisibles' and reformatting it as a monograph. The theory of otaku presented in that book was actually meant to be part of a broader theory of information society.

In a word, what I argued in that broader project was that the essence of information technology lies in the experience of *the uncanny*, and that the metaphor of 'cyberspace' popular in information society theory at the time was incapable of grasping this.

'Cyberspace' is a metaphorical expression which suggests that the network linking computers together can be seen as one 'space'. Although it may have an old-fashioned ring to it today, it was once common parlance, and was translated as *dennō kūkan* [literally 'electro-brain space'] in Japanese.

William Gibson's 1984 novel *Neuromancer* is generally held to be what sparked the currency of the term. Gibson used the term 'jacking in' to describe access to the network, portraying it as if the consciousness of the characters switched from a physical body to an electronic body. In other words, he portrayed the information network of the near future as an electronic parallel world that exists independently and in a different form from the physical reality before our eyes.

This parallel world, dubbed 'cyberspace', is close to today's concept of virtual reality (VR).

Cyberspace and the experience of 'jacking in' are ultimately literary expressions. While we use computers and the internet on a daily basis, these experiences have no effect on our physical bodies. In the sense that they are both 'reading', connecting to the internet to read social media posts and reading a book offline are no different. Indeed, they say that Gibson knew next to nothing about actual computers and the internet when he wrote *Neuromancer*. Cyberspace was completely a product of his imagination.

Nonetheless, the word obviously had an attraction for many readers. Since Gibson's book was published, many novels and films depicting cyberspace have employed similar images. One famous example is *Ghost in the Shell* (1995), a film directed by Mamoru Oshii based on a manga by Masamune Shirow. This trend originating with *Neuromancer* is known in cultural history as 'cyberpunk'. Not only has it come to influence fiction, it has also infiltrated theories of information society in reality.

From the perspective of the history of the genre of science fiction (SF), we might say that there was a certain necessity to the emergence of the concept of cyberspace.

What is SF? Darko Suvin defines SF as a literature that simultaneously produces both 'estrangement' and 'cognition' in the reader.[2] In short, SF refers to a type of literature that incorporates and portrays a reality different from the reality of the 'here and now' in which we live, a reality extrapolated on the basis of a logical supposition. SF based on such a definition dates back to Thomas More's writing in the sixteenth century, but by the twentieth century it had matured into a distinct literary genre. The SF genre is generally held to have emerged in the 1920s—Hugo Gernsback's *Amazing Stories*, the first SF magazine, began publication in 1926.

---

2.   D. Suvin, *Metamorphosis of Science Fiction: On the Poetics and History of a Literary Genre* (New Haven, CT: Yale University Press, 1979), 20. Suvin attempts to classify literature into four categories through two sets of binary oppositions: naturalistic/estranged and cognitive/noncognitive. Naturalistic and cognitive literature is 'realistic' literature (what is called pure literature, or *junbungaku*, in Japan), naturalistic and noncognitive literature is a sub-literature of 'realism' (popular literature), estranged and cognitive literature is SF, and estranged and noncognitive literature corresponds to myth, folktale, and fantasy. Suvin's book was published in 1979, and if we follow his categories, most of the SF published in Japan today would probably be categorised as fantasy.

In the SF genre, what Suvin calls 'estrangement' was originally achieved via outer space and the future. The writers that emerged one after the other during the golden age of SF such as Clark, Asimov, and Heinlein built their narratives upon space and the future. But beginning in the 1970s, this setting became more difficult to use. Space and the future in and of themselves were no longer sufficient as scenarios to stimulate imaginary estrangement. In 1969 Apollo 11 landed on the moon. But in reality, as everyone came to realise, humanity's advancement to the moon changed very little. This set the mood for the 1970s which, even in broader contexts, has been described as the decade during which modernism arrived at its limits. The Club of Rome announced *The Limits to Growth*, Daniel Bell wrote *The Coming of Post-Industrial Society*, and forms of thought that looked upon the values of modernity with suspicion—such as New Ageism, ecology, and postmodernism—appeared everywhere. Scepticism toward space and the future emerged at this point as well.

SF authors were then faced with a difficult decision. Put simply, would they continue to insist on space and the future, knowing full well that these settings no longer served the function of estrangement (that is, would they accept that SF had become sheer fantasy)? Or should they search for a new literary frontier? In my view, although a film rather than a novel, George Lucas's 1977 *Star Wars* consciously chose the former path—and the success of this work decisively changed the place of SF from the 1980s on. Although in Japan this development is linked to anime and the light novel as well, I will leave discussion of this for another occasion. What is important here is that some authors instead chose the other option. Authors such as J.G. Ballard, Brian Aldiss, Samuel R. Delany, and Thomas Disch are together known as the 'New Wave' of SF. Philip K. Dick, who I will discuss below, is also sometimes classified as belonging to this group.

The trajectory of New Wave authors is sometimes described as a shift from 'outer space' to 'inner space'. These authors focused on the interiority and illusions of their characters rather than the depiction of future worlds or space. Inner space essentially refers to the mind, but it bears noting that it applies the metaphor of 'space'. These new SF writers invented a third stage/space of estrangement that succeeded the future and outer space. This movement led to many great works. And yet, because depicting inner space essentially means depicting the mind, the prose of SF works ended up coming closer to pure literature. As a result, although critically acclaimed, in comparison to their predecessors of the golden age, these works declined in character as entertainment. I would venture to guess that my readers are probably less familiar with New Wave authors as well.

Now, when we trace the history of the SF genre, we can concretely understand the context in which the word 'cyberspace' emerged in the 1980s. SF writers needed an estranged world. However, space and the future had already become antiquated, and inner space was lacking in entertainment value. Under these conditions, cyberspace emerged precisely as a fourth stage/space of estrangement, free of these shortcomings. This invention of a new setting/ space invigorated the power of imagination within SF for a long period. While cyberpunk itself became popular in the late 1980s, its influence has persisted far longer. Although *Ghost in the Shell* is a 1995 work, in the world of visual media we might say that the cyberspace imaginary reached its peak with the 1999 film *The Matrix*, directed by the Wachowskis. Thus the invention of cyberspace prolonged the life of SF for twenty years.

Considered from a different perspective, these facts also suggest that the concept of cyberspace is nothing more than a literary or visual apparatus that became necessary in the development of the genre of SF. I repeat: computer networks do not create a different world in reality. No matter how active one's avatar on social media or in massively multiplayer online role-playing games (MMORPGs), one's body, which is its subject of manipulation, continues to exist in the ordinary reality of the 'here and now'. The emergence of cyberspace does nothing to threaten this differentiation between reality and fiction or between player and character.

Despite this, theories of the information society in the 1990s were hamstrung by the metaphor of cyberspace, and seemed to assume that the spread of infor- mation technology would not only change the characters that we control, but would directly alter the bodily sensations of the players themselves. My theory of cyberspace was written out of frustration at this state of affairs.

That doesn't mean that I haphazardly put forward the argument that infor- mation technology does nothing to change the essence of humans and that therefore theories of the information society were meaningless (many who are trained in the humanities make this argument, but I am not one of them). My argument was that, although the spread of information technology certainly has destabilised the boundary between reality and fiction in a certain way that is not without philosophical significance, this shift cannot be grasped through the simple metaphor of cyberspace. And this brings us to the concept of the 'uncanny'. As many of my longtime readers know, the issue of the difference between character and player and the violation of that boundary later became one of the topics of my book *The Birth of Gamic Realism*, the sequel to *Otaku*. As mentioned above, I always intended my theory of otaku to form part of a broader theory of information society.

What is the difference between the experience of cyberspace and the 'uncanny', then? Before entering into an explanation, allow me to mention one more point that made me uneasy at the time. The metaphor of cyberspace, in which the birth of information technology is grasped as the birth of a new setting/space, did more than invite misunderstanding; it also harboured some particular political implications.

Gibson's *Neuromancer* was published in 1984. The ten or so years prior to this had been the period during which personal computers had rapidly become more commonplace. Microsoft was founded in 1975 and the Apple II first went on sale in 1977. The era between the late 1970s and the early 1980s was a revolutionary era in the history of information technology, as Bill Gates and Steve Jobs, who had been building computers in their garages as a hobby, stepped out into the world and found huge success. The Macintosh launched in the year that *Neuromancer* hit bookstores.

At the time, young programmers like Gates and Jobs were known as 'hackers'. While today this word implies criminality, originally it broadly referred to technicians experienced in the manipulation of computers, and in the 1950s to scientifically minded students who skilfully composed programs for expensive mainframe computers at universities and research centres. The unique culture that these hackers created spread beyond the universities in the 1960s and merged with West Coast New Age thought and subcultures, and by the 1980s had grown to become the foundation of massive companies , with the emergence of personal computers.[3]

---

3.   See S. Levy, *Hackers: Heroes of the Computer Revolution, 25th Anniversary Edition* (Sebastopol, CA: O'Reilly Media, 2010). The fact that the first edition of this book was published in 1984 shows that when Gibson published *Neuromancer* in 1984, hacker culture had already fully matured. Of course,

In any case, what is important here is that, as Steven Levy's book *Hackers* tells us, the American information industry didn't develop simply as a business. It has a unique *zeitgeist* as its background. And even deeper in its core there lies a grassroots anti-establishment spirit powerfully influenced by the cultural climate of the West Coast in the 1970s, which is also tied to certain subcultures. These sensibilities resemble the Japanese otaku of that era. Indeed, the early 1980s saw the emergence of the first generation of Japanese otaku such as Hideaki Anno, who would go on to create *Neon Genesis Evangelion*, and other creators of his generation. The otaku was also the group that most passionately embraced 'informationisation' in Japan.

Both hacker culture and otaku culture are new youth cultures that emerged in the postmodern era, were embraced by the same generation, and share a similar spirit. Yet unlike otaku culture in Japan, which in the late 2010s had managed to remain resolutely apolitical, hacker culture was forced to confront political power directly. In the spring of 1990, the United States federal government, fixated on the threat of computer crime, conducted an illegitimate investigation into a gaming company and its related operations. There had been several similar incidents prior to this, and it became clear that the criminal code at the time, drafted prior to the existence of information technology, was being used quite arbitrarily for purposes such as the suppression of the development of certain software. In response to this incident, American hackers founded the nonprofit group Electronic Frontier Foundation and began actively promoting education and lobbying to protect the freedom of engineers. These developments are detailed in Bruce Sterling's non-fiction book *The Hacker Crackdown*.[4] Sterling is a representative novelist of the cyberpunk genre and even co-wrote a book with Gibson, but unlike Gibson he is also an activist with a deep understanding of the realities of the hackers' world. His book details the US context that produced scholars such as Lawrence Lessig, who are not only familiar with law and information technology but are also politically committed (which also helps us understand why such figures are not present in Japan). Lessig himself once sat on the board of the Electronic Frontier Foundation.

the realities of the hackers depicted in Levy's book are significantly different from the fantasies depicted in cyberpunk.

4.   B. Sterling, *The Hacker Crackdown: Law and Order on the Electronic Frontier* (New York: Bantam, 1992).

With such a history, we might say that hacker culture is fundamentally 'anti-establishment', and indeed it is broadly seen in that way. But what is important here is that, unlike the Japanese Left, in America anti-establishment does not necessarily imply anti-American or anti-nationalist. There is an extremely strong tradition of individualism and liberalism in the United States that dates back to the colonial era (libertarianism emerged from this tradition), and it is this that has served as the source of anti-establishment thinking. In other words, in the US there is no contradiction between loving America and criticising the incumbent authorities, between pride in one's country and anger toward the establishment (indeed, we should rather say that the condition of postwar Japan, where the two are never linked, is globally unique).

This link can be observed in hacker culture as well. The clearest case is the short text entitled 'A Declaration of Independence of Cyberspace', written by John Perry Barlow in 1996.[5] The paper was written in opposition to the Telecommunications Act, which had just been passed into law in the US, and which regulated the circulation of indecent information on the internet. At the time the merits of the Act were hotly debated in relation to the freedom of speech. While Barlow demanded an end to censorship on the internet, what is important here is that in doing so, he used the US Declaration of Independence as a model, as is obvious from the title he chose for his text.

Barlow likens cyberspace to the New World, declaring that the information industry is a new frontier, or new world, called cyberspace. America once suffered under the yoke of the Old World, but obtained prosperity through independence—indeed, that is the starting point of the United States. Accordingly, we cannot today apply to the new world of cyberspace the legal order of the old world and of established industries. Just as the US declared independence from the Old World, cyberspace must become independent from the old legal order, Barlow argues. The metaphor of a space called cyberspace thus plays an important role here in linking the reformist (anti-traditional) character of the information industry with patriotism (love of the American tradition).

Cyberspace was nothing more than a literary metaphor. But within a decade or so of the publication of *Neuromancer* it had become a political term used

---

5.   J.P. Barlow. 'A Declaration of Independence of Cyberspace', 1996, <https://www.eff.org/cyberspace-independence>.

to superimpose the future of the information industry onto the history of the United States of America. Calling the internet 'cyberspace' implies that it is seen as the new frontier of capitalism. And history did indeed take this path. Countless 'cyberspace cowboys' (an expression that had already appeared in *Neuromancer*) flooded into the information industry, and the hitherto ownerless internet was divided up into countless private properties. The first comers amassed a staggering amount of wealth. But was this truly the form the internet should have taken?

Taking their cue from Marx and Engels's attack on the 'German Ideology' of the Young Hegelians, British researchers Richard Barbrook and Andy Cameron call the hacker movement 'The Californian Ideology'.[6]

They argue that this ideology is a twisted amalgam of a technological optimism that new technologies will improve society, anti-establishment tendencies influenced by hippie culture, and finally the kind of patriotism referred to above— an uncritical mixture of conservative and liberal tendencies. It was precisely because of that admixture that hackers could naively speak to anti-capitalist ideals without denying the essence of capitalism. Put another way, they were able to act as if they were selfless communists while maintaining their ravenous desire for wealth. While the Americans who develop anti-capitalist buzzwords such as 'open source', 'shareware', and 'freeware' are often also billionaires, they do not seem to struggle with this contradiction.

In the 2016 American presidential elections, more than a few figures from the Silicon Valley elite shocked the world by supporting Donald Trump's candidacy. But we could say that this conservatism was already predicted twenty years prior with the 'Declaration of Independence of Cyberspace'. Californian hackers had always been 'America First', because from the very beginning 'cyberspace' was just another name for America.

2

The word 'cyberspace' is therefore a vehicle for a specific message. In brief, it implies that through the birth of information technology we will come to live in a new world or new space. It is commonly thought that jacking into virtual

---

6.   R. Barbrook and A. Cameron, 'The Californian Ideology', *Mute* 1:3 (1995).

reality is the epistemological expression of this, while its economic expression is 'the new frontier of the information industry'.

Based on this understanding, in my theory of cyberspace I attempted to overcome this entire schema and open up a new possibility for a theory of information society that would no longer be reliant upon the metaphor of space. What emerged from this was the concept of the 'uncanny'.

Very briefly, according to Freud's famous 1919 text, the essence of the uncanny is its mechanism of inversion, whereby something thought to be intimately familiar suddenly changes into an object of estranged fear (for example, a close relative becomes a ghost). The mechanism of the uncanny is triggered when something that is supposed to be singular increases in number or an event that is supposed to be singular happens again and again. Freud argues that this mechanism is deeply related to psychoanalytical concerns such as the death drive and repetition compulsion.[7]

I argued that this sense of the uncanny must be placed at the foundation of information society theory. In short, I argued that when people encounter information technology, rather than entering a different world, *they become possessed by a ghost*.

I then proceeded to juxtapose the 'double' with the 'uncanny',[8] and explored this opposition by superimposing it on the works of Gibson and Philip K. Dick.

---

7.   S. Freud, 'The Uncanny', in *The Standard Edition of the Complete Works of Sigmund Freud Volume 17*, tr. J. Strachey (London: Hogarth Press, 2019), 217–56: 234.

8.   In Freud's text, the double (*doppelgänger*) is a motif that frequently appears as an expression of the uncanny. If this is the case, perhaps it would be more accurate to say that in expressions of the double there are those that create an uncanny effect and those that do not, and that Gibson's cyberspace is an example of the latter kind. Now, in his short article Freud defines the 'uncanny' as a sense that is produced when an experience of an individual or a group at a primitive stage that was once repressed returns: 'It seems as if each one of us has been through a phase of individual development corresponding to this animistic stage in primitive men, that none of us has passed through it without preserving certain residues and traces of it which are still capable of manifesting themselves, and that everything which now strikes us as "uncanny" fulfills the condition of touching those residues of animistic mental activity within us and bringing them to expression.' (Freud, 'The Uncanny', 240–41). What is interesting about this definition in the present context is that it appears to be deeply related both to the family and to the return of gifting (in a higher dimension) discussed in Chapter 5. The family, gifting, and animism once ruled the world in the primitive stages of civilisation, but were later repressed. If you think about it, the family, gifting, and animism are all uncanny. Perhaps we are living in an age of their return, and that is why the solidarity of the multitude (the return of the family) and the sharing economy (gifting returned) are so often discussed and the expressive forms

Gibson is clearly a writer of the 'double': cyberspace is a virtual space into which people dispatch their doubles (avatars). The subject of information society is split between the physical body and the electronic body when it comes into contact with the network and the electronic body is sent into cyberspace. In *Neuromancer*, based on such an image, the essence of information technology is believed to be the generation of an electronic avatar of the self. The power of this imaginary remains stubbornly alive to this day.

Although I will only mention it in passing here, this imaginary in which the subject is split in two or doubled probably has a deep connection to the phenomenon of multiple personality disorder, which became a widely discussed topic around the same time. In her 1995 work *Life on the Screen*, the psychologist Sherry Turkle drew precisely upon both Gibson's work and Lacan's psychoanalysis, issuing a warning on the ways in which, in online communication, people take on multiple personalities.[9] Meanwhile, the historian of science Ian Hacking demonstrated in his book published in the same year, *Rewriting the Soul*, how multiple personality disorder became culturally widespread in the US in the 1980s, its symptoms having been quite rare prior to the 1970s.[10] In other words, the concept of cyberspace and the symptoms of multiple personality disorder were 'invented' around the same time, in North America, and went on to spread rapidly around the world. What this reveals is that analyses which conclude that online communication produces some kind of splitting of the mind are themselves in fact nothing more than an expression of the spirit of the era rather than being the product of objective analysis. In Japan, too, there was a time in the early 2000s when certain writers used the expression 'dividuals'.[11] The term was based on the argument that contemporary people should quit being 'individuals' with

---

of animation and games (the return of animism) are so celebrated. The discussion in this chapter connects to those in Chapters 5 and 7 in this way. Although I was not able to develop this line of thinking here, given that psychoanalysis was the most influential twentieth-century philosophy of the family, if I aimed to reconstruct/deconstruct the concept of the family, I would necessarily have to include a rereading of Freud. If I were to write a continuation of this book, then, it would to some extent probably have to be a discourse on Freud.

9. S. Turkle, *Life on the Screen: Identity in the Age of the Internet* (New York: Simon & Schuster, 1995), 258.

10. I. Hacking, *Rewriting the Soul: Multiple Personality and the Science of Memory* (Princeton, NJ: Princeton University Press, 1995).

11. Suzuki, *Namerakana shakai to sono teki*, 134. See also K. Hirano, *Watashi to wa nanika* (Tokyo: Kōdansha Gendai Shinsho, 2012).

a unified self and become 'dividuals' who change personalities according to the situation. But this too should be understood as an expression of the times rather than as a new philosophy. We are living in an age where people's dreams are strangely full of the split of the subject.

Philip K. Dick, many of whose works have been adapted into Hollywood films, is often credited with predicting the coming of the information society. However, as noted above, he is sometimes categorised as a New Wave author, and is of an older generation than Gibson, active during the 1960s and 1970s. He died two years before the publication of *Neuromancer*. Thus, Dick knew nothing of 'cyberspace'.

How, then, did Dick depict the changes that take place in the subject when it comes into contact with the network? Dick was not necessarily an author who wrote on the theme of computers and the internet. Having died in 1982, he did not live to see the spread of personal computers take off in earnest. Yet his novels, including his very early works, have been highly acclaimed for capturing some of the features of postmodern consumer society, and, since he lived on the West Coast, he came into close cultural proximity with young hackers. For that reason, his works continue to be highly regarded as literature that grasped the characteristics of information society (such as the emergence of surveillance society), even though they do not feature computers or the internet in any detail. In what sense did he anticipate the arrival of a new information society, then?

It is precisely the motif of the uncanny that plays an important role here. The characters in Dick's novels often encounter very peculiar technologies. In *Martian Time-Slip* a hallucinogen alters one's sense of time; in *The Three Stigmata of Palmer Eldritch* a virtual reality kit combines hallucinogens and miniature dioramas; *Do Androids Dream of Electric Sheep?* features androids, and *Ubik* revolves around a technology that revives the brains of the dead. In encountering these technologies, the characters in the novels become engulfed in realities they cannot discern as real or fake, human or non-human, organic or inorganic. They become engulfed in 'simulacra', to express it in the language of contemporary thought. In order to build a sense of these simulacra, Dick depicts the characters' experience of losing their sense of reality over and over again. His fictional worlds are often described as 'nightmarish'.

I believe that this characteristic of Dick's novels is decisively important in imagining a new theory of the information society. Dick's characters do not remove their doubles from reality and send them into cyberspace, into another world. Rather, they are possessed by something uncanny and lose sight of the very boundary separating reality and cyberspace/another world. In other words, where Gibson depicted reality and cyberspace as clearly differentiated worlds, in Dick's work the boundary between them becomes uncertain, and he takes precisely this experience to be the essence of contemporary society. At the time, it occurred to me that this kind of reading of Dick could serve as the foundation for a new theory of the information society in the real sense of the term—that is, one that doesn't grasp the internet as a new frontier or another world.

Searching for a theory of contemporary society in the differences between the works of Gibson and Dick—such an approach might sound strange for readers unaccustomed to the methods of literary criticism. Yet I think that the argument I put forward in my theory of cyberspace is something that many readers can sense and experience today, twenty years later, when social media has become ubiquitous.

Users of social media today (especially in Japan) often use both a 'true account [*hon aka*]' and a 'burner account [*ura aka*]'. The former is tied to the actual name of the user and is treated as the account that actual friends and acquaintances will read, while the latter is cut off from the actual name and is treated as the account with which the user can anonymously pursue any lines of thought and expression they want.

If we employ this distinction in reading Gibson's work, what he depicted was a world in which true account and burner account remain clearly demarcated. The true account is managed by us in reality, while the burner account is managed by our electronic double. 'Jacking in' to cyberspace is essentially like logging in to your burner account. Hampered by the metaphor of cyberspace, the information society theory of the 1990s emphasised only the positive and liberatory aspects of how maintaining a burner account frees human beings. Furthermore, this was also a convenient discourse in our era, one which dreams continually of the splitting of the subject. Hail the great network that will make us all 'dividuals'!

However, as is clear today, the peril of information society lies in the fact that this dream is nothing but a dream: that is to say, we are slowly becoming unable to differentiate between our true and burner accounts. The distinction between the two often does not hold up. The true name of the account holder is exposed and it goes viral—this sort of thing happens every day. But that is not all. What is even more frightening is when the actual person who is supposedly distinguishing between the true and burner accounts slowly becomes unable to do so. When you continue to spew venom in fiction, it will eventually affect reality as well. People cannot so deftly become 'dividuals'. The venom spewed by the double on the burner account adheres to the actual person precisely as an uncanny thing, slowly introducing a distortion in communications at the level of the 'true' account as well. It seems that we are seeing examples of this phenomenon daily in the form of the rise of hate speech and fake news. Dick's novels accurately predict this 'nightmare'. This is why I believe that information society theory should be constructed not on the model of Gibson's cyberspace, but that of Dick's nightmare.

From the double to the uncanny: in that article from twenty years ago, I focused my explanation of this logic on a reading of Dick's novel *VALIS*.

VALIS was published in 1981. The protagonist is modeled after Dick himself, and the book contains strong autobiographical elements. Yet at the same time, it is a strange work that is a mixture of fact and fiction, taking in the author's unique religious philosophy and conspiracy theories, actual experiences of a drug overdose, and New Age and hippie culture. A short synopsis of the story could be as follows: the protagonist produces a double (a split personality named Horselover Fat) by coming in contact with a new information technology, but it is extinguished through an encounter with the uncanny (a girl named Sophia). It was from this story that I derived the thesis of a shift from the double to the uncanny.

I will refrain from explaining my reading in detail here. But given the context of this book, I should add that it may be important that Sophia, who plays the role of the uncanny in this novel, is always depicted along with an image of the family.

The protagonist of *VALIS* is an extremely solitary figure. He is divorced from his wife and his friends suffer from drug addiction and commit suicide one after the other. His children are not close to him either. As I noted earlier, much of this is a projection of Dick's own life experiences. It is in this context that the protagonist encounters a flood of information (network) and develops an illusion about another self. Thus the story of *VALIS* begins, but it is Sophia who dissolves this illusion (although, as with many of Dick's works, this only means entering a higher-level illusion) and provides direction to his life. Sophia is depicted as one who speaks for God and who is an object of veneration, despite being a young child; she dies suddenly in an accident (this is one of the terrifying aspects of Dick's novels). Yet she is also depicted as a young member of a family. Upon their first meeting, the protagonist accepts her as family: '"What a beautiful child," I said, thinking to myself how much she reminded me of my own son Christopher.'[12] Dick clearly incorporates into his novel the opposition of the two motifs: the double (split personality) that heals his solitude is nothing more than a similar image of the self, but the uncanny appears in the form of a child. While this departs a little from the theory of cyberspace I put forward in the nineties, twenty years later I cannot help but think that an important issue is raised here. At the end of the previous chapter I touched upon compassion towards a newborn child. Couldn't we say that newborns are precisely messengers of God and, at the same time, the uncanny?

Today I might read *VALIS* as a novel where Dick, having emerged from the hell of conspiracy theory and drug addiction, attempted to depict the escape from negative theological multitude (solitary solidarity) into postal multitude (family).

3

Understanding the subject of information society as a subject surrounded by the uncanny—readers who have read this book to this point may have found the style of this chapter to be rather too literary.

For that reason, in this section I would like also to introduce my past attempt to diagram what it means for the subject to be surrounded by the uncanny, which I drew upon psychoanalytic theory in developing. Today, updating it from my perspective twenty years later, I can link it to the discussion developed in Part 1. However, I should repeat that my discussion here is nothing more than preparatory work for a future, more fully-fledged exploration.

---

12.   P.K. Dick, 'VALIS', in *VALIS and Later Novels* (New York: The Library of America, 2009), 354.

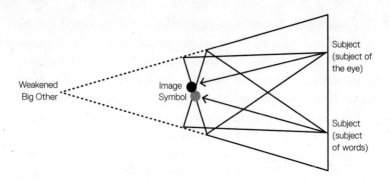

Figure 10. Structure of the subject in the information society (interface subject). Modified version of diagram from 'Saibāsupēsu wa naze sō yobareruka+, 93.

Twenty years ago, I proposed the schema shown in Figure 10. This diagram represents how the subject relates to the world in the postmodern era where ideology has disappeared and the network has been laid down in its place.

This diagram rests upon a particular premise. It is actually a redrawing of a diagram of the structure of the subject as depicted by Jacques Lacan. Some readers may be sceptical about whether the structure of the subject can be demonstrated in such a diagram (and personally I think such scepticism is warranted), but for now I ask you to simply accept that such enterprises exist in the academic field, without thinking too deeply about it.

According to Lacan's psychoanalytical theory, the human subject is made up of the combination of two mechanisms: imaginary identification and symbolic identification.[13]

Imaginary identification refers to identification with an image perceivable with the eye. It originally referred to the activity by which an infant grasps their image reflected on the mirror as the self (the mirror stage), but it is also used in a much broader context in Lacanian theory. It is widely known, for example, that Lacanian psychoanalysis has a great affinity with Film Studies. Lacan's theory of the subject can in part be read as if humans engage the world through the same structure as a movie audience facing the screen. The flipside of this is

---

13.   The difference between imaginary identification and symbolic identification, too, is more easily understood by consulting Žižek's explanation instead of Lacan's books and seminars (his works are known for their difficulty). See the discussion in The Sublime Object of Ideology, 116sq.

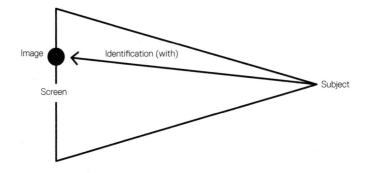

Figure 11. Structure of imaginary identification. Diagram from *Saibāsupēsu wa naze sō yobareruka+*, 93.

that his theories are easily understood if we take film as an example. Readers of contemporary thought probably know that Slavoj Žižek often writes about movies—precisely because Lacan's theory, upon which Žižek relies, has this strong affinity.

Figure 11 is a schematisation of the operation of this imaginary identification. This diagram was created by taking a portion of a figure drawn by Lacan during one of his seminars (Figure 12), and simplifying it.[14] The 'subject' is placed on the right-hand side of the diagram, and on the left is the 'screen'. Think of the screen as the world. At the same time as it models the situation of an audience viewing a screen at the cinema, the figure also models the condition of a human facing the world.

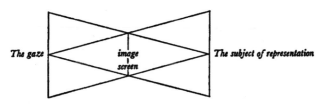

Figure 12. Lacan's original diagram, from *The Four Fundamental Concepts of Psychoanalysis* (1964).

14.   J. Lacan, *The Four Fundamental Concepts of Psychoanalysis*, tr. A. Sheridan (London: Hogarth Press, 1977), 106. In this seminar the two layers of imaginary identification and symbolic identification are expressed as the 'split between the eye and the gaze' (see Figure 12). When we see something, we are at the same time looked at. Lacan's argument is that this split is the basis of the subject. 'The subject of representation' on the right side of the figure refers to the 'subject who is looking at something'.

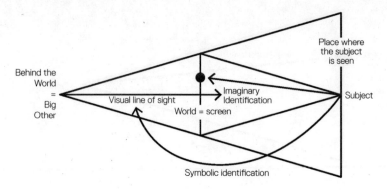

Figure 13. Structure of the modern subject (imaginary identification + symbolic identification), from *Saibāsupēsu wa naze sō yobareruka+*, 81.

Now, I should like to draw your attention to the arrow leading from the subject to a particular part of the screen (image). This arrow represents the operation of imaginary identification. Everybody 'identifies' with someone in the world as they grow up. Concretely speaking, it may be one's parents, teachers, or senior colleagues. This is represented in the diagram as the black dot. People become adults by seeing themselves in the objects of imaginary identification and by mimicking their behaviour. In the case of film, this corresponds to moments at which a viewer thinks, 'Wow, that actor is cool—I want to be like that too', or, 'That actress is beautiful, I want to be like that too'.

But that is not all. According to Lacan, there is another mechanism of identification in humans: symbolic identification.

Figure 13 is a diagram of this operation of symbolic identification. As you will immediately notice, it is an expansion of Figure 11. This diagram is actually closer to Lacan's original. Here, too, the screen represents the world, and the subject is looking at the world/screen. But this diagram is different, in that it shows the structure that lies behind the world/screen. The world/screen isn't something that is simply given to the audience/subject; behind it there lies the order that produces it. In philosophical terms, this would be the 'transcendental subjectivity' that establishes the world or the 'symbolic order' that creates society. In the example of cinema, it corresponds to the film projector or the camera of the film director who captured the scene that is reflected in the film.

This source that generates the world is called 'the big Other' in Lacanian theory. It serves as the apex of the large triangle.

In Figure 13 there are two arrows that extend from the subject. One is the arrow of imaginary identification, as in Figure 11. However, what is important here is that the other arrow jumps over the world/screen and extends towards something called the 'line of sight' which extends from the big Other, through the world/screen, and toward the subject on the right. This represents the operation of symbolic identification. It is an identification with the very mechanism that establishes the world/screen.

Identification with the mechanism that establishes the world might sound excessively abstract. But this, too, is easy to understand through the example of film. Earlier I wrote that imaginary identification consists in identifying with the actor (image) projected on the screen. But why are those actors projected on the screen in the first place? Of course, it is because someone cast them in their roles, and someone filmed them. Symbolic identification consists in identifying with the work of those behind the scenes. In other words, if we continue with the example of film, it would consist in *identifying with the camera*. The 'line of sight' extending straight from the 'big Other' refers to the line of sight of the film director observing the actors.

Symbolic identification is on a 'higher level' than imaginary identification. This, too, is easily understood through the example of film. You have probably experienced being told the following (at least, I have). Whether it is the actors or the plot, so long as you're looking at the content of the film, you're still an amateur. People who truly love film (cinephiles) look not only at what is projected on the screen, but also at what is *not* projected on the screen, that is, the camera's frame or the director's line of sight. This is precisely the difference between imaginary identification and symbolic identification. Amateurs look at the image. Cinephiles identify with the camera. And it is through the latter form of identification that film viewing finally reaches maturity.

Lacanian theory explains the process of subjectivation through the same logic. People cannot become adults simply by mimicking their parents or teachers (i.e. purely through imaginary identification). Only by understanding *why* they behave in the way they do—that is, by understanding the mechanism (i.e. by symbolically identifying) do they finally become adults. This double movement is key to Lacanian psychoanalysis. Put differently, it is by identifying not only with the visible (image), but also with the invisible (symbols or language) that humans can finally become adults (i.e. subjects). Lacan called this visible world the 'Imaginary' and the invisible world the 'Symbolic'. The 'big Other' and 'the Symbolic' have virtually the same meaning.

With all of this in mind, let us now return to Figure 10. Now you should be able to easily see how this figure is a modification of Figure 13. What I tried to show in this figure was my way of responding to the question of how the subject retains the double movement of identification in postmodern society where the Symbolic (the big Other) has been weakened.

This question is actually closely related to the issue of cyberspace discussed above.

The notion of cyberspace emerged in the 1980s. It is generally said that the era defined as 'postmodern' began a little before this, in the 1970s. Although I will not get into details here, the postmodern is an era defined by the loss of any 'grand narrative'. This also means, in the words of psychoanalysis, the disintegration of 'the Symbolic'. Crucial here is the fact that the declining position of 'space' and 'the future' in the history of genre SF can be thought of as the advent of postmodernisation in literature, both in terms of its timing and content. The downfall of space and the future: this is precisely the loss of the grand narrative.

When we sketch out such a history, traversing information society theory, psychoanalysis, and the SF genre, we come to understand that the notion of cyberspace played the role of a new grand narrative, filling a gap in a world from which the grand narrative had disappeared. Cyberspace emerged as a new stage in SF in an era when space and the future had lost their appeal. It also emerged as the frontier of a new industry in an age that called for attention to ecology and the limits of growth. In other words, it emerged as a word that performed the psychoanalytical function par excellence of gathering up the dregs of the grand narrative, the modernism that lingered long after modernity had ended both in literature and in politics. Put flatly, the real world was completely post-modernised, and people were no longer able to harbour grand dreams (space and the future) as in the past; only with cyberspace was there still hope for such dreams—that's what the people of the twentieth century believed, or tried to believe. And that illusion still remains today. There still circulates in information society theory the grand narrative that 'singularity' will arrive in the near future and that the shape of the human and society will completely change through the power of new technology, an idea that reminds one more of nineteenth-century utopian socialism than of the twentieth century. While such discourse is received quite simplistically in the business world, in reality it must be critically reviewed through such perspectives.[15]

Now, as I mentioned above, in the article that I wrote twenty years ago I attempted to develop a theory of information society that would not rely on cyberspace. One of the hints I drew on in doing so was a reading of Dick and the uncanny, and the other was the updating of the Lacanian theory of the subject introduced above.

Exploring the subject of information society without recourse to the concept of cyberspace means exploring the structure of the subject in a way that candidly accepts the weakening of the big Other. And according to Lacanian theory, in order for the subject to be a subject, it must always undergo the double

---

15.   Although I was not able to pursue it in this book, we might say that one of the origins of the argument that human society will completely change through technological evolution, which today takes the form of the theory of singularity, lies in the work of the nineteenth-century Russian thinker Nikolai Fyodorov (along with that of his contemporary, Charles Fourier). Fyodorov developed a unique mysticism that combined Christian eschatology and technological progressivism, and deeply influenced the later Dostoevsky (it is said that the young philosopher Vladimir Solovyov with whom Dostoevsky discussed Fyodorov's philosophy was the model for Alyosha in *The Brothers Karamazov*). Fyodorov argued that at the end of history it should be technologically possible to resurrect the dead, and also planned a massive museum (archive) that would record all of the actions of all people who once lived. These strong interests in immortality and the archive also have an affinity with the discourse of information technology ideologues today. These ideas of Fyodorov became known as 'Cosmism', and influenced a variety of Russian philosophers that followed. Among them was the geologist Vladimir Vernadsky, whose idea of the noosphere (sphere of reason) subsequently entered Marshall McLuhan's *The Gutenberg Galaxy* via Pierre Teilhard de Chardin's *The Phenomenon of Man*, leading to the concept of the 'global village' and, later, 'cyberspace'. In this sense, the issues discussed in Chapter 6 here resonate with those of Chapter 7. Along with the 'end of history', or the end of the grand narrative (the end of the story of communism) that had been passed down from Hegel to Fukuyama through Kojève, at the very same time, also in the US, another 'grand narrative' originating with Fyodorov was experiencing its resurrection in the form of the Californian Ideology. This is a stimulating drama in terms of intellectual history as well. Either way, there are a myriad of influences to the thought of the technological revolution, and since the activities of the information industry directly decides the world order today, it seems to me that a cultural historical study of it is an urgent task. On Fyodorov, see Svetlana Semyonova's biography, *Fyōdorofu-den*, tr. H. Yasuoka and I. Kameyama (Tokyo: Suiseisha, 1998). On Russian Cosmism, see B. Groys, *Russian Cosmism* (Cambridge, MA: MIT Press, 2018).

movement of imaginary identification and symbolic identification. Thus I came to think about how the subject retains this double movement of identification in a postmodern society where the big Other has been weakened. One might say that this is another way of expressing my thoughts on the uncanny.

What, then, was the answer that I proposed? Take a third look at Figure 10. Unlike Figure 13, in this diagram there is no longer a structure behind the world/screen. In the postmodern age, the subject can no longer access the symbolic order (the Symbolic/grand narrative) that supports society, and thus is unable to direct its desire for identity toward this order. To take the example of film once again, this means that there is no longer any director's camera. What I had in mind as I wrote this article twenty years ago was the interface screen on a computer: there is no projector or camera behind a computer screen.

How does one maintain the double movement of identification in such a camera-less condition, then? What I came up with at the time was the idea of doubling the destination. The diagram in Figure 10 depicts how the object of imaginary identification (image) and symbolic identification (symbol) are placed equally and side-by-side on one world/screen. In the postmodern world, the camera of the world is replaced by a situation in which image and symbol, visible and invisible, phenomena and the principle that generates those phenomena, both appear at once on the screen. The subject identifies with both at the same time. As a result, a tension is generated: even though one might identify at times with the image, there is always an intervention from a different identification with the symbol. It is precisely this tension that generates a double movement of the subject particular to the postmodern, one that is similar to, but has definite differences from, the double movement of imaginary identification and symbolic identification in Figure 13. This was my hypothesis.

Twenty years ago, this hypothesis remained abstract. But today I can explain it a little more concretely.

As noted several times in Part 1, in 2011 I published a book entitled *General Will 2.0*. Although its main topic was Rousseau's idea of the general will, I included Figure 14 as a model for future politics in the concluding section of the book.

In this book I argued that the politics of the future must be a combination of deliberations by specialists and a visualised representation of the unconscious of

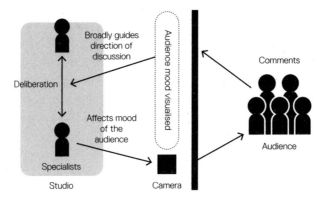

Figure 14. Model of political communication for a new era, reproduced from *General Will 2.0* (Japanese edition), 196.

the masses, that is, the 'database'. The diagram depicts the form in which that combination can take place. On the right side of the diagram is the audience/ people of the nation. On the left side is deliberation among actors or specialists in a studio. The wall that separates them serves the purpose of picking up the voices of the viewers' unconscious and providing them as feedback to the deliberations of the specialists. I called this central wall that connects deliberation and the database (the unconscious of the masses) 'general will 2.0'.

Earlier I noted that Lacanian psychoanalysis resembles the structure of film. In contrast, in creating this diagram I was inspired by the structure of the niconico live stream.[16] Think of the central wall as the nico live screen. The audience watches the deliberation among the specialists. However, at the same time, comments by audience members are shown on the screen. The audience views those as well. What is interesting is that, because comments on nico live are anonymous and short and scroll across the screen and disappear in a short amount of time, they function more as an expression of collective 'feeling' in regard to the space of debate as a whole than as individual 'opinions'. In short, comments on nico live appear as a visualisation of what one would in theory see when one is told to 'read the room'. The specialists, too, will see these comments

---

16.   <http://live.nicovideo.jp>. [Niconico live stream is a live streaming option offered by the video streaming site niconico douga, popular in Japan. Like YouTube and Twitch, viewers can post comments on videos, but in the case of niconico videos the comments scroll on the video screen itself from right to left, at times dominating the visual experience—trans.].

and at times make adjustments to the content of the discussion. The presence of this feedback is what makes nico live attractive. Although I will avoid getting into the details here, on this basis I develop the argument that the possibility of a new politics can be found precisely in this feedback where one can literally 'read the room' in real time through visualisation, and where to some extent this guides the deliberations among specialists. Either way, what is important here is the fact that the central wall/screen serves the function of visualising simultaneously both the deliberation among specialists and the unconscious of the audience (database), and provides it to the audience.

Although I do not mention this in *General Will 2.0*, the structure of Figure 14 actually inherits the subject model of Figure 10. Try superimposing the two graphics by lining up 'audience' in Figure 14 with 'subject' in Figure 10, 'specialist' with 'image', and 'audience mood visualised' with 'symbol'. At the same time that the audience sees the deliberating specialist (image), they also see visualised the mood of the room/the stream of audience comments (language/symbol). There are probably those who have watched nico live and were jolted out of their identification with cast members upon seeing acerbic and cynical comments scroll across the screen. In the world of Figure 14, the audience/subject cannot simply identify with the image. Although they may identify with the cast of specialists at times (imaginary identification), comments continue to scroll across the screen simultaneosly, and in reading these comments they come to identify with the unconscious of the audience (symbolic identification) rather than the big Other, and their simple identification with the specialists is eroded. Understood in this way, we can see that the experience I tried to describe in rather abstract terms twenty years ago—'eyes and words, image and symbol, information communicating the fictive nature of reality and information constructing reality are both visualised on the screen'—has now been realised fairly concretely on the nico live screen.[17] The new double movement of the postmodern subject that could only be discussed hypothetically in the 1990s has now been set into motion in reality.

What kind of subject is the subject of information society? How can humans be subjects (i.e. adults) in the postmodern world in the absence of grand narratives?

17.   Azuma, *Saibāsupēsu wa naze sō yobareruka+*, 92. Emphasis removed.

I think we have arrived at several important hints through the discussion thus far. I would like to leave for another occasion the task of connecting these hints to the theory of the tourist put forward in Part 1.

I will append one more point of discussion in closing. As noted earlier, when I created Figure 10 what I had in mind was a computer interface screen.

Lacanian psychoanalysis grasped the modern subject as a subject who views films. In my view, the postmodern subject must be grasped as a subject who views graphical user interfaces (GUIs) on a computer. Indeed, the invention of the GUI by Alan Kay and others coincided with the arrival of the postmodern era in the 1970s.[18]

Although the movie screen and the computer interface are both planes that display images, their characteristics as media are completely different. The former uses a projector that projects an image and a camera that captures that image, whereas in the latter there is nothing that corresponds to these. Indeed, the computer interface is not a plane containing only images. While only images are projected on to the movie screen, images and symbols (words), or even the codes that exist on a deeper level than the images and words, can all be shown on a computer interface. While this may be difficult to understand precisely because it is so obvious, when one is working on a Microsoft Word document while playing a YouTube video and entering code into a terminal, the screen is displaying three different types of symbols at the same time.

There is a camera behind the movie screen, which also represents the gaze of the director, so the audience can easily identify with it. But behind the interface there is nothing but a series of calculations, so there is no object for the user to identify with there. In other words, whereas in film viewing it is possible for the audience to identify with the director and find in them their own 'doppelgänger' (cinephiles are precisely those who do so), computer users cannot find anyone in their likeness 'behind' a computer. Even if we peek behind the scenes of the interface, unlike the movie screen, all we find there is a mass of source code, an uncanny swarm. Although I was not able to touch upon this point here, this difference in character between the movie screen and the computer interface provides us with a significant hint in considering the difference between the

---

18. The best source for understanding the significance of this invention from the perspective of media theory are the words of Kay himself. A. Kay, *Alan Kei*, tr. Y. Tsuruoka (Tokyo: Ascii, 1992).

modern subject and the postmodern subject. Urry and Larsen, cited above in Chapter 1, grasped the origin of the tourist's gaze together with the origin of the photograph. But couldn't we say that the gaze of the tourist is a gaze that captures the world as a computer interface, rather than as a photograph or a film? In it they find images and symbols and codes that they must interpret.

How should we relate to the world in this age in which, in place of ideology, we are given computers? This is in fact a question that lies behind all the explorations of this book. We can no longer simply say that because there are no more ideologies, we are free and therefore can build a new form of solidarity. Computers now occupy the place where once there were ideologies, and the order of computers rules over us to a far greater extent than the ideologies of the past.

The flat surface of the computer upon which images and symbols are placed side by side with equal status—this must also be the flat surface of the postal multitude that traverses the order of Empire and the order of the nation state. The metaphor of cyberspace serves only to hide these possibilities from view.

7. Dostoevsky's Final Subject

The outline given in this chapter concerns Dostoevsky. By reading the novels of Dostoevsky 'dialectically', that is to say as the self-development of a mode of thought, I will attempt to approach the subject of the tourist (postal multitude) from a different angle. Readers will notice how the thought process of this novelist from one hundred and fifty years ago resonates remarkably with the way in which this book understands our condition.

It is more accurate to describe what follows as unpolished rather than unfinished. The discussion does reach a conclusion, but the argumentation is hurried and contains many gaps. Equally, many points that would normally be developed further are left as is. I ask you to read on with these limitations in mind.

1

Why Dostoevsky? Because we live in an age of terrorism. As I noted in Chapter 1, the age of the tourist is also the age of the terrorist, and many of Dostoevsky's novels deal with the terrorist. Dostoevsky was a novelist fixated on the question of how one could avoid becoming a terrorist in an era where faith and justice have been lost.

Dostoevsky's writing is deeply related to terror, *The Devils,* written between 1871 and 1872, being a prime example. The protagonist of *The Devils*, Nikolai Stavrogin, may well be the most famous terrorist in literary history. *The Devils* depicts the hesitations and internal feuds of a group of young terrorists associated with Stavrogin. The novel is said to have been inspired by an actual event (the Nechayev Incident) which occurred shortly before it was written.

Even when not dealing with terror directly, many of Dostoevsky's novels are written in close proximity to the terrorist psyche. *Notes from the Underground* (1864) gloomily tallies the depraved curses of a man who has failed in life.

Crime and Punishment (1866) tells the story of a young man who develops a drawn-out, sophisticated theory in order to justify his murder of an old woman. The desire of these characters is to unleash their perverse anger upon the world and to destroy the lives of those who live in peace. Dostoevsky's depictions of them are reminiscent of the psychology of homegrown terrorists with no organisation or ideology in the United States and Europe today. As I will discuss below, *The Brothers Karamazov*, written between 1879 and 1880, is also a work whose unwritten sequel, many have suggested, would have featured a protagonist who becomes a terrorist. Dostoevsky thus depicted terrorists in his work up until the very end of his life.

Dostoevsky's style is deeply related to his own life; we could in fact say that he himself was an 'ex-terrorist'.

Dostoevsky appeared on the literary scene in 1846 with *Poor Folk*. It was a celebrated debut for a young writer in his twenties, but three years later he was arrested in connection with an alleged conspiracy to overthrow the state (the Petrashevsky Incident). Although it is said that he only attended meetings and did not participate in any of the planning, Dostoevsky was sentenced to death, only to be granted clemency and exiled to Siberia.

With such a past, even after achieving success as a writer, Dostoevsky remained under surveillance by the secret police for many years. It is said that this situation did not change even after he gained the support of the masses as a representative writer of the nation and came to be viewed as a 'Tzarist' in his later years, expounding patriotic arguments in his essays. Thus, even his counterrevolutionary writings (which made him unpopular among twentieth-century leftist intellectuals) cannot simply be taken at face value. There were many incidents of terror across Russia in the 1870s. Yet it is said that, at the time, when asked what he would do if he heard of a plan to assassinate the Tsar, Dostoevsky replied that he would do nothing.[1] Although Dostoevsky loved Russia and was a conservative writer who loved the Orthodox Church, this did not prevent him from sympathising with terrorists. The Japanese scholar of Russian literature Ikuo Kameyama speculates that, concretely speaking, Dostoevsky's unique sense of language, which Mikhail Bakhtin, in *Problems of Dostoevsky's Poetics*,

---

1.   I. Kameyama, *'Karamazofu no kyōdai' no zokuhen o kūsō suru* [*Imagining the Sequel to 'The Brothers Karamazov'*] (Tokyo: Kōbunsha, 2007), 44.

called 'polyphony'—that is, a method in which many contradicting voices seem to reverberate within one expression—was cultivated through his struggles with the censors.[2] Maybe if Dostoevsky were alive today in 2017 he would be taking an ambiguous, precarious position as an opinion leader expressing some sympathy with the anti-foreigner arguments of the authorities (as a Trump supporter, for example), while at the same time publishing a novel featuring a protagonist who is a Muslim terrorist. At the very least, he certainly wouldn't limit himself to just showing up at demonstrations.

In this chapter, then, I would like to think about how the tourist or postal multitude may feel sympathy for the terrorist without falling into terrorism, by exploring the works of Dostoevsky. With establishment and anti-establishment voices alike now coming increasingly close to the logic of mobilisation, to me this question seems extremely important both in theory and in practice.

2

Dostoevsky's *Notes from the Underground* is commonly held to be one of the original sources of existentialist literature. Existentialism refers to the search for a universal human truth, beyond nationality or era. Indeed, a part of what gives this novel its power is the thoroughness of the anger of the protagonist (known as the Underground Man), who protests against even the laws of mathematics and nature:

> Twice-two-makes-four is, in my humble opinion, nothing but a piece of impudence. Twice-two-makes-four is a farcical, dressed-up fellow who stands across your path with arms akimbo and spits at you. Mind you, I quite agree that twice-two-makes-four is a most excellent thing; but if we are to give everything its due, then twice-two-makes-five is sometimes a most charming little thing, too.[3]

The Underground Man's anger transcends his own particular era.

2.   I. Kameyama, *Dosutoefusukii: chichigoroshi no bungaku ge* [*Dostoevsky: Literature of Parricide, Vol. 2*] (Tokyo: NHK Bukkusu, 2004), 28. On polyphony, Bakhtin writes of '[a] plurality of independent and unmerged voices and consciousnesses', and claims that 'a genuine polyphony of fully valid voices is in fact the chief characteristic of Dostoevsky's novels.' M. Bakhtin, *Problems of Dostoevsky's Poetics*, tr. C. Emerson (Minneapolis: University of Minnesota Press, 1984), 6.

3.   F. Dostoevsky, 'Notes from the Underground', tr. D. Magarshack, in *Great Short Works of Fyodor Dostoevsky* (New York: HarperCollins, 1968), 291.

At the same time, the novel carries the mark of its age. Indeed, it was written as a response to the bestselling novel *What Is to Be Done?* published around the same time by Nikolai Chernyshevsky, a socialist writer seven years younger than Dostoevsky.

In *What Is to Be Done?*, Chernyshevsky trumpets a typical nineteenth-century idealism according to which, through the enlightenment and proper rationalisation of the people, poverty and war disappear and the world approaches utopia. Dostoevsky hated this idealism, and *Notes from the Underground* was his riposte to it.

The philosophy of Chernyshevsky and other socialists of his era is today known as utopian socialism, as distinct from Marxism, that is scientific socialism, which came later. This is a critical moniker which labels their position as a utopianism lacking any scientific analysis of class struggle, and thus incapable of really achieving revolution. Yet this mode of thought played a significant role in the mid-nineteenth century. Chernyshevsky's novel was widely read at the time, inspiring many a youthful reader. Lenin famously admired the book and, in fact, went on to write a book with the same title.

So what kind of novel is *What Is to Be Done?* It is rarely read today, but we can make several interesting observations if we read it from today's perspective.

In today's terms, the plot of *What Is to Be Done?* makes it essentially a workplace novel [*oshigoto shōsetsu*]. The protagonist is a young woman named Vera who aspires to run her own dressmaking shop—as a result, the book has sometimes been called the world's first feminist novel.

Vera possesses a clear vision of an ideal shop. In order to realise this vision, she recruits seamstresses from other shops by offering higher wages, organises an 'association' with her fellow seamstresses, and rents a communal apartment, changing the workshop into something they run on their own. This progression is a key element in the book's narrative, and it is interesting to note that Chernyshevsky depicts in detail the problems Vera encounters in that process of reform, and her solutions to them. For example, the workers experience some rainy weather. They must report to work rain or shine, but who should supply the umbrellas for their commute? Vera concludes that if the workshop were to purchase umbrellas in bulk and share them, it would be cheaper than each worker purchasing their own, and the umbrellas would be used more efficiently as well. Thus, the umbrellas should be supplied as a welfare benefit. *What Is to Be Done?* features many depictions of such issues, complete with concrete monetary figures. Although I do not know precisely how these scenes were read at the time of publication, it seems as if the novel itself were written to function as a manual for a movement or for starting a business. In fact, the dressmaking shop in mid-nineteenth century Russia was a cutting-edge industry, much like IT in today's economy. In other words, *What Is to Be Done?* is a novel in which a young woman establishes a venture start-up and elaborates a managerial philosophy while living in a communal shared house. It's no surprise that it became a bestseller.

At the same time, *What Is to Be Done?* is a romance novel. And in this respect too it expounds rather progressive views. This was likely another reason why the book was widely appreciated by younger readers.

At the beginning of the novel Vera has a lover, but they differ in their respective philosophies. Then a different man appears, and after a series of events Vera chooses him instead. However, the former lover is neither jealous nor sad; he accepts everything, gets along with the new lover, and ultimately the three live together. These developments, which seem odd on the surface, are described in the story as relating to the 'new man': as Vera and her friends repeat, in building a new society, humans, too, must become new. The protagonists themselves, who abandon exclusivist private property and share not only their belongings but also their lovers, serve as the model for this newness. At one point Vera says the following (using a metaphor that may seem to have sexual connotations):

> [Jealousy] shouldn't exist in a developed person. It's a distorted emotion, a false feeling, a despicable one, an outcome of the sort of thing that would make me refuse to let anyone wear my underclothes or use my cigar holder. It's the result of regarding a person as my own property, as an inanimate object.[4]

One further noteworthy point is that Chernyshevsky mentions Rousseau's *The New Heloise* as an example of a pioneering work that depicted a new woman

---

4.   N. Chernyshevsky, *What Is to Be Done?* tr. M.R. Katz (Ithaca, NY: Cornell University Press, 1989), 305.

like Vera.[5] Often referred to as the original modern romance novel (although it too is rarely read today, at the time of its publication it was a major bestseller, more widely read than *The Social Contract* or *Confessions*), *The New Heloise* also depicted the dream of a woman and two men living together. I will return to the significance of this commonality below.

Now, throughout *Notes from the Underground* Dostoevsky includes critical passages that appear to target Chernyshevsky.

Especially noteworthy in the context of this book is the fact that the words 'Crystal Palace' appear frequently. Dostoevsky uses these words to symbolise the ideal society that the Underground Man rejects.

> You believe in the Crystal Palace, forever indestructible, that is to say, in one at which you won't be able to stick out your tongue even by stealth or cock a snook even in your pocket. Well, perhaps I am afraid of this palace just because it is made of crystal and is forever indestructible, and just because I shan't be able to poke my tongue out at it even by stealth.[6]

Recall that this Crystal Palace, the massive glass building constructed for the 1851 Great Exhibition in London, was mentioned in Chapter 1. Chernyshevsky employs the image of the Crystal Palace as the symbol of the great wealth of future society. He depicts a scene in which Vera dreams of a future society where people live in a crystal and cast-iron structure and lead a rich life liberated from labour.[7] Although the name of the Crystal Palace itself does not appear, it is quite identifiable, and in fact we know that Chernyshevsky himself saw the Crystal Palace in London.

At the risk of repeating what was said in Chapter 1, let us take a moment to review some of the details. The London Great Exhibition was an important moment in the cultural history of the nineteenth century. In tandem with the progression of the Industrial Revolution, England saw a major shift in values, from beauty to technology. The goals of the Exhibition, too, emphasised the trumpeting of the industrial power of each nation rather than the exhibiting of

---

5. Ibid., 365.
6. Dostoevsky, 'Notes from the Underground', 292.
7. Chernyshevsky, *What Is to Be Done?*, 370.

the grandeur of power through the amassing of beauty. The Crystal Palace was precisely the building that exemplified this shift in values. However, there was in fact no architectural specialist involved in its design. The designer, Joseph Paxton, a former gardener and a 'self-made man', was what we would today call an engineer. In other words, the Crystal Palace was the product of a cutting-edge engineering project based not on the principle of beauty, but on the principle of technology. Chernyshevsky framed this building as a symbol of future society, and Dostoevsky criticised it in this capacity.

Furthermore, and echoing what was said in Chapter 1, the Crystal Palace is significantly related to the origins of the shopping mall. A massive steel frame and glass construction, the Crystal Palace is similar to the 'arcades' of the Paris of that era. According to Walter Benjamin, the arcade was a phantasmagorical space that traversed reality and fiction, imbued with the dream of a middle-class utopia. Concretely speaking, this was realised through 'the intoxicated inter-penetration of street and residence'—in other words, a spatial design that was neither indoors nor outdoors;[8] the Crystal Palace was constructed with the same architectural grammar, with features such as an indoor fountain. It was precisely these Parisian arcades that Fourier consulted as a model in designing the buildings of the ideal society. Both Chernyshevsky, who employed the Crystal Palace as the symbol of an ideal society and Dostoevsky, who criticised it, were likely aware of this fact.

To put it in today's terms, the Crystal Palace symbolised a utopian theory according to which new technology and new consumption would lead to an ideal society.[9] It was this very ideal that the 'Underground Man' spat upon.

---

8. Benjamin, *The Arcades Project*, 423.

9. New technology and new consumption will lead to an ideal society...in fact, I myself was making similar arguments just a few years ago. I made such an argument by focusing on the shopping mall, the descendent of this very arcade and of the Crystal Palace, and developed it around the issue of the new publicness generated by malls. See H. Azuma and A. Kitada, *Tokyo kara kangaeru* [*Thinking from Tokyo*] (Tokyo: NHK Bukkusu, 2007), and H. Azuma and K. Ōyama, *Shoppingu mōru kara kangaeru* [*Thinking from the Shopping Mall*] (Tokyo: Gentōsha shinsho, 2016). Thus, we could say that, by positing my previous views as aligned with those of Chernyshevsky and tracing Dostoevsky's dialectic, I am embarking upon a self-criticism as well as an updating of those views. As I wrote in the preface, this book was originally published as a preparatory issue of *Genron* and the final issue of *Shisō chizu ß*. The feature focus of the first issue of *Shisō chizu ß* was actually the shopping mall (the feature title was 'Shopping Mall / Pattern', and in the editor's remarks I wrote the following: 'A twenty-first century world transformed by networks of consumption. New politics. New classes. New bodies and new world views. And a new reality that is both global and local, beyond the dichotomy of real and fake. To sum up in explicitly abstract terms, *Shisō chizu ß* is founded for all people who encounter

When we summarise it in this way, we can see how the issues raised in *Notes from the Underground* not only concern the universal hardship of existence but are also deeply related to the society of the era—and that these issues can also be connected to the present day.

Today, on the one hand, we are fed a vision of a future in which everything is connected, everything is shared, and artificial intelligence will eliminate the need for work—a vision resembling utopian socialism. As noted in the previous chapter, this has also been called the 'Californian Ideology'. On the other hand, we live in a world in which similar shopping malls are built in many countries regardless of differences in religion or ideology, and tourists crisscross the world encountering the same clothes, the same food, the same music, and the same brands. It is as if the theme of Prince Albert's speech at the Great Exhibition in London, 'the unity of mankind', has been realised.[10] To borrow Kojève's metaphor, we are now living in an animal utopia.

However, in *Notes from the Underground* Dostoevsky created a character who rejects all of this. The Underground Man accepts neither IT nor shopping malls. He refuses the very premise that all of mankind can live wisely and happily.

Crucially, this is no simple rebellion. The Underground Man is criticising neither the content nor the possibility of Chernyshevsky's argument. He writes that if a utopia is going to be realised, then fine, let it be realised, and if everyone is going to be happy, then fine, let everyone be happy. Be that as it may, the Underground Man declares that *he himself wants no part of it*. In other words, he demands his right to remain unwise and unhappy:

> I cannot help thinking, gentlemen, that you look upon me with pity; you go on telling me over and over again that an enlightened and mentally developed man, such a man, in short, as the future man can be expected to be, cannot possibly desire deliberately something which is not a real 'good,' and that, you say, is mathematics. [...] But I repeat for the hundredth time that here is one case, one case only, when man can deliberately and consciously desire something that is

---

this reality.' H. Azuma (ed.), *Shisō Chizu β, Volume 1* (Tokyo: Contectures, 2011), 8. In this first issue, I thus affirmed the Crystal Palace and the multitude, and the shopping mall. However, in the end, this affirmation means nothing unless it is set out in a quite complex way. In the present work I attempt to take this prior affirmation and 'recover it in a higher dimension'.

10.   Matsumura, *Suishōkyū monogatari*, 58.

injurious, stupid, even outrageously stupid, just because he wants to have the right to desire for himself even what is very stupid and not be bound by an obligation to desire only what is sensible.[11]

Notes from the Underground is made up of two parts. Part 1 is a record written by a middle-aged man in his forties, and Part 2 is a memoir written by the same man reminiscing about his failures in his twenties. In Part 1 The Underground Man is no longer a young man. He has received an inheritance from relatives and quit his job in the civil service. Growing bored, he begins to pen a record of his life, and becomes agitated about 'twice-two-makes-four'. That in itself is pathetic, but his memoir of twenty years ago is even worse: he ruins a friend's party because of his own persecution complex, hires a prostitute, goes so far as to confront the woman with his own sense of guilt, and is overwhelmed by self-condemnation and shame.

Even twenty years later, the Underground Man is unable to let go of this 'cringe' experience. Indeed, he believes that forgetting that shamefulness would mean losing his pride as a human being. *Notes from the Underground* was in effect written in order to protect this *right to cringiness*. 'And, really, here am I already putting the idle question to myself—which is better: cheap happiness or exalted suffering? Well, which is better?'[12] Here we find the archetype of a logic that rejects animal utopia.

3

In today's terms, we could say that Chernyshevsky's standpoint is close to that of the somewhat liberal intellectuals who place their hopes in information technology and globalism—the point of view according to which an ideal society is possible through the accumulation of rational thought. At the root of this point of view is the utopian socialism of the nineteenth century.

Thus, in the twenty-first century, the opposition between Chernyshevsky and Dostoevsky corresponds to the opposition between internationalist intellectuals who support globalism and dispirited citizens who tend towards anti-globalism.

---

11.   Dostoevsky, 'Notes from the Underground', 286.
12.   Ibid, 376.

In fact, this opposition is being played out in the US through the clash between IT companies and the Trump administration.

But that is not the end of it. We cannot lose sight of the fact that Dostoevsky, who criticised socialist ideals, was himself a socialist just like Chernyshevsky. As I wrote earlier, Dostoevsky joined a circle of revolutionaries in his youth, was arrested, and sent to Siberia. Records tells us that he worshipped Fourier, just like Chernyshevsky.[13] Thus, the opposition between Chernyshevsky and Dostoevsky is not so simple; the relationship between them is more twisted.

Just as the Underground Man's refusal and curses are the inevitable fruit of the ideals of socialism, the terrorist's refusal and curses are the inevitable fruit of the ideals of globalism. It was precisely insight into the existence of this circuit that Dostoevsky gained in his fifteen years of experience from the time he was sent to Siberia. It was because Chernyshevsky naively sang the praises of utopia without noticing the existence of this circuit that Dostoevsky expressed such agitation.

But why does such a circuit exist? Allow me to introduce three studies of Dostoevsky to assist our exploration here.

The first is Freud's essay, 'Dostoevsky and Parricide'. Written about ten years after 'The Uncanny', this essay is a celebrated work in Dostoevsky studies. As the title suggests, in this essay Freud interprets Dostoevsky's literature as being driven by the desire for parricide. It has been said that Dostoevsky's own father was killed by a servant, and his final work *The Brothers Karamazov* is overtly about parricide. For that reason, Freud's interpretation became quite influential.

The second is *Resurrection from the Underground* by the French philosopher René Girard, published in 1963. Two years prior to this, Girard had published *Deceit, Desire, and the Novel* (the original title was *Romantic Lie and Romanesque Truth*), where he analysed 'triangular desire', which involves desiring the desire of others—put simply, this means the desire for a so-called 'triangular relationship', where one falls in love with one's friend's lover. Girard focuses on the fact that such triangular desire is depicted many times in the works of Dostoevsky. Dostoevsky's first novel *Poor Folk* is a tragicomic story in which the protagonist falls in love with a woman, but ultimately she is taken

---

13.   Kameyama, *Dosutoefusukii: chichigoroshi no bungaku jō*, 74.

from him by another person. His last novel, *The Brothers Karamazov*, is a story in which a father and his sons fight over a woman and the father is killed as a result. It is known that the author himself lost women he loved to other men on several occasions.

The third is Ikuo Kameyama's 2004 book *Dostoevsky: The Literature of Parricide*, already cited above. This work is a comprehensive attempt at reading all of Dostoevsky's work through the lens of jealousy and masochism by combining Freud's focus on parricide and Girard's focus on triangular desire.

In Kameyama's view, Dostoevsky is an impotent writer who failed in his parricide and was 'castrated'. His real father was killed by a servant before Dostoevsky could kill him. Even in the case of the symbolic father, the Tzar, he was arrested before he could participate in the assassination. For that reason, Dostoevsky exhibits a unique masochism which consists in the perversion of feeling pleasure in castration itself. This perverse pleasure reaches an apex at the moment of 'cuckolding' when the woman he loves is taken by another man and he is denied fatherhood/manliness. According to Kameyama, this is precisely why Dostoevsky repeatedly set up triangular relationships and consistently depicted scenes in which the protagonist loses the woman he loves, and why he became involved in such romantic relationships in reality.

Researchers seem divided on this reading, but it provides a significant hint for our discussion here. What I would like to focus on specifically is the fact that Kameyama interprets the shift in Dostoevsky's work from socialism to the Underground Man as a self-conscious masochism.

As I noted regarding *Poor Folk*, Dostoevsky depicts triangular relationships even in his early works. However, at that time what he envisioned was the dream of three people living together, as depicted in *What Is to Be Done?* Indeed, the protagonist of *Poor Folk* remains a 'devoted servant' to the woman who has been taken away by another man. But according to Kameyama, over the course of Dostoevsky's career the perverse pleasure that lurks behind the servitude slowly rears its head. The turning point in his real life was meeting Appollinaria Suslova upon his return from exile in Siberia. At the time Dostoevsky was married to an older woman who had fallen ill, but he fell head over heels for this young woman with a somewhat sadistic personality, and after having been pushed around by her, was left broken-hearted. According to Kameyama, his romantic experiences with Suslova provided insight into the 'masochism of undergoing an inversion into self-sacrifice at the apex of humiliation and jealousy', preparing him for *Notes from the Underground*, 'a work that was the literary fleshing out of the thesis that "suffering is pleasure"'. According to Kameyama, '[t]he discovery of sadomasochism carried with it a destructive power that fundamentally overturned the philosophical foundations he had relied upon up to that point.'[14]

When a utopian socialist awakens to their inner masochism, they turn into an underground man. Rather than believing in ideals and serving the world, they become someone who exposes the perversion lurking behind such service, and spew curses. Precisely because they once believed in the ideals of utopia, they prove harsh against those that pervert them. Kameyama's reading reveals another dimension of Dostoevsky's critique of Chernyshevsky. *What Is to Be Done?* depicted the communal life of two men and one woman as an ideal. Dostoevsky did not simply criticise this as unrealistic; he confronted it with the cruel observation that, of course, it is not simply fine for a man to lose a woman to another man—to think so, one would have to be a pervert who finds excitement in seeing his beloved fornicate with another man.

The Underground Man is not simply criticising socialists. If that were the case, one could convert the Underground Man by preaching to him the wonderful virtues of socialism. This indeed was Chernyshevsky's strategy (and has been that of leftists ever since).

Instead, the Underground Man is pointing out the hypocrisy of socialism. He has noticed the perverse pleasure lurking within the ideals of utopia—an *erotic pleasure in doing the right thing*. Thus, he demands the right to not get involved—and there is a logic to this demand. The political and sexual circuit that connects the socialist to the Underground Man—this was Dostoevsky's discovery. This discovery retains all of its lustre today. In 2017 we are surrounded by the very curses that expose the hypocrisy of liberals. They are the curses that hoist up Trump as a hero. This is why I thought that we should reread *Notes from the Underground* at this very moment.

No matter how close to utopia the world comes, and no matter how closely that utopia approximates perfection, so long as humans are humans and utopia is

---

14.   Kameyama, *Dosutoefusukii: chichigoroshi no bungaku jō*, 173, 175.

utopia, terrorists who reject all of it will always emerge. This is the issue that our world is confronting today. The essence of the issue does not have to do with politics; it has to do with literature. Yet its product, terrorism, is a political issue.

A socialist becomes an underground man. An idealist becomes a masochist. Such a reading is possible because Dostoevsky's novels exhibit a dialectical structure. The protagonists in his major works are shaped as if they are an overcoming of the protagonist of the previous work. Therefore we may consider there to be a 'logical development' from *Notes from the Underground* to *Crime and Punishment*, to *The Devils*, to *The Brothers Karamazov*. As Girard writes: 'It is remarkable that Dostoevsky, from his adolescence to his old age, would have traveled through all the moments of a mythology of the Self that are displayed over almost three centuries in Western Europe.'[15]

But where does this dialectic of Dostoevsky's ultimately lead? This is where the interpretation of Dostoevsky intersects with the themes of the present work.

Notes from the Underground was published in 1864. Later in that decade Dostoevsky would write some of his major works including *The Gambler*, *Crime and Punishment*, and *The Idiot*. The protagonist of *Crime and Punishment*, Raskolnikov, is especially connected to the Underground Man. But if we are looking for a character that inherits the problem-consciousness of the Underground Man but changes into a different type of character, we must first examine Nikolai Stavrogin of *The Devils*.

The Devils was published between 1871 and 1872 and, as mentioned above, its narrative focuses on infighting and murder among young terrorists, and is modelled on an actual incident. Stavrogin arrives at the provincial town that serves as the setting of the novel midway through the narrative and is the leader of these terrorists.

Unlike the Underground Man, Stavrogin is young and handsome. He is also calculating and smart. He gracefully waltzes into social circles and skilfully manipulates others' desires. As the narrative progresses, he is pampered by many powerful people, shares his bed with many women, and ultimately, manipulated by

---

15.   R. Girard, *Resurrection from the Underground: Feodor Dostoevsky*, tr. J.G. Williams (East Lansing, MI: Michigan State University Press, 2012), 47.

his words, the activists end up killing one another and even set the town ablaze. Despite this, Stavrogin's motives are never clear. Although he issues commands to his comrades, he is actually not interested in revolution, nor does he make any secret of this fact. He remains cold in the face of everything. This chronic demeaner of others is described as a 'disease of indifference' in the novel,[16] and it is this disease of indifference that is the principal theme of *The Devils*.

Stavrogin is a sadist, not a masochist. He is not a cuckold, he makes cuckolds of other men; he does not curse the world, he is indifferent to it. For this reason, on the surface it seems as if he is moulded in opposition to the Underground Man. Indeed, they are opposed to one another in the narrative. The characters in *The Devils* that correspond to the Underground Man are Kirilov and Shatov, who hang around Stavrogin and are manipulated by him at will. Although the underground masochists can point out the hypocrisy of socialists, they cannot oppose the sadist's disease of indifference.

However, what is interesting here is that Dostoevsky simultaneously furnishes Stavrogin with a backstory that reminds one of the Underground Man. His past is revealed in a chapter entitled 'At Tikhon's' (also known as 'Stavrogin's Confession', the chapter was removed at the time of the initial publication of *The Devils*). It tells of how Stavrogin deliberately commits a sordid act, reproaches himself for its sordidness, and simultaneously hurts another person—a series of actions identical to those committed by the Underground Man in his youth. Thus, Stavrogin does not simply stand in opposition to the Underground Man. Rather, it would be better to understand his sadism as a product of the Underground Man's masochism ballooning to its limits until it bursts, inverting everything. In other words, Stavrogin is an Underground Man who avoided becoming a wilted middle-aged man, one who chose to become a sadist rather than deepening his masochism. Interested readers should consult Kameyama's book on how Dostoevsky depicted this shift from masochism to sadism,[17] but in any case, it seems to me that, even for someone who has not read *The Devils*, this is a recognisable psychological phenomenon: when hope and expectation for the world (masochism) balloons to the extreme, it may suddenly invert into cold indifference. Furthermore, it is not uncommon for those afflicted with such

---

16.   F. Dostoevsky, *The Devils*, tr. D.D. Magarshack (London: Penguin, 1953), 685.
17.   Kameyama, *Dosutoefusukii: chichigoroshi no bungaku jō*, 79.

'coldness' to also be charismatic at times. That is how Stavrogin was able to become a leader of terrorists without having any faith in either God or ideals. Girard writes: 'Whoever revolts against God in order to adore himself always ends up adoring the Other, Stavrogin.'[18]

From the socialist to the Underground Man, to Stavrogin; from an idealist to a masochist, to a sadist. From one who hisses, red in the face, that calling for social change is nothing more than lip-service, to one who boasts that they couldn't care less whether the world changes or not and will do as they like either way. Dostoevsky's dialectic arrived at this third subject in *The Devils*.

Above I compared Chernyshevsky to today's internationalist intellectuals and the Underground Man to today's terrorists. As an extension of this, I consider the best analogue to Stavrogin to be not the terrorist, but rather the libertarian IT entrepreneur or engineer. As I noted at the beginning of this chapter, Stavrogin is depicted as a terrorist in the novel. However, in reality he himself does not dirty his hands with destructive acts, whether murder or arson. He only manipulates the desires of the group members. Moreover, he has no motive for doing so—he simply manipulates them because he can. Even at the end of the novel, Stavrogin shows no sign of regret (he commits suicide, but it cannot conceivably be out of regret for his acts), nor is he prosecuted for any violation of law. This depiction is completely different from that of, say, Raskolnikov in *Crime and Punishment*.

The essence of Dostoevsky's Stavrogin lies neither in the will to social reform nor in a hatred for idealism, but in the disease of indifference. He manipulates the fate of others, and he does so simply because he can, without motive. Today, the only people who can maintain such a nihilistic relation to the world are businessmen who move millions of dollars every day through financial markets, or engineers who move tens of thousands of people at will through internet services. With the slightest touch of their fingertips, countless terrorists detonate suicide bombs on the other side of the globe. That is the state of our world today. Girard compares Stavrogin's philosophy to Nietzsche's philosophy of the superhuman.[19] Indeed, perhaps terrorists/revolutionaries were once superhumans. However, there is no trace of the superhuman in the young people who are blowing themselves up in Turkey, Syria, Iraq, or in developed

---

18.   Girard, *Resurrection from the Underground*, 41.
19.   Ibid., 47sq.

nations in response to those actions. Today, terrorism is nothing more than the expression of the desperate curses of underground men. Stavrogin is far more powerful than them. Thus, in the twenty-first-century world, we can no longer compare Stavrogin to the terrorist.

From socialist to the underground man to the superhuman. From utopian to terrorist to the cynical elite. The tragicomedy of those who once were passionate about ideals of social reform and engaged in radical movements becoming nihilists somewhere along the line can be found in Japan today as well. Dostoevsky's literature depicts this quite recognisable dialectic of the psyche with far more precision than any book of philosophy.

There is a dialectic to Dostoevsky's works, and this is actually a very important characteristic of them. Although this is somewhat of a tangent, I should like to make a simple comparison to Rousseau here.

It is sometimes said that Rousseau and Dostoevsky are similar writers. Indeed, similar motifs are developed throughout their respective works. However, the structures of the totality of their respective oeuvres are very different.

Earlier I touched upon the fact that Chernyshevsky mentions *The New Heloise*. Like Chernyshevsky, Rousseau dreamed of a world without jealousy. In fact, this is an argument that appears in his philosophical texts as well. To that extent, he is an idealist and a socialist. But there was a different side to Rousseau as well, an aspect of him that was more underground man than socialist. As I noted in Chapter 2, Rousseau was a very jealous, cringy man with something of a persecution complex. There are many passages in his *Confessions*, *Reveries of the Solitary Walker*, and his correspondences with contemporaries that read as if they were written by none other than the Underground Man himself.

Then how are these two Rousseaus integrated with one another? To cut a long story short, in Rousseau's own work they are not. As I pointed out in Chapter 2, Rousseau is generally understood to be a contradictory philosopher who argues both that humans are originally solitary beings and have no need for society (the Underground-Man-like aspect), and that the individual will must submit to the general will (the socialist aspect). In *General Will 2.0* I attempted to resolve this contradiction—indeed, my argument there is that there is no contradiction, but readers will no doubt sense a contradiction if they read his work straightforwardly.

This is precisely the major difference between Rousseau and Dostoevsky. As noted above, in the case of Dostoevsky the contradiction between the socialist and the Underground Man is resolved dialectically through the developments in his works. There is a transition by way of which the Underground Man overcomes the socialist, and another in which Stavrogin overcomes the Underground Man. But there is no such transition in Rousseau. To the very end he suffered from his own contradiction between the socialist self and the underground self, the self that wants to improve the world and the self that believes that all such thoughts are deceptive. Even in his final years he wrote a self-splitting text titled *Rousseau, Judge of Jean-Jacques*. Girard expresses this lack of dialectic in Rousseau by saying that while Dostoevsky followed *The Insulted and Injured* with *The Eternal Husband*, Rousseau's *New Heloise* was met with no equivalent of the latter.[20]

But why was there no dialectic in Rousseau? Here it may be helpful to remember that, as Freud pointed out, the theme of parricide always haunted Dostoevsky's writings.

Like Dostoevsky, Rousseau engages with the issue of sexuality. He too is possessed of a triangular desire. Indeed, so far as we can tell from his biography, Rousseau's masochism seems to have been more perverse than Dostoevsky's and quite out in the open. For example, in *Confessions* he confesses with brutal frankness that he exposed himself in public in his youth. But there is no issue of parricide in Rousseau's texts or biography. If Rousseau harboured any kind of complex, it probably had to do with his mother. He lost his mother soon after birth, and—as is also recorded in his *Confessions*—tended to be attracted to older women. The issue of parricide occurs in one and not in the other. It would be an interesting phenomenon if it was this difference between the two that created the difference in their way of thinking.

4

Let us return to Dostoevsky. The socialist was overcome by the Underground Man and the Underground Man was overcome by Stavrogin. That being the case, does Dostoevsky conclude that we must all become like Stavrogin?

---

20. Girard, *Resurrection from the Underground*, 45sq.

Of course, that cannot be the case. Stavrogin is not depicted at all positively in *The Devils*. In fact, he commits suicide at the end of the book. Stavrogin was indeed the protagonist of *The Devils*, but unlike Raskolnikov in *Crime and Punishment* and Myshkin in *The Idiot*, his position was that of the antihero. We should instead think that with this novel Dostoevsky appealed to the need to be liberated from Stavrogin's disease of indifference. In other words, in the path that leads from the socialist to the Underground Man and then to Stavrogin, there is one further, final stage: the final subject that appears beyond Stavrogin's nihilism.

The consideration of this final subject harbours great significance for the project of this book.

In Chapter 4 I wrote that today in the twenty-first century there are only two philosophies that can claim to be logically consistent: communitarianism—that is, nationalism—and libertarianism—that is, globalism—while liberalism, lacking in universality, has lost its place. In order to reconstruct a place for the universal in a different form, I argued for the incorporation of misdelivery generated by the tourist/the postal multitude. In other words, the liberalism of the past has lost its efficacy and only communitarianism and libertarianism remain, but this is unacceptable, so we need a fourth line of thought. The dialectic of Dostoevsky explored in this chapter follows this very schema. Chernyshevsky is a liberal, the Underground Man is a communitarian, and Stavrogin is a libertarian. Liberals are hypocrites, communitarians bask in masochistic pleasures, and libertarians suffer from the disease of indifference.[21]

---

21. My conclusion here that the communitarian (essentially synonymous with the nationalist in my usage) basks in the pleasures of masochism may be difficult to grasp. Therefore, I will provide a simple supplementary explanation here. According to Ōsawa's *Origins of Nationalism*, mentioned above, nationalism was an ideology that first appeared as a type of reaction to the movements of capitalism that invalidate all transcendence—in Ōsawa's words, 'judgement by a third party'. Capitalism invalidates God. The nation state was constructed as a substitute. For that reason, while the nation state is the most intimate thing to people, it can at the same time function as something absolutely alien as well. In fact, nation states sometimes have their origins 'outside' of the country: for instance, the origins of Japan are in the South Pacific and the Asian continent (see *Origins of Nationalism*, 377). In Deleuze's terms (see below, 219n29), Ōsawa is saying that nationalism has essentially the same psychoanalytic structure as masochism. The masochist creates a master where there is no master (super-ego). Similarly, the nationalist creates a nation state where there is no God (super-ego).

Once we have overcome Chernyshevsky's hypocrisy and escaped the trap of the Underground Man's pleasure, how can we peel ourselves away from Stavrogin's nihilism? To put it in the terms of Part 1, once we have overcome the hypocrisy of liberalism and escaped the trap of nationalism's pleasure, how can we peel ourselves away from the nihilism of globalism? In our contemporary age, this is an extremely real and practical, yet at the same time philosophically and politically important question.

What kind of subject is Dostoevsky's final subject? I would like to conclude the explorations of this book by giving an answer to this question.

At this point we encounter the need to take a risk. In fact, the discussion that follows is rather precarious as a reading of Dostoevsky. This is because what I am about to read is not a novel that Dostoevsky wrote, but a *novel that he did not write*. In what follows, I will refer to Ikuo Kameyama's 2007 work *Imagining the Sequel to The Brothers Karamazov*.

Why do such a thing? After *The Devils*, aside from a few short stories in a periodical that he himself published (in fact, in his later years he was quite passionate about running his periodical, and his commentary on current events helped him rise to fame), Dostoevsky only wrote two novels: *The Adolescent* in 1875, and *The Brothers Karamazov*, published between 1879 and 1880. He then died suddenly, only two months following completion of the latter. Thus, common sense would tell us that Dostoevsky's dialectic finds its endpoint in *The Brothers Karamazov*. Indeed, today the novel is recognised as a masterpiece in literary history.

However, this novel is actually incomplete. *The Brothers Karamazov* in its existing form is written in such a way that it can be read as a complete piece, and in fact there is nothing unnatural in considering it as an independent novel. But Dostoevsky clearly states in the preface that it is only a 'first novel', to be completed by the forthcoming 'second one'. Therefore, I would like to include the plan for that sequel in my consideration of Dostoevsky's dialectic. What kind of narrative was planned for that sequel, then? Kameyama's book speculates on its possible content, based purely on 'imagination', the author says. Since Dostoevsky left no clear manuscripts or notes on the plan, technically speaking we have no choice but to call it a product of imagination. Yet, to me, Kameyama's prediction seems precise and convincing enough for me to want to consider Dostoevsky's final subject on its basis.

In my view, Dostoevsky's dialectic did not conclude with the existing *Brothers Karamazov.* It reaches its final conclusion in Kameyama's imaginary novel (the unwritten sequel). Such an approach would not be permissible were this chapter merely an attempt to analyse the work of Dostoevsky. But I think it may be permitted if it were instead an attempt to interpret the potential of his philosophy. What I am interested in here is not just the reality of what Dostoevsky was thinking, but also what he *would have been able* to think.

Let me briefly summarise the content of Kameyama's speculative schema. The existing *Brothers Karamazov,* in other words Volume 1 (the first novel) was a story of parricide. Kameyama speculates that, extrapolating from this, Volume 2 (the second novel) would have been a story of parricide as well. So what kind of father would be killed in it? Based on a number of biographical testimonies, Kameyama predicts that it would have been a story of killing the 'symbolic father'—that is, a tale of regicide (the assassination of the Tzar).

Next, on the basis of several pieces of evidence, Kameyama speculates that the second volume would have been set thirteen years after the events of the first volume. Volume 1 of *The Brothers Karamazov* features Fyodor Karamazov and his four sons, Dmitri, Ivan, Alyosha, and Smerdyakov (whom I include here for sake of simplicity). Since by the end of the first volume the father and three of the sons have either died, gone mad, or been arrested, the focus of the second volume would inevitably be Alyosha. Now, in Volume 1, Alyosha is depicted as a devout Christian. So does he undergo conversion in Volume 2 and suddenly become a terrorist? Many prior studies have speculated that this would be the case.

However, Kameyama argues that this is mistaken. In the preface to the existing first volume, Dostoevsky, writing with the second volume also in his purview, states that the protagonist of the first volume, Alyosha, remains an unknown figure to the end. In which case, the theory that Alyosha becomes an assassin cannot stand. How could a man who killed the Tzar remain unknown? So who tries to assassinate the Tzar if not Alyosha? Kameyama focuses on a boy named Kolya Krasotkin. Indeed, toward the end of Volume 1 there is a section in which many boys appear for the first time and begin interacting with Alyosha (Part 4, Book 10: 'The Boys'). It is a rather abrupt development if we read it solely in the context of the existing book (Volume 1), and indeed some critics have argued that it is a failure in terms of composition. But Kameyama believes, in contrast, that this very 'failure' proves that this chapter foreshadows Volume 2. Based on the age of the boys and other circumstantial evidence, he concludes that Kolya becomes the protagonist in Volume 2 and that it is he who attempts to assassinate the Tzar.

What is the plot of Volume 2, then? According to Kameyama's speculation, in Volume 2 Kolya creates a secret society and attempts to kill the Tzar. Judging by Dostoevsky's relationships in his later years and Kolya's name, at the core of the secret society would be a strange, Russian socialist mysticism influenced by Nikolai Fyodorov (Kolya is the diminutive form of Nikolai).[22] At the same time, Alyosha must still be part of the picture as well. Based on another piece of foreshadowing in Volume 1, we can speculate that he would emerge from a Christian sect (the Khlysts) to form his own sect and become its leader. The narrative of Volume 2 would begin with Kolya inviting his former teacher Alyosha to join his secret society. From there the novel would develop through the clash of concepts: Alyosha and Kolya, teacher and disciple, heretical religionist and heretical revolutionary....

Now, what is important about Kameyama's speculation is that it pushes forward the dialectic of Dostoevsky charted above.

The Brothers Karamazov is composed as if it were the culmination of his dialectic, leading from the socialist to the Underground Man to Stavrogin. The respective placements of the characters of the novel are quite clear when viewed through the lens of this dialectic.

As noted above, the four brothers Dmitri, Ivan, Alyosha, and Smerdyakov appear in *The Brothers Karamazov*. If we place each of them within the schema developed so far, we could say that Dmitri and Smerdyakov correspond to the Underground Man and Ivan corresponds to Stavrogin. There are no characters that correspond to the socialist.

---

22. On the philosophy of Nikolai Fyodorov, see above, 187n15.

The fact that there are two underground men is easily understood if we think of one of them as inheriting the Underground Man of *Notes from the Underground*, while the other inherits the underground men of *The Devils*. Dmitri is depicted as an awkward young man, unhinged by jealousy, who cannot hold a conversation, a figure reminiscent of the Underground Man. On the other hand, Smerdyakov is a servile masochist who worships Ivan. Ivan is a nihilist who declares that everything is permissible if God does not exist. The relationship between Ivan and Smerdyakov is comparable to that between Stavrogin and the terrorists. In fact, Smerdyakov faithfully follows Ivan's unconscious incitement and commits a terrorist act (parricide). Even though they are both underground men, Dmitri is incapable of committing parricide while Smerdyakov is quite capable of it. Here we see the stamp of the transition from *Notes from the Underground* to *The Devils*. In other words, we can read *The Brothers Karamazov* as a novel that synthesised the dialectical movement from *Notes from the Underground* to *The Devils* and attempted to go further.

From this perspective, Dostoevsky's clear statement in his preface that Alyosha is the protagonist of his novel—'In starting out on the life of my hero, Alexei Fyodorovich Karamazov, I feel somewhat at a loss'[23]—is quite significant. *Notes from the Underground* was Dmitri's story, *The Devils* is Ivan's and Smerdyakov's, and *The Brothers Karamazov* is Alyosha's. This being the case, it would be natural to conclude that this very Alyosha embodies the new stage in the dialectic. If Dmitri's spirit was inherited by Smerdyakov, and Smerdyakov's spirit is dominated by Ivan's spirit, perhaps Ivan's spirit, too, is overcome by Alyosha in some way. And perhaps this is precisely where we can find, through this narrative, the answer to the question of how to overcome the hypocrisy of Chernyshevsky, escape the trap of the Underground Man's pleasure, and finally tear ourselves away from Stavrogin's nihilism too.

However, if we read the existing *The Brothers Karamazov*, this hope is unceremoniously betrayed. As things stand, Alyosha's role is quite vague. Unlike the other three brothers, there are few scenes where he expounds any philosophy of his own. In most scenes he serves as a listener, and in general plays the role of an interlocutor who moves the narrative forward. When we compare this to his importance as declared in the preface, this vacuousness seems suspicious.

---

23.   F. Dostoevsky, *The Brothers Karamazov*, tr. A.R. MacAndrew (New York: Bantam Books, 1970), 1.

Why did Dostoevsky mould such a character? The answer is not to be found in the existing *Brothers Karamazov*, and therefore we must look to the non-existent second volume.

5

Let us then finally begin our reading of the imaginary Volume 2. Kameyama predicts that the title of Volume 2 would have been *The Children of Karamazov*,[24] in reference to Kolya and the other boys introduced in the first volume.

For various reasons, Kameyama predicts that in Volume 2 Kolya would become a character comparable to Ivan in Volume 1—that is to say, a Stavrogin-like figure. Thus, we can say that he would have become the lead conspirator in the Tzar's assassination. In fact, even in 'The Boys' he describes his friend (Ilyusha) as 'slavishly devoted' to him and brags that he 'helped him develop his mind'.[25] Although still young, his attitude resembles that of Stavrogin. The relationship between Kolya and the other boys in *The Brothers Karamazov* is a repetition of that between Stavrogin and the terrorists in *The Devils*. The nightmare of underground men manipulated at will by a superhuman is repeated once more, this time in the context of a massive conspiracy to assassinate the Tzar.

However, there is a decisive difference between *The Devils* and *The Brothers Karamazov*: the presence of Alyosha. Stavrogin had no one by his side, whereas Kolya passionately desires the presence of Alyosha. This passion is already clear in Volume 1: 'Oh, Karamazov, I've been so anxious to meet you for such a long time! Did you really think about me too?'[26] In a word, Kolya is a Stavrogin who needs Alyosha.

Why does Kolya need Alyosha so much? What we cannot lose sight of is the fact that Kolya is not seeking Alyosha alone, but rather the construction of a *familial community* with Alyosha as a pseudo-father. In fact, many of the boys who appear in the section 'The Boys' have family issues. Kolya does not have a father. Ilyusha's mother has gone mad, and the family is falling apart. But they all come together to form a kind of pseudo-family, in which Alyosha appears as the one they hope will fill the role of father. These hopes of the boys are clearly

24.   Kameyama, '*Karamazofu no kyodai' no zokuhen o kūsō suru*, 216.
25.   Dostoevsky, *The Brothers Karamazov*, 641.
26.   Ibid., 669.

displayed in the final scene of the existing *The Brothers Karamazov* when they shout 'three cheers for Karamazov!' at the funeral of Ilyusha (who has succumbed to illness).[27] Even though it is Ilyusha's funeral, they do not cheer for Ilyusha or Snegiryov (Ilyusha's family name), but for Karamazov. It almost seems like a ritual for the foundation of *a new Karamazov family* with Alyosha as father and Kolya as eldest son, in the wake of the old Karamazov family, now crumbling to the ground, with Fyodor killed, Dmitri arrested, Smerdyakov a suicide, and Ivan insane. The story of the Karamazov family begins anew at the end of Volume 1.

Volume 2 follows this conclusion. So we can postulate that Alyosha becomes a father and creates a pseudo-family (society) with Kolya. This becomes the new Karamazov family, and the narrative of this process will drive *The Children of Karamazov*.

Will this family succeed? According to Kameyama's forecast, it seems not. In the end Alyosha cannot become a father. He does not become the leader of the society, nor can he stop the plan to assassinate the Tzar. Kolya and his followers follow through with the plan, fail, and are sentenced to death. At the end of the narrative, they are granted a reprieve from the Tzar and escape death. While this is the climax of Volume 2 as predicted by Kameyama, despite the fact that Kolya desperately needed Alyosha, as seen in Volume 1, Alyosha is able to exert very little influence on the incident. He cannot even save Kolya; it is ultimately the Tzar who saves Kolya's life.

Stavrogin needs a father; *but it is an impotent father*—an impotent father surrounded by underground men/children who cannot even save him. Kameyama imagines *The Children of Karamazov* as a narrative of impotence.

Herein lies the decisive importance of Kameyama's speculative image. Again, *The Brothers Karamazov* and *The Children of Karamazov* deal with the philosophical or spiritual logic through which Alyosha overcomes Stavrogin/Ivan. As I noted earlier, many scholars believe that in Volume 2 Alyosha himself would attempt to assassinate the Tzar. In other words, they conclude that Dostoevsky's final subject overcomes Stavrogin/Ivan's disease of indifference and ultimately becomes a terrorist cloaked in religiosity.

---

27. Ibid., 936.

Kameyama suggests a completely different logic. He completely removes such agency from Alyosha in Volume 2, arguing that Alyosha becomes an impotent father—but it is that very impotence that makes the overcoming of Ivan/Kolya possible.

Although Kameyama's logic may at first appear somewhat acrobatic, it is actually quite convincing, because it suggests the return of the Dostoevskyian dialectic that we have been surveying to its starting point, and thus a closing of its circle. This dialectic, as noted above, began with the author's experience of symbolic castration when he was arrested on suspicion of attempting to topple the government when he was still in his twenties. He was sentenced to death and survived precisely through the grace of the Tzar (who granted him a pardon). Kameyama imagines Dostoevsky's steps in returning to that experience and attempting to overcome it, and believes that this must have been the significance of Dostoevsky's return to the theme of regicide in his later years—an attempt to repeat the castration of the past in the form of fiction. Castration returns to castration. The libertarian afflicted with the disease of indifference who has forgotten the fact of castration, too, ultimately returns to castration. It is in this way that Kameyama understands Dostoevsky's dialectic.

In reality, *The Children of Karamazov* was never written. Thus, we do not know how Dostoevsky actually planned to depict Stavrogin/Kolya's 'craving for the impotent father'. Maybe such a thing cannot be depicted. However, had he been able to depict this craving then, very probably, by the end of *The Children of Karamazov* there would have appeared a new subject beyond Stavrogin: Dostoevsky's final subject. That is precisely where Alyosha would have become the true protagonist.

How does one overcome the hypocrisy of Chernyshevsky, escape the trap of the Underground Man's pleasure, and finally tear oneself away from Stavrogin's nihilism? I will answer this question here by saying: only by becoming an impotent father. After overcoming the hypocrisy of liberalism, escaping the trap of the pleasures of nationalism, and finally tearing oneself away from the nihilism of globalism, one ultimately arrives at the impotent subject surrounded by children. And this is precisely the subject of the tourist.

One follows Stavrogin by becoming a subject that accepts castration. However, this doesn't simply mean being powerless, nor does it necessarily mean giving up on changing the world. As I have been saying thus far, this final subject is surrounded by children, and it is the children who will change the world.

I would like to close this book by considering the significance of the child in Dostoevsky's dialectic by returning once more to his actual novels.

Thus far we have considered Alyosha's overcoming of Ivan as an entry point for thinking about Dostoevsky's final subject. Yet Ivan and Alyosha actually clash head-to-head in the existing *Brothers Karamazov*. The scene appears in Part 2 of Book 5, 'Pro and Contra', and features a long dialogue, the theme of which is the suffering of children.

This dialogue between Ivan and Alyosha is quite famous and has given rise to many interpretations. Thus I will limit my description of it here, but essentially, Ivan develops the following line of argument to challenge Alyosha's faith: Perhaps God does exist; maybe salvation exists as well. Perhaps hundreds or thousands of years from now a day will come when all sinners will be forgiven, all of the dead will be resurrected, and murderers and victims will tearfully embrace one another. But the issue is that there are many innocent children being hurt and shamed *here and now*. Their pain and humiliation cannot be atoned for through future salvation. How does God answer to this problem?

Alyosha actually loses this debate. At the very least, he appears to skirt the question. Alyosha simply kisses Ivan on the cheek and walks away. He cannot overcome Ivan.

However, what is crucial here is that the very existence of this dialogue reveals Ivan's weakness. Ivan was supposed to be afflicted by the disease of indifference. Indeed, he boasts that God does not exist. But even he cannot overlook the existence of children's suffering. That is precisely why he challenges Alyosha to a debate.

The superman can withstand all injustices, but cannot stand the suffering of children. This schema is actually inherited from *The Devils*. In *The Devils*, too, there is a scene where Stavrogin confesses an experience that he found 'unbearable'. Like the aforementioned dialogue in *The Brothers Karamazov*, it is a very famous passage. It appears in a reminiscence of the past incorporated into the chapter 'At Tikhon's', discussed above.

Stavrogin encounters a young girl at his lodgings. She is still a pre-teen and is abused by her mother every day. On a whim, Stavrogin has a sexual encounter with her and just as quickly loses interest. A few days later, feeling betrayed, the girl commits suicide. She stares him down and enters an unoccupied shed by herself. Stavrogin foresees her suicide, but does nothing to stop her, and the girl hangs herself. Stavrogin soon forgets even this. However, several years later he begins to suffer visions of the child. And, as he confesses, he feels no remorse; he would do the same again if given a chance. But he admits that 'what I find so unbearable is the image of her standing on the threshold and threatening me with her small raised fist, just the way she looked at me then, just that shaking of her head. It is this that I cannot stand'.[28]

Deleuze once wrote that, while the masochist only has the ego, in contrast the sadist only has the superego.[29] Having only the superego means having only a system that is beyond the ego. When I refer to the libertarian as a sadist, it is based on this understanding of sadism. The libertarian/sadist/Stavrogin has no self. There is only an existence beyond the self. There is only the necessity of the world, thus there is no desire. All things are obtainable, yet nothing is desired. The disease of indifference signifies the lack of self.

Therefore we might be able to say that here Stavrogin is finally able to regain the self through his vision of the girl. The illusion (ghost) of the child is the return of the lost self. In the terms of the previous chapter, it is the 'uncanny'. The return of the uncanny eats away the superego of the superhuman from within.

The suffering child is Ivan/Stavrogin's greatest weakness. Yet Alyosha was not able to strike that weakness in their direct conversation. Thus, in this chapter we needed Kameyama's imaginary sequel in order to explore Alyosha's overcoming of Ivan.

The critic Mutsumi Yamashiro has suggested yet another possible reading. In his 2010 book *Dostoevsky*, he attempts to build a rebuttal of Ivan's argument through a close reading of the aforementioned section 'The Boys'.

Yamashiro's argument is quite complex, so here I would like to merely introduce the core of his logic by consulting Satoshi Bamba's summary of it

---

28.   Dostoevsky, *The Devils*, 696.

29.   G. Deleuze, 'Coldness and Cruelty', in *Masochism* (New York: Zone Books, 1991), 123sq.

in his 2012 book *Dostoevsky and the Questions of the Novel*, in addition to Yamashiro's writing itself.[30]

According to Yamashiro and Bamba, what we must pay particular attention to in 'The Boys' is actually the scene of the 'resurrection' of the dog Juchka. Ilyusha was fond of a wild dog that he named Juchka. However, he was tricked by Smerdyakov into feeding it a piece of bread with a pin in it. Juchka squealed around and ran off whimpering. Ilyusha is worried about this on his sickbed. And so Kolya finds an identical dog and decides to give it to Ilyusha. The new dog he finds is named Perezvon and is presented as *not* being Juchka. Yet Ilyusha takes one look at Perezvon and is convinced that it is Juchka himself, and is overjoyed. Nobody knows whether that dog was actually Juchka, and it seems that there are various theories among scholars as well (the fact that there are such studies is itself surprising).

How does this story become a rebuttal of Ivan's argument? The issue that Ivan raises is framed as an issue of the particularity of being—that is, even if salvation comes in the future, the suffering of *this* child can never be healed. We can think of the anecdote of Juchka and Perezvon as depicting precisely the moment where such 'thisness' itself is disassembled and dissolved.

Ilyusha loved Juchka. And the Juchka he loved was only *that* Juchka. To that extent, the scar from Juchka's disappearance will never heal. Indeed, at the beginning Ilyusha rebuffs all suggestions of finding another dog. And yet here Dostoevsky depicts the miraculous moment when this very scar is healed. As Yamashiro and Bamba both point out, it is no longer important whether Ilyusha believes Perezvon to be Juchka or whether Perezvon is indeed Juchka. What is important is that Perezvon can be Perezvon at the same time as being Juchka,

---

30. M. Yamashiro, *Dosutoefusukii* (Tokyo: Kōdansha Bungei Bunko, 2015). S. Bamba, *Dosutoefusukii to shōsetsu no toi* (Tokyo: Suiseisha, 2012). I refer to the final chapter in Yamashiro's book, which is actually entitled 'The Children of Karamazov' (although he does not refer to Kameyama). In this book, Yamashiro cites an article on Aleksandr Solzhenitsyn that I wrote nearly twenty-five years ago titled 'The Tactility of Probability (*Kakuritsu no tezawari*)' (in H. Azuma, *Yūbinteki fuantachi beta* [*Postal Anxieties ß*] [Tokyo: Kawade Bunko, 2011]). There I referred to the very same dialogue between Ivan and Alyosha I discuss here, and developed the key concept of 'probability' that would later lead to the 'postal'. Bamba incorporates my nearly twenty-year-old book *Ontological, Postal* in his explanation of Yamashiro's arguments concerning Juchka through the theoretical framework of the proper name. In other words, in the above works Yamashiro and Bamba both touch upon my previous work in reading Dostoevsky and attempting to overcome Ivan's arguments. My discussion in this chapter is a response to them and an attempt to push their arguments further.

and that Ilyusha noticed the possibility of that kind of thinking. The very fact that Juchka was Juchka was itself only a chance occurrence. It was only a wild dog in the first place. Thus, even after Juchka's death, we can once again seek *something Juchka-esque* and build a new relationship—and moreover, we *must* do so. That is what living entails. As Yamashiro states, '[b]y Perezvon being Juchka, [the relationship between Ilyusha and Kolya] is replaced by a completely new and different relationship—a Karamazovic brotherly love. What Arimasa Mori calls "resurrection" is this new relationship as an event brought about by the "coincidence" of Perezvon, Kolya, and Ilyusha.'[31]

Because I am only *this* I and Juchka is only *that* Juchka, this scar will never heal with the salvation of a future I or a different dog. It is for this reason that the Underground Man rejected utopia and Ivan/Stavrogin denied the existence of God. Alyosha cannot logically rebut this. However, what Dostoevsky is trying to demonstrate here is the possibility of a different thinking that can break through the impasse—this is Yamashiro and Bamba's reading.

Moreover, this different thinking once again plays a decisive role in the aforementioned final scene of *The Brothers Karamazov* at Ilyusha's funeral. Ilyusha's father laments the death of his son. 'Why did that Ilyusha have to be the Ilyusha that died? Why is my child my child?'[32] This lament will never be healed. It sequesters people into solitude, and ushers Ivan/Stavrogin toward nihilism.

If that is the case, just as Juchka's death was overcome through the introduction of Perezvon, another path of overcoming must be demonstrated in the death of Ilyusha. Yamashiro and Bamba believe that it is for precisely this reason that Dostoevsky ultimately had Kolya shout 'Three cheers for Karamazov'. Bamba writes: 'The very fact that Ilyusha was Ilyusha was itself a complete contingency. It should be sufficiently possible for a new "good child" to arrive and start a new relationship with the father. Just as the resurrected Juchka came back as Perezvon, a new Ilyusha, too, will arrive as a contingent, exchangeable body, and set in motion a new movement that changes contingency into necessity together with the father.'[33] A child is born from chance and dies by chance. And then a new child is born from chance and before you know it changes into

---

31.   Yamashiro, *Dosutoefusukii*, 587–88.

32.   Ibid., 606.

33.   Bamba, *Dosutoefusukii to shōsetsu no toi*, 319.

a necessary being. Ilyusha's death is overcome through such a movement. We generally call this movement *family*.

Thus, the impotent subject surrounded by children may be impotent, but is certainly not powerless. Children will change the world for us. By tearing their bodies from the gravity of 'this'-ness that entraps them in solitude and entrusting their fate to children, humans can finally escape the nihilism of Ivan/Stavrogin.

Kameyama suggested that Alyosha could overcome Ivan by becoming an impotent father. We might say that this image of the non-existent sequel constructs, in narrative form, the above speculation by Yamashiro and Bamba regarding the existing first volume.

6

From the socialist to the Underground Man, to the superhuman, to the impotent father surrounded by children. From liberalism to communitarianism, to libertarianism, to the tourist. Or, from universalism to nationalism, to individualism, to the space of misdelivery. In this chapter I abstracted these four subjects from Dostoevsky's works and attempted to approach the philosophy of the tourist from a different angle by clarifying the mechanism by which one transitions into the next.

Allow me to state one more time in closing: one of the messages I wanted to communicate in this chapter is that in approaching the world, we ought to approach it not as an underground man or as a Stavrogin, but as a parent approaches a child. To put it another way, we should approach others not as communitarians or libertarians, but as we would approach a newborn based on familial similarity.

I began this book with a discussion of the Other. We live in an age where narrow-minded underground men continuously point out the hypocrisy of liberalism, and libertarian sadists rule the world order.

In the past, liberalism advocated a logic of the Other, but this no longer holds any power. At the same time, neither of the thriving credos of communitarianism (nationalism) and libertarianism (globalism) possess a viable logic of the Other either. Today in 2017, familial similarity and 'misdelivery' are just about the only philosophical principles that support tolerance toward others. That is my understanding. And that is why I believe that philosophy must more seriously and comprehensively engage with the ideal of family and its possibilities. This is the case philosophically, regardless of the individual issue of whether you, the reader, have a family or have children or not. That is why I wrote this second part of the book.

The figure of the child is closely related to the uncanny. The face of a newborn is in fact uncanny. Children are beings that are at once the most intimate to us and at the same time scatter, proliferate, and before we know it arrive at an unknown place and come to tear down our lives from within.

Philosophers, regardless of their era, hate children. However, we were all once children. We were all uncanny. We were all children of chance. The existence of each of us will indeed end; death is a necessity. However, birth is not necessary, and none of us were existences when we were born. Thus, we cannot complete our lives unless we expose ourselves to the chance of also becoming parents who give birth to the next generation, and do not simply become existences that arrive at necessity. So long as we think as children, we cannot escape the three choices of Chernyshevsky, the Underground Man, and Stavrogin. Heidegger's mistake was that he built his philosophy not from the standpoint of the parent who gives birth to multiple children, but from the standpoint of one single child who will die alone.

Don't simply die as a child; live as a parent too. In a word, that is what I want to say in this second part of the book. Of course, 'parent' here does not necessarily mean a biological parent. Symbolic or cultural parents exist too. Indeed, perhaps those kinds of parents are closer to the concept of the parent referred to here. Because being a parent means making a misdelivery and being surrounded by children of chance.

I hope that my work here, too, will give birth to as many children of chance as possible, and will make way for philosophies of the future.

Arendt, Hannah. *The Human Condition*. Chicago: University of Chicago Press, 1998.

Azuma, Hiroki. *Sonzaironteki, yūbinteki*. Tokyo: Shinchōsha, 1998.

———, 'Jōhō jiyūron', *Jōhō kankyōronshū Azuma Hiroki korekushon S*. Tokyo: Kōdansha BOX, 2007.

———, *Geemuteki riarizumu no tanjō*. Tokyo: Kōdansha gendai shinsho, 2007.

———, *Otaku: Japan's Database Animals, tr. J.E. Abel and S. Konio*. Minneapolis and London: University of Minnesota Press, 2009.

———, *Saibāsupeesu wa naze sō yobareruka+*. *Tokyo: Kawade Bunko, 2011*.

———, *Yūbintoki fuantachi heta*. Tokyo: Kawade Bunko, 2011.

———, (ed.) *Shisō Chizu β, Volume 1*. Tokyo: Contectures, 2011.

———, *Sekai kara motto chikaku ni*. Tokyo: Tokyo Sōgensha, 2013.

———, (ed.) *Cherunobuiri daaku tsūrizumu gaido*. Tokyo: Genron, 2013.

———, *General Will 2.0: Rousseau, Freud, Google*, tr. J. Person and N. Matsuyama. New York: Vertical, 2014.

———, *Yowai tsunagari—kensaku wādo o sagasu tabi. Tokyo: Gentōsha, 2014*.

———, (ed.) *Fukushima Daiichi Genpatsu Kankōchika Keikaku*. Tokyo: Genron, 2013.

———, (ed.), *Genron 3*. Tokyo: Genron, 2016.

———, and Akihiro Kitada. *Tokyo kara kangaeru*. Tokyo: NHK Bukkusu, 2007

———, and Ken Ōyama. *Shoppingu mōru kara kangaeru*. Tokyo: Gentōsha shinsho, 2016.

———, and Hiroshi Kainuma. 'Datsu "Fukushima-ron"', *Mainichi Shimbun*, 2015, <http://mainichi.jp/correspondence>.

Bakhtin, Mikhail. *Problems of Dostoevsky's Poetics*, tr. C. Emerson. Minneapolis: University of Minnesota Press, 1984.

Bamba, Satoshi. *Dosutoefusukii to shōsetsu no toi*. Tokyo: Suiseisha, 2012.

Barbrook, Richard, and Andy Cameron. 'The Californian Ideology', *Mute* 1:3 (1995).

Barlow, John Perry. 'A Declaration of Independence of Cyberspace', 1996, <https://www.eff.org/cyberspace-independence>.

Beck, Ulrich, and Anthony Giddens and Scott Lash. *Reflexive Modernization: Politics, Tradition, and Aesthetics in the Modern Social Order*. Stanford, CA: Stanford University Press, 1994.

Benjamin, Walter. *The Arcades Project*, tr. H. Eiland and K. McLaughlin. Cambridge, MA: Belknap Press, 1999.

Boorstin, Daniel J. *The Image: A Guide to Pseudo-Events in America*. New York: Harper Colophon, 1961.

Buchanan, Mark. *Ubiquity: The Science of History... Or Why the World is Simpler Than We Think*. New York: Crown, 2000.

Burke, Edmund. *Reflections on the Revolution in France and Other Writings*. New York: Knopf, 2015.

Calichman, Richard F. (ed.). *Contemporary Japanese Thought*. New York: Columbia University Press, 2005.

Cassirer, Ernst. *The Question of Jean-Jacques Rousseau*, tr. P. Gay. Indianapolis: Indiana University Press, 1963.

Chernyshevsky, Nikolai. *What Is to Be Done?* tr. M.R. Katz. Ithaca, NY: Cornell University Press, 1989.

Deleuze, Gilles. 'Coldness and Cruelty', in *Masochism*. New York: Zone Books, 1991.

———, 'Postscript on the Societies of Control', *October* 59. (Winter 1992), 3–7.

———, and Félix Guattari. *A Thousand Plateaus: Capitalism and Schizophrenia*, tr. B. Massumi. Minneapolis: University of Minnesota Press, 1987.

Dick, Philip K. 'VALIS', in *VALIS and Later Novels*. New York: The Library of America, 2009.

Diderot, Denis. 'Supplement to Bougainville's "Voyage"', in *Rameau's Nephew and Other Works*, tr. J. Barzun and R.H. Brown. Indianapolis: Hackett, 2001.

Dostoevsky, Fyodor. *The Devils*, tr. D.D. Magarshack. London: Penguin Books, 1953.

———, 'Notes from the Underground', tr. D. Magarshack, in *Great Short Works of Fyodor Dostoevsky*. New York: HarperCollins, 1968.

———, *The Brothers Karamazov*, tr. A.R. MacAndrew. New York: Bantam Books, 1970.

———, *The Adolescent*, tr. R. Pevear and L. Volokhonsky. New York: Vintage, 2003.

———, *A Writer's Diary*, tr. K. Lantz. Evanston, IL: Northwestern University Press, 2009.

Dugin, Alexander. *The Fourth Political Theory*, tr. M. Sleboda and M. Millerman. Budapest: Arktos, 2012.

Eidin, John, and David Edmonds. *Rousseau's Dog: Two Great Thinkers at War in the Age of Enlightenment*. New York: Harper Perennial, 2006.

Foucault, Michel. *The History of Sexuality, Vol. 1: An Introduction*. New York: Vintage, 1990.

Freud, Sigmund. 'The Uncanny', in *The Standard Edition of the Complete Works of Sigmund Freud Volume 17, tr. J. Strachey*, 217–56. London: Hogarth Press, 2019.

Friedman, Michael. *Capitalism and Freedom, 40th Anniversary Edition*. Chicago: University of Chicago Press, 2002.

Friedman, Thomas L. *The World is Flat: A Brief History of the Twenty-first Century*. London: Picador, 2005.

Fukuyama, Francis. *The End of History and the Last Man*. New York: Free Press, 1992.

Girard, René. *Resurrection from the Underground: Feodor Dostoevsky, tr. J.G. Williams*. East Lansing, MI: Michigan State University Press, 2012.

Groys, Boris. *Russian Cosmism*. Cambridge, MA: MIT Press, 2018.

Habermas, Jürgen. 'Beyond a Temporalized Philosophy of Origins: Jacques Derrida's Critique of Phonocentrism', in T. McCarthy (ed.),*The Philosophical Discourse of Modernity*. Cambridge, MA: MIT Press, 1987.

Hacking, Ian. *The Taming of Chance*. Cambridge: Cambridge University Press, 1990.

——, *Rewriting the Soul: Multiple Personality and the Science of Memory*. Princeton, NJ: Princeton University Press, 1995.

Hardt, Michael, and Antonio Negri. *Empire*. Cambridge, MA: Harvard University Press, 2001.

——, *<Teikoku>, tr. K. Mizushima et al*. Tokyo: Ibunsha, 2003.

——, *Multitude: War and Democracy in the Age of Empire*. London: Penguin, 2004.

——, *Maruchichūdo (ge), tr. S. Ikushima*. Tokyo: NHK Bukkusu, 2005.

——, *Declaration*. Independence, KS: Argo Navis, 2012.

Hegel, Georg Wilhelm Friedrich. *Elements of the Philosophy of Right, tr. S.W. Dyde*. Cambridge: Cambridge University Press, 2003.

Hirano, Keiichirō. *Watashi to wa nanika*. Tokyo: Kōdansha Gendai Shinsho, 2012.

Hiromatsu, Wataru (ed.). *Iwanami tetsugaku, shisō jiten*. Tokyo: Iwanami Shoten, 1998.

Hirukawa, Hisayasu. *Tomasu Kukku no shōzō*. Tokyo: Maruzen, 1998.

Itō, Jōichi. 'Sōhatsu minshusei', tr. Kumon Shunpei, *Kokusai Daigaku GLOCOM*, 2003, <https://www.glocom.ac.jp/wp-content/uploads/2020/10/75_02.pdf>.

Japan Society for Tourism Studies, 'Gakkai no kiroku', 2012, <https://jsts.sc/archive>.

Kainuma, Hiroshi. *Hajimete no Fukushima-gaku*. Tokyo: Iisuto Puresu, 2015.

Kameyama, Ikuo. *Dosutoefusukii: chichigoroshi no bungaku ge*. Tokyo: NHK Bukkusu, 2004.

————, *Dosutoefusukii: chichigoroshi no bungaku jō*. Tokyo: NHK Bukkusu, 2004.

————, *'Karamazofu no kyōdai' no zokuhen o kūsō suru*. Tokyo: Kōbunsha, 2007.

Kant, Immanuel. 'Critique of Practical Reason', in *Practical Philosophy*, tr. M. Gregor. Cambridge: Cambridge University Press, 1999.

————, 'Perpetual Peace', in *Kant On History*, ed. L.W. Beck. Indianapolis: Bobbs-Merrill, 2001.

Karatani, Kōjin. *Tankyū I*. Tokyo: Kōdansha Gakujutsu Bunko, 1992.

————, *The Structure of World History: From Modes of Production to Modes of Exchange*, tr. M.K. Bourdaghs. Durham, NC: Duke University Press, 2014.

Kay, Alan. *Alan Kei*, tr. Y. Tsuruoka. Tokyo: Ascii, 1992.

Kojève, Alexandre. *Introduction to the Reading of Hegel*, tr. J.H. Nichols, Jr.. Ithaca, NY: Cornell University Press, 1980.

Lacan, Jacques. *The Four Fundamental Concepts of Psychoanalysis*, tr. A. Sheridan. London: Hogarth Press, 1977.

Laclau, Ernest, and Chantal Mouffe. *Hegemony and Socialist Strategy: Towards a Radical Democratic Politics*. London: Verso, 2001.

Leed, Eric J. *The Mind of the Traveler: From Gilgamesh to Global Tourism*. New York: Basic Books, 1991.

Leibniz, Gottfried Wilhelm. *Theodicy*. Chicago: Open Court, 1985.

Lennon, John, and Malcolm Foley. *Dark Tourism: The Attraction of Death and Disaster*. London: Continuum, 2nd Edition 2000.

Lévi-Strauss, Claude. 'Jean-Jacques Rousseau, Founder of the Sciences of Man', in T. O'Hagan (ed.), *Jean-Jacques Rousseau*. Aldershot: Ashgate, 2007.

Levy, Steven. *Hackers: Heroes of the Computer Revolution 25th Anniversary Edition*. Sebastopol, CA: O'Reilly Media, 2010.

Lyon, David. *Surveillance Society: Monitoring Everyday Life*. Maidenhead: Open University Press, 2001.

MacCannell, Dean. *The Tourist: A New Theory of the Leisuire Class*. New York: Schocken, 1976.

————, *The Ethics of Sightseeing*. Oakland, CA: University of California Press, 2011.

Masuda, Naoki. *Watashitachi wa dō tsunagatte irunoka*. Tokyo: Chūkō shinso, 2007.

————, and Norio Konno, *'Fukuzatsu nettowāku' to wa nanika*. Tokyo: Kōdansha burūbak-kusu, 2006.

Matsumura, Masaie. *Suishōkyū monogatari*. Tokyo: Chikuma Gakugei Bunko, 2000.

Miyadai, Shinji. *Sabukaruchā Shinwa Kaitai*. Tokyo: Kadokawa Bunko, 2001.

Morimura, Susumu. *Jiyū wa dokomade kanō ka*. Tokyo: Kōdansha Gendai Shinsho, 2001.

———, (ed.) *Ribatarianizumu dokuhon*. Tokyo: Keisō Shobō, 2005.

Morohoshi, Daijirō. *Kanata yori*. Tokyo: Shūeisha Bunko, 2004.

Mulhall, Steven, and Adam Swift. *Liberals and Communitarians*. Oxford: Blackwell, 1996.

Murakami, Yasusuke, Shunpei Kumon, and Seizaburō Satō. *Bunmei toshite no ie shakai*. Tokyo: Chūō Kōron sha, 1979.

Nozick, Robert. *Anarchy, State, and Utopia*. New York: Basic Books, 1974.

Okada, Atsushi. *Gurando tsuā*. Tokyo: Iwanami shinsho, 2010.

Okamoto, Nobuyuki. *Kankōgaku nyūmon*. Tokyo: Yūhikaku Aruma, 2001.

Otsuka, Eiji. *Teihon Monogatari Shōhi-Ron*. Tokyo: Kadokawa, 1989.

Ōsawa, Masachi. *Nashonarizumu no yurai*. Tokyo: Kōdansha, 2007.

Ōyama, Ken. 'Cherunobuiri wa 'futsū' datta', *Daily Portal Z*, 2016, <https://portal.nifty.com/kiji/161118198099_1.htm>.

Rawls, John. *The Law of Peoples*. Cambridge, MA: Harvard University Press, 2001.

Rorty, Richard. *Contingency, Irony, and Solidarity*. Cambridge: Cambridge University Press, 1989.

Rousseau, Jean-Jacques. *The Social Contract and Other Later Political Writings*, ed. V. Gourevitch. Cambridge: Cambridge University Press, 1997.

———, *On the Origin of Inequality*, tr. G.D.H. Cole. New York: Cosimo Classics, 2005.

Saito, Jun'ichi. *Kōkyōsei*. Tokyo: Iwanami Shoten, 2000.

Satake, Shin'ichi S. 'Tsūrizumu to kankō no teigi', in *Osaka Kankō Daigaku kiyō*. Tokyo: Kaigaku jyusshūnen kinengō, 2010.

Schmitt, Carl. *The Concept of the Political*, tr. G. Schwab. Chicago: University of Chicago Press, 1996.

———, *Political Theology*, tr. G. Schwab. Chicago: University of Chicago Press, 2010.

———, *Dictatorship*, tr. M. Hoelzl and G. Ward. Cambridge: Polity, 2014.

Semyonova, Svetlana. *Fyōdorofu-den*, tr. H. Yasuoka and I. Kameyama. Tokyo: Suiseisha, 1998.

Singer, Peter. *Practical Ethics*. Cambridge: Cambridge University Press, 1993.

———, *One World: The Ethics of Globalization*. New Haven, CT: Yale University Press, 2002.

———, *The Life You Can Save: Acting Now to End World Poverty*. New York: Random House, 2009.

Sokal, Alan, and Jean Bricmont. *Fashionable Nonsense: Postmodern Intellectuals' Abuse of Science*. New York: Picador, 1999.

Sterling, Bruce. *The Hacker Crackdown: Law and Order on the Electronic Frontier.* New York: Bantam, 1992.

Suvin, Darko. *Metamorphosis of Science Fiction: On the Poetics and History of a Literary Genre.* New Haven, CT: Yale University Press, 1979.

Suzuki, Ken. *Nameraka na shakai to sono teki.* Tokyo: Keiso Shobō, 2013.

Todd, Emmanuel. *La Diversité du monde: Famille et modernité.* Paris: Seuil, 1999.

———, *Sekai no tayōsei,* tr. F. Ogino. Tokyo: Fujiwara Shoten, 2008.

———, *After the Empire: The Breakdown of the American Order,* tr. C. Jon Delogu and M. Lind. New York: Columbia University Press, 2006.

———, *Lineages of Modernity: A History of Humanity from the Stone Age to Homo Americanus,* tr. A. Brown. Cambridge: Polity Press, 2019.

Thaler, Richard H. and Cass R. Sunstein. *Nudge: Improving Decisions About Health, Wealth, and Happiness.* London: Penguin, 2009.

Turkle, Sherry, *Life on the Screen: Identity in the Age of the Internet.* New York: Simon & Schuster, 1995.

Ueno, Chizuko. *Kafuchōsei to shihonsei.* Tokyo: Iwanami Gendai Bunko, 2009.

———, *The Modern Family in Japan: Its Rise and Fall.* Victoria: Trans Pacific Press, 2009.

Urry, Jonas, and John Larsen. *The Tourist Gaze 3.0.* London: Sage, 2011.

Voltaire. *Candide and Other Stories,* tr. R. Pearson. Oxford: Oxford World's Classics, 2006.

Wakabayashi, Mikio. 'Tayōsei, kinshitsusei, kyodaisei, tōkasei', in M. Wakabayashi (ed.), *Mōruka suru toshi to shakai.* Tokyo: NTT Shuppan, 2013.

Watts, Duncan J. *Small Worlds: The Dynamics of Networks Between Order and Randomness.* Princeton, NJ: Princeton University Press, 1999.

Wittgenstein, Ludwig. *Philosophical Investigations,* tr. G. E. M. Anscombe. London: Macmillan, 1953.

Yamaguchi, Masao. *Chi no enkinhō.* Tokyo: Iwanami Shoten, 1978.

———, *Bunka to ryōgisei.* Tokyo: Iwanami Gendai Bunko, 2000.

Yamazaki, Masakazu, and Kushida Magoichi, *Akuma to uragirimono.* Tokyo: Chikuma Gakugei Bunko, 2014.

Yamashiro, Mutsumi. *Dosutoefusukii.* Tokyo: Kōdansha Bungei Bunko, 2015.

Yoshikawa, Hiromitsu. *Rifujin na shinka.* Tokyo: Asahi Shuppankai, 2014.

Žižek, Slavoj. *The Sublime Object of Ideology.* London: Verso, 2009.